SOCIETY, RELIGION AND PATRIARCHY

Society, Religion and Patriarchy

Exploring Medieval Punjab through *Hir Waris*

ISHWAR DAYAL GAUR

MANOHAR
2009

First published 2009

ISBN 978-81-7304-826-5

Published by
Ajay Kumar Jain *for*
Manohar Publishers & Distributors
4753/23 Ansari Road, Daryaganj
New Delhi 110 002

Typeset by
Kohli Print
Delhi 110 051

Printed at
Salasar Imaging Systems
Delhi 110 035

To
Dr. Amrik Singh

Contents

ILLUSTRATIONS

Acknowledgments

The present study is dedicated to Dr. Amrik Singh who inspired me to work on medieval Punjabi society and culture. During the long walks, which we undertook at Chandigarh, Patiala and Delhi over a period of about ten years, he enlightened me on Islam, Punjabi literature and history of the Punjab. I am also indebted to my teacher, late Dr. Satish K. Bajaj who taught me to approach history from the viewpoint of sociology and anthropology. I am thankful to Dr. Mohinder Singh, Director, National Institute of Panjab Studies, Bhai Vir Singh Sahitya Sadan, Delhi, for funding the project on a socio-cultural study of *Hir Waris*. I also thank Prof. Sutinder Singh Noor who shared my enthusiasm for studying medieval Punjab through Punjabi literature.

My thanks are due to Prof. Surinder Singh, Department of History, Panjab University, Chandigarh, for placing his personal library at my disposal. He taught me the methods of reading medieval India from the cultural perspective and suggested the ways to situate *Hir Waris* within the broader medieval milieu. Whenever I faced any difficulty in locating information in the Persian and Urdu sources, he readily offered his expertise. He read the preliminary and final drafts of the manuscript and offered numerous suggestions for improvement.

My gratitude is due to Prof. Nahar Singh, Prof. Jagjit Singh and Dr. Yog Raj Angrish, Department of Punjabi, and Prof. Rana Nayar, Department of English, for providing me the material for my study of *Hir Waris* and helping me appreciate a historic relationship between folklore, literature and history. I am also thankful to S. Harnek Singh Ghuruana for providing the photographs of Waris Shah and the mausoleums of Hir-Ranjha, which he had brought from Pakistan. I also wish to express my special thanks to Shri S.A. Ali, the founder-member of Jamia Hamdard for making an arrangement for my stay at the Scholars House,

Hamdard Nagar, New Delhi. I am beholden to Prof. Iqtidar Husain Siddiqui who approved the format of the present study and paved the way for its publication.

I am grateful to the staff of the libraries of the Nehru Memorial Museum & Library, Jamia Hamdard and Jamia Millia Islamia, Bhai Vir Singh Sahitya Sadan (all at New Delhi); Punjabi Sahit Akademi Reference Library, Ludhiana; A.C. Joshi Library, Panjab University, Chandigarh; Institute for Development and Communication, Chandigarh; Centre for Research in Rural and Industrial Development, Chandigarh; and the Punjabi University, Patiala.

I take this opportunity to acknowledge my roots in the rural soil of Malwa in Punjab, where I was born and brought up. The socio-cultural ambience of the Malwa region and the warmth of kinship relationships motivated and encouraged me, first, to versify in my own vernacular the cultural collage of the Punjab under the titles of *Surmedani* (1999) and *Charkha Bole Sain Sain* (2006); and second, to unfold the nature of Punjabi society and culture through folk literature like the *qissa* of Hir-Ranjha. Before reading this *qissa* in print, I had heard it from my mother who used to sing it while I was growing up.

The book has taken a long time to write. Owing to a number of other preoccupations, both academic and personal, the work on *Hir Waris* could be pursued in phases. However, I am thankful to Shri Ramesh Jain and Shri Ajay Jain for their readiness to publish the manuscript.

ISHWAR DAYAL GAUR

CHAPTER 1

The Narrative

Friends came one day and made a request
That the tale of Hir be told anew

WARIS SHAH

The Punjabi love legend of Hir Siyal and Dhido Ranjha is central to my study of medieval Punjabi society. Hir, the legendary rebellious heroine, is said to have been born around AD 1425 and to have died in 1452. Thus she lived for twenty-seven years in the time of the Delhi Sultanate. Hir was the daughter of Chuchak, a chief (*sardar*) of the Siyal clan. This clan is said to have embraced Islam during the time of Baba Farid (1175–1265), the celebrated Chishti sufi of Punjab. Hir's parental or native village was Chuchakana on the confluence of the Jhelum and Chenab. Jhang Siyal, generally identified as her native village, is said to have been founded in 1462 by Mal Khan, the nephew of Chuchak who bequeathed his entire domain (*riasat*) to him.[1]

Although a number of *qissa-kars* (poet-narrators) versified this legend, Waris Shah made it popular when he versified it in 1767. This popular version of the legend is narrated below.

Mauju[2] of the Ranjha clan was the chief (*chaudhari*) of Takht Hazara village in western Punjab. Respected by his fraternity and honoured by all, he lived in wealth and happiness with his family of eight sons and two daughters. Dhido, the youngest of his children, was carefree and handsome, fond of playing the flute (*vanjhli*). His brothers hated him. For fear of their father they could not wound him openly, but their secret taunts hurt him. When Mauju died, Dhido was the only unmarried member of the family. He now had to face the hard realities of life. His brothers and their wives redoubled their taunts, saying, 'You eat the bread of idleness and drink two men's share of whey (*lassi*)'. They thought about how to get rid of him. So the elder brothers called the *panchs* or village assembly and the *qazi* (the local judge) to measure and distribute their father's land among them. They greased the palms of these functionaries, who awarded fertile land to seven brothers, but the least productive parcel to Dhido, commonly called Ranjha after the name of his clan. Unaccustomed to the hard life of an agriculturist, Dhido was now obliged to work for his living. He could not till the barren and hard land. In the scorching sun, his hands were blistered and his body began to ache. He held his sisters-in- law, who often bullied and made fun of him, responsible for what had happened. They would often tell him he ate too much and that he was a blot on the family. They did not like his idleness. They said, 'You prowl about the village making eyes at the girls. The other women of the village taunt us at female spinning parties (*trinjan*)[3] and say we are in love with you. Day and night the women run after you. Your love has ruined many households.' One day they taunted him to marry Hir of the Siyal clan or to elope with her. As Ranjha could not put up with the banter, he prepared to leave the house. However, his brothers and their wives came out to dissuade him. He left, nevertheless.

Ranjha travelled towards Jhang Siyal, the village of Hir. At night he stayed in a mosque, where the *mullah* first refused to allow him to stay the night because of his un-Islamic bearing. He called Ranjha a cad. Ranjha retorted, 'You have a long beard like a venerable Shaikh, yet you behave like a devil. Why do you send innocent travellers and poor faqirs like me away? You sit in the pulpit with the Quran in front of you, yet your mind is bent on iniquity. You lead the village women astray; you are like a bull among cows.' After this heated exchange, Ranjha was permitted to stay in the mosque on condition that he would rise from his slumber and 'slink away before the morning spreads itself'. The next day he reached the river Chenab. Many travellers were assembled at the ferry crossing, waiting for Luddan, the ferryman. Ranjha, who had no money, requested Luddan to ferry him across. Luddan, a muscular man known to have two beautiful wives, was proud and arrogant, and refused. So Ranjha sat there sadly and played his flute. The two wives of Luddan, taking a fancy to him, began to press his feet. Luddan became angry and muttered, 'This youth is a wizard. He has cast a spell over my wives.' He appealed to the villagers around saying, 'Save us from the wiles of this Jat. He will beguile all our womenfolk.' However, the people did not pay attention to him because of the enchantment of Ranjha's flute. After having soothed his soul with music, Ranjha plunged into the river. The folk cried, 'Sir, go not down into river, the stream of the Chenab runs deep and strong!' Luddan's wives too begged him to return. Eventually, the people caught him and brought him back, saying, 'Friend, enter not the river or you will be drowned. We ourselves will carry you on our shoulders.' So they caught Ranjha by the arms and put him into a boat.

On the other bank, Ranjha met Hir. She had come there along with sixty girls for a boat ride. Hir and Ranjha fell in love. Hir swore by the name of Khwaja Khizar, the legendary guardian saint of the river and of sailors, to remain loyal to him. Hir took Ranjha to her father, Chuchak, the sardar of the Siyal clan. She requested him to appoint Dhido as a herdsman (*chaak*). Her father agreed, and Hir began to carry food to Ranjha when he was grazing the cattle in the pastures (*bela*) around the river, and began to enjoy romantic intimacy with him. All day long Ranjha would play his flute and the animals gamboled and wagged their tails in ecstasy. The lovers were blessed by the five *pirs*: Khwaja Khizar, the lord of all waters, Shakarganj (Farid) of Pakpattan, Zakariya of Multan, Shahbaz Qalandar of Uch, and Saiyyid Jalaluddin Bukhari whom people also call Makhdum Jahanian. By the grace of God and the five pirs, Hir was bestowed on Ranjha. The five pirs were gracious to Ranjha. Khizar gave him a turban tuft, Saiyyid Jalal a dagger, Zakariya a thick blanket, Shahbaz a ring, and Shakarganj a handkerchief. Hir and Ranjha created a world of their own, but this was fated to be shattered. Beyond the boundaries of the pastures, the scourge of the patriarchy was active. Kaido, a lame uncle of Hir, spied the romance between the daughter of the sardar and his servant, and told the family about it. Very soon, the love affair became a scandal in the village. Hir was advised by the qazi, Shamsuddin, to stay at home spinning. Later she was threatened with the fatal consequences. But the warnings of father, mother, brother and qazi were all futile. Hir continued to see Ranjha. The lovers even managed to locate a safe rendezvous in the house of a barber. Hir would go there at night and stay until one watch of the night remained, and then slip back to her own house. In the morning Ranjha drove the buffaloes out to graze in the forest. Under the pretence of bathing, Hir and her maids used to meet him in the forest on the banks of the Chenab. The river banks shook with their merry making. Ranjha played his flute and Hir and her maids sang the merry songs of the Chenab.

Much perturbed, Malki, Hir's mother, asked her husband to terminate the services of the herdsman. Ranjha was thrown out of his job. But later Malki entreated her husband to reinstate him for the people of the village were cursing them: the buffalos were not properly looked after. So the services of the herdsman were restored. As Hir kept arranging clandestine meetings with him, her father shared his concern with his kinsmen and expressed his desire to marry Hir with the herdsman. But the Siyal fraternity (*biradari*) told him that the Siyals had never formed a matrimonial relationship with the Ranjhas: the latter were inferior to them in social status. Eventually Hir was betrothed to Saida, the son of Ajju of the Khera clan of Rangpur village. Hir now suggested to Ranjha that they elope, but he was reluctant.

The Kheras consulted a Brahman to fix the date of the marriage. The qazi was invited to perform the *nikah* or marriage ceremony on the auspicious day. After a long debate with the qazi on the issue of love, Hir refused to agree to marry Saida. Nevertheless, she was forcibly pushed into the palanquin (*doli*) as the wife of Saida. Ranjha saw Hir being carried off by the Kheras. He wandered in the wilderness in shocked dismay and misery. Hir for her part pined for Ranjha, and resolved to reject Saida Khera. She persuaded Ranjha to come to Rangpur in the guise of a mendicant (*jogi*), and Ranjha visited the hillock (*tilla*) of Balnath, the disciple of Guru Gorakh Nath, to become a jogi. Dressed in the garb of a jogi, he rushed to Rangpur, the village where Hir had been married. He went to Ajju's (Hir's father-in-law) house for alms. Here he became involved in a discussion with Sahiti, Hir's sister-in-law, who teased him and called him a fake jogi. This eventually led to a quarrel. Sahiti and her friends, in the presence of Hir, beat Ranjha. Finding no way out, he ran away and took shelter in a garden (Kala Bagh) on the outskirts of the village. Hir appeased her sister-in-law and made her relent. Later, Ranjha's fame as a jogi with miraculous powers spread through the town. Women visited him in large numbers. Sahiti also went to the garden to offer him sugar, butter, and five rupees, as a token of devotion and reverence. She sought his blessings for the consummation of her love with a Baloch youth, named Murad. The jogi undertook to further the love of Sahiti and Murad, and Sahiti in turn promised to help Hir and Ranjha. The jogi asked her to send Hir to the garden which she did. A plan to elope was then chalked out.

One day Hir and Sahiti, in the company of the village girls, went to the fields to pluck and gather cotton buds. Hir cried out and pretended that a snake had bitten her. Since it was all pre-planned, all efforts to cure her proved abortive. At last Sahiti pleaded with her father to call in the jogi (Ranjha). As soon as he arrived, he told the family that an isolated place was required to cure her. He instructed the family that no one except a maid could stay with Hir when she was being treated. Ranjha, Hir, and Sahiti were accommodated in the house of a *doom* (a low caste menial). At night Sahiti eloped with Murad, and Hir with Ranjha. When the Kheras found that a fraud had been played on them, they followed the fugitives on horses. Hir and Ranjha were caught on the way and Ranjha was given a sound beating. The lovers were produced before the king, named Adli. The case was handed over to the qazi who ordered Ranjha to part with Hir. Ranjha appealed to God to cause a calamity to befall the town of the king, and soon the town was in the grip of fire. To appease God and to cool His wrath, the king restored Hir to Ranjha. The couple then started their journey to Takht Hazara. But the parents of Hir asked Ranjha to go to his village and come back in a ceremonial way along with a *barat* or marriage party. Ranjha complied; but Hir's family, who still refused to accept the matrimonial relationship with the Ranjhas, poisoned their daughter. Hearing about her death, Ranjha also breathed his last. The tomb of Hir is situated outside the city of Jhang. According to the legend, Hir and Ranjha lie buried in the same grave.

NOTES

1. With reference to Maulvi Nur Muhammad's *Tarikh-i-Jhang* (1862), Jit Singh Sital suggests that Chuchakana was the native village of Hir, and Jhang came into being later on. Jit Singh Sital, *Hir Waris*, Patiala, n.d., pp. 10–11. Syed Abdul Quddus is of the same view. *Punjab: The Land of Beauty, Love and Mysticism*, Karachi, 1992, p. 393. However, Jagtar Singh is of the view that Jhang was in existence when the story of Hir–Ranjha actually happened. See *Heer Damodar*, Patiala, 2000, p. 9.
2. Mauju is vernacularization of Muizzuddin, the name given in some of the Persian Hir–Ranjha *masnavis*.
3. Spinning parties were a famous institution of the Punjab village. Young girls sat together spinning and competed with one another in skills and scandalous gossip.

CHAPTER 2

Culture of the People

> I have long had a favourite theory that the average villager one meets in Punjab and Northern India is at heart neither a Muhammadan nor a Hindu, nor a Sikh, nor of any other Religion, as such is understood by its orthodox—or to speak more correctly authorized—exponents. . . .
>
> R.C. TEMPLE, *The Legends of Punjab*, vol. II, p. xxi

I present in this book a historical narrative implanted in the society and culture of medieval Punjab. An in-depth reading of *Hir Waris*, and of the direct and indirect references to the Islamic and Hindu religion, history and mythology in it, obliged me, first, to identify it as an indigenous Punjabi text, historically rooted in the soil, and second, to illumine the cultural fusion that made Muslims a specific vernacular component of medieval Punjabi society. (This phenomenon has so far remained unexplored.) Indeed, the qissa of *Hir* is a fabric woven by Waris Shah out of distinct threads of Punjabi soil and space.

IDENTITY: ETHNICITY AND RELIGION

It needs to be mentioned at the outset that the appellation 'Muslim' assigned to one of the communities of Punjab does not signify any watertight communal compartmentalization of the medieval society. Strictly bounded categories were then absent, though they came to be conspicuously present in colonial Punjab. The term Muslim has been used simply to explain and highlight the holistic and open-ended nature and character of the socio-religious and cultural ethos of those people of Punjab who, in the context of the Great Islamic Traditions (or in the imperialist census reports), are situated in the standardized category of 'Muslims'. It is interesting to note that the 'Muslim' characters of the qissa *Hir* are known either by the names of their respective clans (Ranjha, Siyal and Kheras) or by the names of their clan-villages (Takht Hazara, Jhang).[1]

With the political split of Punjab in 1947, the problem arose of defining, determining, and demarcating Punjabi identity (or the description of culturally circumscribed characteristics) and that of its component social sections, labelled in religious terms. Since then the problem has persisted. Politicization and communalization of the identity, both in the east and the west Punjabs, have transfigured the socio-cultural diversities into religious differences. Like religion, state, nation and nationality have been presented as single organic wholes. Critiquing the religion-oriented discourse of vernacular identity, Bipan Chandra observes,

> Not only did Hindus or Muslims or Sikhs or Christians *not* form a nation or a nationality, they did not even form a distinct and homogeneous 'community' except for religious purposes. That is, they did not separately form a 'monolithic social structure' or a cohesive unit on a religious basis with common economic, political, social and cultural interests, or bonds or outlook. The religious coordinates did not coincide with class, ethnic, linguistic, or cultural coordinates.[2]

During medieval times too, one needs to remember that (i) the Timurids, Ottomans, Safavids, and Mughals 'had no need to accept even theoretical allegiance to an Imam or Khalifa outside their states',[3] (ii) and that religious discourse, for example of *dar-ul-Islam* or *dar-ul-harb*, was not followed by Abul Fazl to describe the polity of his times. He would have us believe that Akbar's state could be designated as *dar-ul-sulh*, because his conquests were not inspired by a spirit of aggrandizement, but were part of a larger plan to establish an all India polity based on justice and tolerance.[4] During the seventeenth century the Mughals were 'keen to maintain the separate identity of the various ethnic sections comprising the Mughal nobility—the Mughals, the Shaikhs, the Afghans, the Rajputs, the Deccanis, and so on'.[5] Between them 'religion could no longer provide a common means of communication'.[6] It needs to be observed that discourse of identity that emerges from the

Babar Vani of Guru Nanak in the first quarter of the sixteenth century is not religious but ethnic. Babur, the invader, and the Lodis, the rulers of Punjab/Hindustan are not 'Muslim', but Turk and Pathan, as addressed by Nanak. The purpose of citing these observations is to underline that for determining the regional, local, or ethnic character of a community, religion was marginal. Religion may be understood as the defining characteristic of a *Muslim* Punjabi, but not of a *Punjabi* Muslim. Let me explain.

The Shahmukhi and Gurmukhi scripts of Punjabi language (*zuban* or *boli*) and the three social components of Punjabi society, Hindus, Sikhs and Muslims, have been decisive enough to serve and strengthen the communal ideology of colonial and post-colonial forces. This was the 'principal basis for differentiation in Punjab, followed by the script, so that the historic movement has been towards the congruence of Muslims, Urdu, and the Persian script; Hindus, Hindi, and Devnagri script; Sikhs, Punjabi, and the Gurmukhi script'.[7] With reference to the acculturative movements in Punjab like the Arya Samaj, Singh Sabha, and the Ahmadiyahs, it has been observed that 'by the end of the nineteenth century, religious identity was in the process of expressing itself in combinations of symbols based on language, script and religion'.[8] Thus (mis)appropriation of the religious traditions of Hinduism, Sikhism, and Islam made by the communitarian forces, poses a perennial challenge to the concept of vernacular Punjabi identity, both in India and Pakistan. On the map of Punjab we have Muslim-majority western Punjab, the Sikh-majority Punjabi Suba, and Hindu-majority Punjab in the form of present-day Haryana and Himachal Pradesh.[9] The tendency to present, propagate and promote Punjab history and culture in the communitarian perspective has prevailed since the annexation of Punjab to the British Raj in 1849. A number of conflicting discourses of cultural fission can be discovered in the historiography of Punjabi language, literature and culture and writings on Punjab history. Socio-cultural profiles of Punjabi people are being probed in *religious routes*, instead of looking at them from the viewpoint of *indigenous roots*. We cannot approve of the narratives of those scholars who emphasize the high cultural heritage and assume that those who write in Shahmukhi (Persian script) are the real 'Muslim' Punjabis.

Root and Route

In this study, Punjabi Muslim social structure, religious ethos, and practice (as recorded in the text of *Hir Waris*) have been explored in the social and cultural contexts of Punjab. *Hir Waris* is a popular literary document about the medieval Punjabi Muslims who *lived* Islam in their *own* vernacular way.[10] Thus instead of understanding them solely via the standardized Islamic *route*, I have also tried to understand them through their own *roots*, i.e. the historically evolved indigenous cultural canvas of Punjab.[11] As stated by Metcalf, 'Islam in India has found its own expression in both local and cosmopolitan contexts'; and both these levels have 'shaped Muslim religious thought and practice'.[12] Nevertheless, the local context is indispensable for studying the Muslims of the diverse regions of India. The converted Muslims inheriting their Rajput/tribal/Jat legacies were different from Arabs, Turks, Persians, Afghans and even Mongols who had migrated to northern India at different points of time. Hence, it is suggested that the 'outsider' Muslims and Indian Muslims of various tribes had not yet reached a stage of homogeneous culture. They had their own distinctive history, culture, dialects, and literature.[13] The sense of roots in terms of caste, clan, and village (equivalent to a *des* or *vatan* or country) was so strongly prevalent in Punjab in medieval times that, for instance, Hir during her first meeting with Ranjha on the shores of the river Chenab, asks, 'What is your caste and country (*vatan*) and after what clan are you known.'

Speaking from the viewpoint of vernacular identity of Punjabi Muslims (or for that matter of the Hindus and the Sikhs), the root vision of identity stands in opposition to the homogenizing project of the route approach to the identity question. The promotion of a universal Muslim identity is a bid for culture as a system—a self-enclosed totality. Such an agenda proceeds by the elimination of those vernacular or indigenous customs and habits that do not fit the monolithic model of a Muslim/Islamic community—a model that, in anthropological parlance, 'constitutes' a Muslim, and does not 'dissolve'[14] him or her. Instead of identifying, historicizing and emplotting the divergent vernacular profiles of Muslims, the route approach reduces them all to an imagined monolithic community across the world. Critiquing the 'genetic fallacy' involved in this approach, Eaton states, '. . . many theorists of the nineteenth and twentieth centuries assumed that each civilization's qualities were stamped on it at the moment of its birth and persisted throughout all times. Such a reductive and ahistorical approach attributed special significance to a civilization's place of origin, for only there could it be constructed as truly indigenous and hence genuinely authentic.'[15]

Let it be understood that the people of Punjab, in view of their respective Great Religious Traditions and their historically evolved common indigenous culture, constituted a pluralistic–cultural Punjabi whole, not a multi-communitarian society ridden with socio-cultural conflicts. It is in this holistic space that cultural praxis of the people of Punjab took birth and was manifested in sacred spaces (*khanqahs, gurdwaras*), at fairs and festivals (*Jarag Da Mela, Chhapar Da Mela, Jagravan Di Roshni, Haider Shaikh Da Mela, Hola-Mohalla, Baisakhi, Teeian, Gugga Naumi, Basant, Lohri, Diwali*, etc.), in specific literary genres (such as *qissa, kafi* and *baramaha*), in folk religion (the worship of local tiny brick-mausoleums, i.e. *marhis*, of Sitla Devi, Sanjhi Devi, Gugga Pir, Khwaja Khizar, and of elders, i.e *jathere* and ancestors i.e. *pittar*), in veneration of folk heroes (like Raja Rasalu, Dulla Bhatti), in folk dance (*giddha, bhangra, luddi, jhumar, samin*), and in folk art (like *phulkari*).

The identity of a society is ultimately rooted in a more or less invariant network of social relations and is developed and sustained by and through human interaction.[16] The route approach suppresses this network and interaction, and ignores the needs, aspirations and ambitions one has by virtue of being grounded in indigenous space, a concrete historical reality.

Let me illustrate how the route approach serves as a foundation to those who construct the historiography of divergent socio-cultural patterns of Muslims from the viewpoint of the grand narrative of Islamic civilization. Ishtiaq Husain Qureshi in his *The Muslim Community of the Indo-Pak Subcontinent* tends to maintain the universal and normative Islamic character of various local Muslims, instead of presenting their pluralistic and specific vernacular identities. First, he imagines and hence assumes that when groups were converted to Islam, the primordial caste and tribal associations were immediately severed. Second, he underscores Urdu as the *lingua franca* of all Muslims and hence sets aside the historical existence of the vernacular languages and dialects. Third, he believes that the Indo-Muslim culture remained basically Islamic and mostly Islamic and Central Asian in spirit. Fourth, to him at all times the Muslims of the subcontinent were resolute in refusing to be assimilated to the local population and made conscious efforts to maintain their distinct character.[17]

Similarly Abdur Rashid, a protagonist of the 'route'-oriented historiography laments that Indian contact 'adversely affected the spiritual purity and homogeneity of the Muslim community which is essentially monolithic in religion and egalitarian in its social structure'. To him Islam in India 'fell *a victim* to the creeping influence of Hindu caste system'.[18]

Such historiography does not appreciate the dialectical evolution of culture. Its protagonists seem to believe in the 'total' negation of a thesis and do not believe in synthesis. They also exclude from their craft of history writing the existence of the vernaculars spoken by Muslims, and discount the indigenous cultural profiles of South Asian Muslims. Thus the historiographic discourse disentangles Punjabi Muslims from their local cultural moorings and ignores their space-specific sensitivities or what in ethnography is called their 'essential ways of life'. S. Nurul Hasan drops some methodological hints in this connection, when he warns, us that the 'understanding of the significant trends of historical change in the country [India] would remain sadly incomplete unless the details are studied at the regional level'.[19] Thus the root approach offers important opportunities to a social historian to appreciate the local contexts of Indian Muslim belief and action that transcend normative expectations, as is evident from *Hir Waris*, the folk text under study.

Culture and its Communication

A study of a folk legend like that of *Hir* enables us to draw a distinction between the conscious projection of a culture and its spontaneous expression. The former tends to cause communitarian biases and boundaries in the craft of writing history. Unlike the spontaneous expression of culture, it remains remote from the lived experience. It needs to be realized that both the nature of the source material selected for the construction of the said craft and the language of narration play a vital role in constituting the craft of history writing and its ideological nature. Due to the manipulation of these two factors, the true holistic cultural picture of a society becomes distorted and splits into sectarian cultures. As a matter of fact, the way the phenomenon of socio-cultural fusion evolved in the land of the five rivers is something a student of cultural history discovers by using people's sources rather than the *non-people* sources of the archives. Protagonists of the history of subalterns like Antonio Gramsci (AD 1891–1937) consider it essential to do away with the prejudice that philosophy is the exclusive domain of 'systematic philosophers'. Gramsci suggests the necessity of projecting through history that all men are 'philosophers'. For that purpose he looks upon folklore as a source of history.[20] To him folklore needs to be studied as 'view of the world', a reflex of the life of the common folk. The lived experiences of the folk are not necessarily in harmony with the official or elite view. Notwithstanding the fact that in folklore or folk culture there might be conservative tendencies, one also observes a creative and progressive series of innovations, often spontaneously determined by the forms and conditions of life and in contradiction to (or just different from) the cultural characteristics of the hegemonic class and its allies.[21] Stuart Blackburn, therefore, rightly considers folklore a 'source of identity and pride' for small groups, families, and even region.[22] Autonomous tendencies reflected in popular culture also make folklore an 'ideological discipline'.[23]

The study and analysis of folklore, hence, may help us construct a new discourse in the writing of the history of the communities of the Punjab—a discourse which reveals the outlook of the people, different from that which a professional historian appreciates through elite and religious routes. *Hir Waris* treasures a community memory of Punjab people. It is their collective document, their own expression about themselves, just as Richard C. Temple asserts that the folk tale is the 'true reflex of consciousness of the community'.[24] The legend is a felt literature, true as well as real, an unbiased and unadulterated expression of the self of the community. Cultural history based on such material becomes the history of the entire community in which the common folk are seen as people, one united group, and as human beings in their kinship relationships. It is also a history in which people are historians as well as a part of history, telling their own story in their own words—every person's history for each person to read.

Scholars have either projected Waris Shah as a master of the genre of qissa or have reproduced the society as reflected in his *Hir*.[25] But their reproduction does not seem to be well grounded historically. Perhaps these scholars overlook the fact that folklore and history are organically linked. Even when they construct a class-discourse during the course of their analysis of *Hir* within the milieu of feudalism, they do not take into account the autonomous identity of 'the religious' rebelling ideology of the sufis and the Sikh gurus and bhaktas who elicited tremendous response from the people of Punjab. Nor do these scholars situate their analysis within the boundaries of historically evolved Punjabi cultural fusion—fusion being distinct from composite culture or the co-existence of Hindu culture, Muslim culture and Sikh culture. The study of *Hir Waris* reveals the fact that the elite discourse of composite culture tends to undermine the phenomenon of the Punjabi identity of Muslims/Sikhs/Hindus. It appears that by and large studies on *Hir* have proceeded from pre-conceived conclusion to data. In such studies deduction predominates, which means that an analysis proceeds from a general theory to facts, which are examined in accordance with a set of postulates. What is being suggested is that in the analysis of a folk tale like *Hir*, one can use only the inductive method, and proceed from data/evidence to conclusion.

The objective of historical research is to determine the historically evolved meaning and significance of the legend of Hir, rather than to establish the legitimacy of pre-determined concepts. It is equally important to discover the historical conditions in which such a cultural text originated and why it has gone so deep into people's minds and hearts. The love tale of Hir and her struggle against patriarchy constitute the constants or an old element in Punjabi society, history, and literature. It ceases, therefore, to be a 'simple' story of 'the folk or savages', once it is studied in the historical perspective of the fifteenth century when it is said to have happened, or was made a piece of folk literature in the seventeenth and eighteenth centuries by qissa-kars such as Damodar Gulati, Waris Shah, and others. The legend becomes history told through a qissa. It no longer remains 'only' a folk tale. Rather its versification by different qissa-kars makes it a generic story, a cultural narrative of Punjabi society, particularly of Punjabi Muslims. Waris Shah complicates and modulates the legend, weaving in social life through the institutions of the joint family, marriage, kinship relationships and that of the patriarchs and priestly class as hegemonic socio-religious forces.

The selection of *Hir* as an unconventional source of social history is a methodological departure, particularly when the intervention of political ideologies in writing a history of the people has been active for a long time and second, when the semantic of culture has shifted from diversities to differences. In view of the latter, we have been offered the grand or meta history of 'Muslims', 'Hindus' and 'Sikhs' constructed by their respective ideologues or by those who identify these communities with specific geographical boundaries/spaces or routes. Under the spell of the discourse of 'the other', attempts are being made to situate the divergent religious communities in diametrically opposed categories. As a result, in their research pursuits, a section of historians and social scientists are drifting away from the history of, for instance, Punjabi Muslims who shared a common and indigenous socio-cultural space with Punjabi Hindus and Sikhs. A strong desire among folk to save their own socio-cultural life and space is yet to be realized by historians of social history. They must express their concern for people's literature. It has always been in danger of extinction because people are not in power.[26] Let me conclude this section with the following statement of Barker:

> One of the central arguments of cultural studies is that culture is a domain in which competing meanings and versions of the world have fought for ascendancy . . . cultural studies have sought to play a deconstructive and de-mystifying role by pointing to the fabricated character of cultural texts. It has aimed to highlight the myths and ideologies in texts in the hope of producing subject positions, and real subjects, who are enabled to oppose subordination. Deconstructing texts helps us to understand how they work and in particular to be aware of their political implications. Thus we are enabled to grasp the culturally constructed nature of the descriptions that regulate our understanding of the world and their possible consequences in terms of politics, values and purposes.[27]

A Cultural Bearer from Below

Waris Shah exemplifies the vernacular perceptions of Punjabi Muslims and thus counters those who consider them as exclusive or alien, or look upon them as a monolithic group. Hence, it may be premised that *Hir* is the most remarkable cultural narrative constructed by an 'insider'. It treasures a number of Islamic references, but the 'Islamic' profile of Punjabi Muslims is not the major concern. No such concern is in fact available in the entire medieval Punjabi literature. *The Lay of Nadir Shah* may be cited here as an illustration. It is said to have been versified round 1740–50 by Najabat just after the invasion of Nadir Shah in 1739. Najabat was a contemporary of Waris Shah. Although the poet is 'Muslim', his references to the *Ramayana* and the *Mahabharata* spontaneosly travel in the narration of the war between Nadir Shah and the Mughals, testifying to the existence of a historically evolved cultural fusion in Punjab, not simply the 'influence' or 'impact' of Hindu environment on the Muslims and vice versa. Najabat is the product of this fusion. What I also wish to suggest is that in Punjabi vernacular qissas and vars the focus is on the characters, situation, events and legends: religion is not the issue.

Waris Shah's *Hir* is a significant literary construction mainly for four reasons. First, it was written when the Muslim (here it also means medieval) political domain had begun to shrink; second, when Bulleh Shah (1680–1758) in his *kafis* had condemned the orthodox religious formalism of the Hindus and Muslims, and when Ali Haider (1690–1785) in his *siharfi* had expressed his anguish over the failure of the Mughal state to confront Nadir Shah; third when both the Mughal and Afghan claims to Punjab were being successfully challenged by the people of Punjab under the leadership of the Khalsa; and fourth, during this period Shah Waliullah (1703–62) of Delhi attempted to revive Islamic orthodoxy. An in-depth study of *Hir Waris* crystallizes the anti-thesis between civilization and culture or between route and root. Civilization denotes a *universal*, eminently *transferable*, process of growing mastery over barbarism, stressing human capabilities rather than specific works; culture refers to a *particular* pattern of life, ultimately unimportable, with a focus on specific 'meaningful' historical *products* rather than on general capabilities.[28] Thus Waris Shah seems to suggest that the problem of characterizing a local community crops up when its communitarian configuration—in terms of the religious nomenclatures—is allowed to prevail upon the indigenous cultural character that history has conferred on it. Such a vernacular character and identity had been a matter of anxiety for pan-Islamic intellectuals such as Shaikh Ahmad Sirhindi (1564–1624) and Shah Waliullah (1702–63), protagonists of a single and standardized Islamic civilization. In one of his letters, Shaikh Ahmad Sirhindi writes:

> To seek help from idols and demons for the cure of diseases and other miseries, which are prevalent amongst Muslims on one pretext or the other is another name for *shirk* and heresy. Praying for the fulfilment of one's need to the chiselled or unchiselled stone is solely an act of *kufr* and a denial of the existence and overlordship of the Almighty. . . . Showing respect to the sacred days of Hindus and performing the ceremonies prevalent among them are nothing but *kufr*. For instance, during the Dewali of the *kafirs*, the ignorant amongst the Muslims, particularly the women, perform the ceremonies of *kufr*. They celebrate it like their own *id* and send presents to their daughters and sisters like the *kafirs* and *mushriks*. They colour their pots during these days like

kafirs, fill them with red rice and send them as presents. They attach much importance and weight to this season. . . . Similarly women [Muslim] keep fast after the names of Pirs and Bibis.[29]

We must note that socio-cultural diversities prevalent among Muslims gave birth to contending discourses on the social meaning of Islamic beliefs. The theologians advocated the cause of universal or monolithic conception of the Muslim community, whereas the sufis did not entertain such a view. The contention between the two schools of thought had its bearings on the political issues in the seventeenth and eighteenth centuries. While the state, for instance in the context of Akbar's religious open-endedness, pursued a policy of communitarian harmony, an influential section of theologians did not favour it. Among the latter, Shaikh Ahmad Sirhindi, who claimed to be the *mujaddid* (the renewer of Islam), was the most prominent. He looked upon Hinduism and Islam as mutually exclusive. He was critical of the Mughal state for its cosmopolitan culture. As a reformer of Islam, he launched a vigorous campaign to persuade the Mughal authorities to follow the policies befitting an Islamic state. He urged rulers and nobles to impose the poll tax on non-Muslims, to permit cow slaughter, to remove non-Muslims from administrative offices and to impose *shariat* in every way.[30] His follower Shah Waliullah adopted the same line in the eighteenth century. Conversely, the sufis were 'accommodationists'. It is significant to note that in view of the pluralistic composition of the Muslims of India, the idea of universal or unified Muslim identity was not historically viable. It was plurality that conditioned the relation of the Mughal state with Muslim religious life.[31]

In view of this communitarian discourse on the definition and character of a particular religious community *vis-à-vis* that which emerges in *Hir Waris*, an attempt has been made to recognize that Islamic civilization is not a monolithic entity.[32] The study of folklore suggests a 'diffuse plurality of communities' that differ over time and space.[33] My study also shifts from 'generalization' to 'particularization' in writing the socio-cultural history of a community. As the canvas is wide in extent, deep in historical time, wide in magnitude, and kaleidoscopic and complex in nature, it is difficult to analyse all those aspects on which *Hir Waris* throws light. A qissa, as we are aware, is all-embracing and as such presents a comprehensive view of a society, even when its direct purpose is not to construct these aspects. Therefore I have taken up a few conspicuous socio-religious features of medieval Punjabi Muslim society that emerge in the text.

SUGGESTIONS

The multi-directional and multi-dimensional historical account of Punjabi culture and its identity needs to be woven into a historical sequence, chronologically as well as thematically. The said account also needs to be substantiated by a critical study of data supplied by a variety of archival and non-archival sources. The discourse deduced from these sources further needs to be directed in favour of conflict-resolution, ultimately aimed at presenting a systematic and creative exposition of Punjabi or indigenous identities of the 'Muslims/Sikhs/Hindus'. It would be helpful in building an argument that along with the 'constructed' geographical and religious boundaries, the historically evolved Punjabi identities also exist. They cut across the notion of the communitarian identities, which have a limit. The proposed construction (of Punjabi identities in a historical perspective) supports and substantiates the fact that the people of Punjab had a common cultural space of their folk religion, myths, legends, and literary traditions. However, this space is complex and cannot be appreciated easily, particularly by the outsider.[34]

Grounded in the historical cultural fusion, the concept of Punjabi community means the primacy of Punjabi identities over all others, caste, community, and political. Punjabi communities and their identities came into being historically, having transcended these standardized boundaries. The people of Punjab evolved a multi-layered community after centuries of common joint endeavour, struggle, dreams, hopes, and aspirations. Punjabi identity began to reflect itself in the collective response of the people of

Punjab to the ideas and the movements launched by their protagonists—jogis, sufis, bhaktas, and Sikh gurus who spoke against parochialism and patriarchy. Baba Farid's *dohas*, the Sikh Gurus' *bani*, Shah Husain's and Bulleh Shah's *kafis*, Waris Shah's *Hir* and Shah Muhammad's *Jangnama Hind-Punjab* help us appreciate the nature of Punjabi identity. The Punjabi identity of Muslims, Sikhs and Hindus crystallized, first, in the collective struggle of the people of Punjab (particularly in the eighteenth century under the leadership of the Khalsa) against oppression and invasions, second, in their full-fledged participation in the Khalsa Raj established by Ranjit Singh (1799–1839), and, third, in their armed resistance to the British in the two battles, (mis)characterized as Anglo-Sikh Wars.

Apart from the aforesaid creative and collective discourses of Punjabi identity, a number of discourses of fission—imperialistic, Hindu-centric, Sikh-centric and Muslim-centric—also emerged predominantly in the post-Ranjit Singh period. Since then, divergent academic methodologies, theories, techniques, and ideologies have been actively involved in the characterization of Punjabi culture. Most of these discourses attempt to marginalize, nay, negate each other. As a result, the people of Punjab find themselves situated in the bottlenecks of religious, provincial, and sovereign-state boundaries. The minority–majority syndrome marks a new social construction or rehabilitation.

In this study, I have used the *Hir Waris* edited by Jit Singh Sital and published by Navyug Publishers, Delhi, in the second edition of 1973. For the English version, I have relied upon *The Love of Hir Ranjha* by Sant Singh Sekhon, published by Punjab Agriculture University, Ludhiana, 1978. Only the numbers of the original verses of the Punjabi text (in Gurmukhi script) quoted in this study are recorded in the footnotes. For the Punjabi verses, the reader may consult the text I have used. Throughout this book, I mean by *Hir Waris*, in italics, the name of the text. Hir, not in italics, is the proper name. All Indian-language words, when they first occur in the text, are italicized. If used subsequently, they are printed in normal type-face. The reader may remember that in many texts, creative and critical, Hir has been also spelled as 'Heer'.

NOTES

1. For the historiographic implications of linguistic and religious identity see Richard M. Eaton, ed., *India's Islamic Traditions, 711–1750,* New Delhi, 2003, pp. 10–11.
2. Bipan Chandra, *Communalism in Modern India,* New Delhi, 1992, p. 13.
3. Satish Chandra, *Essays on Medieval Indian History,* New Delhi, 2003, p. 35.
4. Ibid., p. 52.
5. Ibid., p.53.
6. Ibid., p.36.
7. Paul R. Brass, *Language, Religion and Politics in North India,* Delhi, 1974, p. 407.
8. Kenneth W. Jones, *Socio-Religious Movements in British India,* New Delhi, 1999, p. 121.
9. Mohinderjit Singh, ed., *Punjabi Sabiachar: Pehchan Te Shakti* Ludhiana, 1998, pp. 30–63 and 122–36.
10. In his conversation with Bruce B. Lawrence, Dr. Tawfik Abdullah identified three Islams: 'the popular Islam which anthropologists are fond of studying, mostly as curious spectators; the public Islam with which political scientists, journalists and policy makers identify, mostly as adversaries; and the academic Islam in which Orientalists delight, whether as art historians, linguists, or religion scholars, each studying artifacts esteemed by their guild'. Bruce B. Lawrence, *Shattering the Myth: Islam Beyond Violence,* Karachi, 2000, p. 4.
11. In cultural studies the route refers to the path 'from the place of origin to elsewhere', and 'this place by default must be "outside", "peripheral", or "marginal" to the "core", "centre", or "birthplace" '. By 'roots' we refer to multiple local contexts. See Peter Gottschalk, 'Mapping Muslims: Categories of Evolutionary Difference and Interaction in South Asia', in Imtiaz Ahmad and Helmut Reifeld, eds., *Lived Islam in South Asia: Adaptation, Accommodation and Conflict,* Delhi, 2004, pp. 12–13.
12. Barbara Daly Metcalf, 'Approaches to Indo-Muslim Studies', in Louis A. Jacob, *American Understanding of India: A Symposium,* New Delhi, 2001, p. 49.
13. A. Yusuf Ali, 'Social and Economic Life in Medieval India', *Islamic*

Culture, 4 April 1930, p. 210. Bernard S. Cohn, *India: The Social Anthropology of a Civilization*, New Delhi, 2000, p. 67.

14. Claude Levi-Strauss makes us appreciate the meaning of 'dissolve': 'I am not blind to the fact that the verb "dissolve" does not in any way imply the destruction of the constituents of the body subjected to the action of another body. The solution of a solid into a liquid alters the disposition of its molecules. It also often provides an efficacious method of putting them by so that they can be recovered in case of need and their properties be better studied. The reductions I am envisaging are thus legitimate or indeed possible', provided the 'phenomenon subjected to reduction must not be impoverished'. Claude Levi-Strauss, *The Savage Mind*, Chicago, 1969, p. 247.
15. Richard M. Eaton, ed., *India's Islamic Traditions, 711–1750*, p. 11.
16. Zygmunt Bauman, *Culture as Praxis*, New Delhi, 2000, p. 87.
17. Ishtiaq Husain Qureshi, *The Muslim Community of the Indo-Pak Subcontinent (610-1947)*, Delhi, 1985, pp. 48, 101, 111–12.
18. Abdur Rashid, *History of the Muslims of Indo-Pakistan Sub-Continent (1707-1806)*, Lahore, 1997, pp. 1–17.
19. S. Nurul Hasan, 'Medieval Punjab', in Harbans Singh and N. Gerald Barrier, eds., *Essays in Honour of Dr. Ganda Singh*, Patiala, 1976, p. 73.
20. Antonio Gramsci, *Selections from the Prison Notebooks*, ed. and tr. Quintin Hoare and Geoffrey Nowell Smith, London, 1971, p. 323.
21. For theoretical insights see Alastair Davidson, 'Gramsci, the Peasantry and Popular Culture', *The Journal of Peasant Studies*, vol. 11, no. 4, 1984.
22. Stuart Blackburn, *Print, Folklore, and Nationalism in Colonial South India*, Delhi, 2003, p. 4.
23. Vladimir Propp, *Theory and History of Folklore*, tr. Ariadna Y. Martin and Richard P. Martin, Manchester, 1984, p. 1.
24. Richard C. Temple, *The Legends of Punjab*, Patiala, 1963, vol. I, p. 1
25. Sutinder Singh Noor reviews the different discourses on *Hir Waris* in *Heer Waris –Jagat Te Jugat*, New Delhi, 1999, pp. 7–16; also see Jaswinder Kaur, *Heer Waris Shah Da Chehan Vigianik Adhian*, Delhi, 1988, pp. 15–34.
26. Barbara Christian, 'The Race for Theory', in Linda Kauffmann, ed., *Gender and Theory*, Oxford, 1989, pp. 225–36.

27. Chris Barker, *The Sage Dictionary of Cultural Studies*, New Delhi, 2004, p. 41.
28. J.G. Merquior, *The Veil and the Mask: Essays on the Culture and Ideology*, London, 1979, p. 42.
29. As quoted in S.A.A. Rizvi, *Muslim Revivalist Movements in Northern India in the Sixteenth and Seventeenth Centuries*, Delhi, 1993, pp. 252–4.
30. For detail see Yohanan Friedmann, *Shaykh Ahmad Sirhindi: An Outline of his Thought and a Study of his Image in the Eyes of Posterity*, Montreal and London, 1971, p. 73.
31. Ira M. Lapidus, *A History of Islamic Societies*, Cambridge, 1989, pp. 461–3.
32. Richard M. Eaton, *Essays on Islam and Indian History*, Delhi, 2000, p. 12.
33. Ibid.
34. N.Gerald Barrier, 'Sikh Identity in Historical and Contemporary Perspective', in Pashaura Singh and N. Gerald Barrier, eds., *Sikh Identity: Continuity and Change*, New Delhi, 2001, p. 34.

CHAPTER 3

The Cultural Confluence in Context

> Secular scholars have too often acquiesced to the conflation of religion to nation. For instance, the electronic version of the *Encyclopedia of Religion*—the standard work for historians of religion—contains a synoptic outline table of contents that list a number of regions and, with each, a selection of religions supposedly of that area. Despite the fact that India represents the third most Muslim-populated nation in the world, Islam does not appear under the heading of 'Indian religions', the implication being that Muslims do not practice an Indian religion. Islam, according to the outline listing, is a Middle Eastern religion, identified as such, one assumes, by its genetic origin . . . this bias privileges the *routes* of a group rather than its *root.*
>
> PETER GOTTSCHALK[1]

> Diversity is less a function of the isolation of groups than of the relationships which unite them.
>
> CLAUDE LÉVI-STRAUSS[2]

In order to understand the open-ended social, cultural, and religious profile of Punjabi Muslims as narrated in *Hir* by Waris Shah, it is necessary to read the following short sketch of the social landscape as it had evolved.

PRE-MEDIEVAL PUNJAB

The advent of the Aryans in the second millennium BC and that of Islam and its spread from the eighth to the fourteenth century, the emergence of Sikhism in the fifteenth–sixteenth century, and the establishment of the Khalsa Raj in the eighteenth century, are generally the significant pre-colonial historical milestones in the development of Punjabi society and culture. These references help scholars constitute paradigms for constructing the history of cultural *differences* (conflict) as well as of *diversities* (conflict-resolution). In other words, these references are projected either as ruptures that tend to underscore 'parochial' great socio-religious traditions or interconnected phases of Punjab culture, which speak of cultural exchange and conflation. My reading of the Punjab cultural matrix reveals that it evolved through the process of socio-cultural reciprocity among the divergent forces, both insider and outsider. The boundaries of Punjab shifted in the past. In the Vedic period, Punjab was known as Sapt Sandhu.[3] When the Greeks occupied it, they called it Pentapotamia.[4] Punjab was also styled Taki, derived from the tribe of Taks or Takkas who were once the undisputed lords of Punjab.[5] Every historical change in the political setup resulted in a concomitant change in the territorial boundaries of Punjab. It is suggested, therefore, that the etymology of the term Punjab (land of five rivers) is 'not meant to be taken literally' because when the term 'became current in the reign of Akbar in the late sixteenth century, it was synonymous with the province of Lahore and, therefore, actually smaller than the area lying between the rivers Indus and Sutlej',[6] i.e. the area which actually corresponds with the etymology of the term Punjab. The lack of a single geographical identity called into being a number of prefixes to denote a particular Punjab: 'Mughal' Punjab, 'cis-Sutlej' Punjab, 'trans-Sutlej' Punjab, 'British' Punjab, 'West' Punjab and 'East' Punjab'. The main cultural stream includes those outside its geographical boundaries, but who have close proximity with the Punjabis, for instance, the people of Hazara district of North-West Frontier Province, of Kashmir, Sind, Rajasthan and Balochistan.[7]

Obviously there was no one-to-one correspondence between the evolutionary growth of Punjabi culture and political boundaries.[8] History conferred on Punjab cultural infusions from Greeks, Parthians, Shakas, Kushanas and many other 'outsiders'. There were inter-racial and inter-religious marriages, producing mixed castes and this contributed to diluting the rigidity of the caste structure and ideology. Sanskrit was no longer popular in this region. Religion and philosophy ceased to be the monopolistic domain of the

Brahmans. Religious standards and conventions also underwent change. People no longer followed the old cults of Vedic sacrifices. The cult of the burial mounds, Buddhist *stupas*, Scythian graves and terraced sepulchres triumphed over the orthodox religion of Brahmanical altars and shrines.[9] The fusion of so many foreign races would not have been feasible under the Brahmanical caste scheme based upon birth.[10] The diet and attire of the people of Punjab was also influenced by cultural exchange and fusion. A large number of Iranian and Chinese plants, vegetables, and fruits (the pistachio, walnut, pomegranate, peach, apricot, coriander, shallot, garlic, onion, asafoetida, oak-galls, cumin, almond, fig, watermelon and carrot) crept into the dietary habits of the people. The food habits of the people of Punjab did not conform to the orthodox Vedic norms. They ate the flesh of pig, fowl, cow, donkey, camel, and sheep; they drank the milk of the animals. The Shakas introduced a fad for excessive drinking. Distilling and selling wine gradually became popular to the extent of forming a new caste named Kalal associated with this profession. These traits reflect the addition of nomadic Asiatic elements to the population of Punjab.[11] Many Punjabi castes are said to owe their origin to the Scytho-Iranian tribes, an important tribe being the Arjunayana. Arjun stands for white colour. It appears that the modern survival of this tribal name is Kapur, which also signifies whiteness. The Virk Jats are said to owe their origin to the Virka tribe. Similarly, the term *thakura*, which implies the ideas of nobility and stands for the Rajputs in Punjab, is related with the Tokhi caste found in the north-west. The name of Sikka caste is the reminiscent of 'Scythian'. The Khatri sub-caste of Sahni reminds one of Sahanushahi, the title of the Kushanas. The Solgi and Solkah Jats of Multan region, and the Sud, Sudgi, and Suri Khatris of Amritsar, Ludhiana, and Macchiwara regions represent the remnants of Sogdians who were Iranians in race and speech. Khanna, another prominent caste of the Khatris, represents the Khionites, a Central Asiatic tribe of Iranian affinity.[12] It was during this period that people of Punjab wore the *kurtau* (coat), *sukhthana* (trousers), boots, and belts. In military technology the metal ring armour, the long sword and pike, the horseshoe, and the stirrups were introduced.

Professional and mercenary soldiers had been spreading and growing.[13]

This brief survey reveals that the society of Punjab was free of Brahmanical hegemony, particularly the taboo of pollution. On its cultural space several diverse races and cultures met and coalesced. Persians, Greeks, Parthians, Scythians, Kushanas and Huns came in an unending sequence. They created temporary upheavals, but each ethnic group contributed to the evolution of cultural fusion in Punjab.[14] The institutions generally associated with the Aryans—the Hindu king and his Brahman advisers—developed in the Ganga Valley to the east; and their influence over Punjab was far less than over the rest of India. The caste system and the Brahmanical rituals were strong in the towns and amongst the literary classes. In the villages, on the other hand, it was tribal feeling that remained powerful. Tribal solidarity came from joint ownership of the village, respect for military prowess rather than ceremonial sanctity, and customary tribal law, which owed more to the morality of kinship than to Brahmanical innovation.[15] In the *Mahabharata* Punjab is a land of irreligious inhabitants: 'One should not go to the Vahika in which the five rivers and the Indus as the sixth flow and which is excommunicated, as it were, by the Himalayas, by the Ganges, by the Yamuna and by the Sarasvati, and is devoid of true religion and cleanliness.'[16] Presenting a panoramic view of ancient Punjab, Buddha Prakash characterizes it thus:

> . . . this region not only played an important part in the history of India but also acted as the crossroads of many movements of culture, commerce and peoples in Asia. Thus it became a cockpit, a crucible and a confluence, in which there was an unending amalgamation of communities and cultures resulting in a broad, pragmatic, experimental and utilitarian outlook and a robust, clear-cut and comprehensive commonsense view, which cut at the root of all sorts of dogmas, conventions and conservatism.[17]

The Turks and the Delhi Sultanate

It was in this 'less Hinduized' region that Islam, and especially sufism, appeared.

The first lasting contact of this region with the Islamic world was established after the Turks founded the state of Ghazni in the heart of Afghanistan in AD 962. East of Ghazni lay the powerful Hindushahi kingdom of Ohind, which extended from Lamghan to the Chenab during the reign of Jaipal. The Hindushahis did not exercise sway over the whole of Punjab, but offered stubborn resistance to the Ghaznavid onslaught for half a century. Sultan Mahmud of Ghazni (998–1030), during the course of his several invasions,[18] realized the significance of Punjab for his larger designs on India. He formalized the annexation of Punjab in 1022 and struck a coin at Lahore, renamed Mahmudpur.[19] The Ghaznavid occupation of Punjab lasted for more than a century and half. Internal conflicts in the ruling family and the rising power of the Seljuqs however, prevented the former from consolidating their rule in Punjab. Not surprisingly, a confederacy of three local potentates ousted the Turkish garrisons from Hansi, Thanesar and Nagarkot (1043). Following in their footsteps, three local chiefs besieged Lahore for seven months, but without success.[20]

As Ghaznavid rule stabilized towards the close of the eleventh century, the governor of Punjab felt strong enough to penetrate deep into the northern plains. Fifty years later, the emergence of the Ghuri forced the Ghaznavids to leave Ghazni and fall back on Punjab. The latter continued a miserable existence till 1186, when it was annexed to the expanding Ghurid possessions. For the Ghaznavids, Punjab served as a base for raids deep into the Ganga plain,[21] and also a place of refuge when faced with hostile forces in Ghazni. By controlling the region, the Ghaznavids appear to have achieved one of their objectives, capture of the commerce between India and Afghanistan, Iran, and Central Asia.[22] Ghaznavid occupation created circumstances for cultural exchange between Punjab and lands lying to the west of the Indus.

Over three decades (1175–1206) Sultan Muizzuddin of Ghur and his generals annexed large parts of the Indo-Gangetic plain and laid the foundation of the Delhi Sultanate.[23] Immediately after the death of the Ghurid ruler (1206), the control of Punjab was contested by his three slave officers, Qutbuddin Aibak in Delhi, Tajuddin Yaldoz in Ghazni, and Nasiruddin Qubacha in Multan and Sind. Aibak (1206–10) took the initiative by occupying Lahore and marched up to Ghazni, but could not solve the dispute in his lifetime. His successor, Shamsuddin Iltutmish, secured a victory (1215–16) over Yaldoz and gained a precarious hold over Punjab, because the situation was complicated by the arrival of the fugitive Khwarizmian prince Jalaluddin Mangbarni, followed by a vast Mongol army under Chengiz Khan. It was only by 1228 that Iltutmish gained control over Punjab with a combination of vigorous military measures and clever diplomatic moves.[24] Iltutmish was credited with introducing several administrative institutions, yet the Delhi Sultanate failed to move on the path of consolidation for two reasons. On the one hand, a persistent conflict within the nobility resulted in political instability and factional conspiracies. On the other hand, the Mongol invasions posed a serious threat to the very existence of the Sultanate.

As a result of Mongol pressure,[25] the north-western boundary of the Sultanate receded from the Indus to the Chenab in 1239, the Ravi in 1241, and the Beas in 1257. Disgruntled princes and nobles sought Mongol assistance to achieve their ambitions. The sultans of Delhi were constrained to forego territorial expansion and divert their resources to check the Mongol advance. The most efficient commanders—Sher Khan Sunqar, Prince Sultan Muhammad and Ghazi Malik—were appointed to frontier outposts at Dipalpur, Multan, and Uch.[26] In 1260, Ghiasuddin Balban (who would be Sultan from 1266 to 1286) opened diplomatic channels with Halaku (the grandson of Chengiz Khan), while Jalaluddin Khalji permitted 4,000 Mongols to settle near Delhi. There were six Mongol invasions from 1296 to 1306, during which period Delhi was besieged on two occasions. Though the Mongols failed to capture the capital, the Delhi Sultanate appears to have been reconciled to the loss of west Punjab beyond Lahore, until the enthronement of the Tughluqs.

A new phase began with the enthronement of Jalaluddin Firuz Shah Khalji (1290–6) and continued to the death of Muhammad bin Tughluq (1351). The rulers attempted to establish a large, centralized and bureaucratic state. All political and military resources were channellized to achieve this objective. The Turkish domination of the state, which was the cause of much conflict in the ranks of nobility, was terminated once and for all. Recruitment to the various rungs of the bureaucracy was henceforth based on loyalty and efficiency, and not on ethnic identity.[27] The doors of the bureaucracy were thrown open to non-Turkish individuals, Indian and foreign. As a logical continuation of this trend, several individuals belonging to socially inferior groups—gardeners, barbers, weavers, distillers, cooks and slaves—were appointed to such high offices as the head of *diwan-i-wizarat* and as provincial governors. Similarly, foreign migrants and sufi families were assimilated into the bureaucracy.[28] This trend caused much heart-burn among those aristocratic families who had been serving the state for many generations. On the positive side, territorial expansion was revived on a massive scale. Vast areas in Rajputana, Malwa, Gujarat, and Maharashtra were annexed. Regular military expeditions were sent to the southern kingdoms, which were reduced to subjugation and forced to pay tribute in precious metals, slaves, horses, and elephants. The most significant change, however, was brought about in the agrarian economy. The area under cultivation was measured, the state share was expressed in cash, the farmers were obliged to sell half their produce at the price fixed by the state, and village level statistics were recorded on paper.[29] A special department was established to frame schemes for the promotion of agriculture. As state policy was based on healthy pragmatism, Muslim theologians were denied a say in these matters.

During the second half of the fourteenth century, the Delhi Sultanate implemented major socio-economic changes in the south-eastern and south-western Punjab. A large network of canals—from the Sutlej, Ghaggar, and Yamuna—was laid in the dry tracts of modern Haryana. New areas were brought under cultivation, winter crops were introduced, new villages were settled. Apart from Hissar Firoza and Firozabad, a number of urban centres emerged in Fatehabad, Firozabad, Tughluqpur, Jaunpur and Firozpur.[30] Urban growth was manifest in the construction of forts, palaces, tanks, markets, seminaries, mosques, and tombs. A network of canals was developed in the Multan region, when the waters of the Ravi and Beas were harnessed with the active collaboration of local elements.[31] With such positive developments under way, it was paradoxical that the authority of the Sultanate began to be eroded. During the reign of Firuz Shah Tughluq (1351–88), there was a reaction. Two military campaigns failed to recover Bengal, while no attempt was made to improve the organization of the army. In order to remove discontent among nobles, state offices were made hereditary. The local elements—chiefs and intermediaries—were freed from the state controls. A massive increase in the number of states-owned slaves placed a huge strain on the exchequer and sowed the seeds of political instability. Forces of orthodoxy recovered lost ground and began to influence the policies of the state.

During this severe internal crisis, the Sultanate suffered an invasion of unprecedented magnitude and ferocity. Amir Timur Gurgan, the ruler of Transoxiana (modern Uzbekistan and Tajikistan), occupied Afghanistan and sent his grandson Pir Muhammad with an army towards south-west Punjab. Pir Muhammad occupied Uch and besieged Multan, which was defended by Sarang Khan. Timur himself crossed the Indus on 20 September 1398, secured the submission of the inhabitants of Koh-i-Jud, and defeated Shihabuddin Mubarak Shah on the Jhelum. Moving east, he plundered the town of Talumba and overpowered Jasrath Khokhar on the Beas. He joined the army of Pir Muhammad, which had suffered owing to an epidemic among the horses. Timur did not allow his soldiers to plunder Ajodhan, as the shrine of Shaikh Fariduddin Ganj-i-Shakar sanctified the town. The inhabitants of Dipalpur, having struck with panic, fled to the fort of Bhatner. Rai Dulchin, the local chief, offered stiff resistance in which 10,000 defenders were killed. As the victims rushed towards Delhi, the inhabitants of intervening places—Fatehabad, Tohana, Kaithal, Samana, Asandi, Tughluqpur and Panipat—also fled to the capital for shelter. Entering Delhi on 8 December 1398, Timur occupied the fort of Loni and defeated a force of 10,000 soldiers, which was led by Mallu Iqbal Khan. Timur ordered the massacre of the 100,000 people who had been imprisoned during his march from the Indus to Jamuna. On 18 December 1398 he defeated an Indian army led by Sultan Nasiruddin Mahmud and Mallu Iqbal Khan. Timur failed to maintain discipline among his soldiers, who fell on the local populace and inflicted cruel atrocities.

After occupying the fort of Meerut, Timur entered the Doab and fell upon Haridwar. In spite of the fear and panic, the local chiefs mobilized their people—Hindus and Muslims—to offer a resolute opposition to the invader. During the course of his northward march through the Dun between the Shiwaliks and the Himalayan foothills, Timur was forced to fight as many as twenty battles. On 27 February 1399 he defeated the ruler of Jammu, who embraced Islam to display his submission.[32] Sikandar Shah, the ruler of Kashmir, had already offered to pay tribute along with the promise of allegiance. The invaders occupied Lahore, extracted a fine from the inhabitants, and captured Shaikha Khokhar who was put to death. Before leaving for Samarqand, Timur marked his sovereignty over north-western India with the appointment of Khizar Khan as governor of Lahore, Multan, and Dipalpur.

After the departure of Timur, the political stage in Punjab was dominated by two persons—first by Khizar Khan and then by Jasrath Khokhar. The former had his headquarters in Multan and appointed his nominees to administer various places in Punjab. Having gained considerable resources and political pretensions, he clashed with Mallu Iqbal Khan who remained in control of Delhi for seven years (1398–1405), because Sultan Nasiruddin Mahmud had voluntarily retired to Qanauj. When Mallu Iqbal Khan failed to recover Gwalior and Qanauj, he marched north to Samana and killed its administrator, Behram Khan. In a battle fought near Ajodhan (14 October 1405) by Mallu Iqbal Khan and Khizar Khan, the former was killed. Though Sultan Nasiruddin Mahmud was restored in Delhi, his authority did not extend to Punjab. On the other hand, Khizar Khan divided the province among his adherents—Qiwam Khan at Hissar Firoza, Bairam Khan Turkbacha at Sirhind and Zirak Khan at Samana and Sunam.[33] He frustrated the Sultan's attempt to recover part of southern Punjab. He led military expeditions to Doab and Mewat, besides organizing an unsuccessful siege of Delhi. Some time after the death of the Sultan, Khizar Khan defeated his successor Daulat Khan Lodi and thus laid the foundation (6 June 1414) of the Saiyyid dynasty, which ruled Delhi from 1414 to 1451. Punjab became an integral part of the Sultanate.

After military expeditions in Uttar Pradesh and Rajputana, the Sultan sent his son, Prince Muazzam, to consolidate the administration in the area between the Sutlej and Jammu. The imperial forces carried out punitive measures against such rebellious elements as Tughan Rais, relatives of the late Bairam Khan Turkbacha, and a self-styled Sarang Khan. The reign of Khizar Khan's successor Mubarak Khan (1421–34) saw the rebellion of Jasrath Khokhar, and the opposition of Bhatinda-based Faulad Turkbacha, while the former's Kabul-based ally Shaikh Ali also attracted the attention of contemporary chronicles.

This account of political developments will remain incomplete without a corresponding analysis of rural society and agrarian relations. That the ruling class and its allies thrived was due to a surplus extracted from the peasantry. The uppermost layer of the rural society was composed of the rural aristocracy—*rais, ranas* and *rawats*—which had descended from the hereditary feudal lords (*samants*) of the Rajput period and, owing to their possession of military resources, fought against the Turkish invaders in the late twelfth and early thirteenth century. In every village and hamlet, the peasants were represented by headmen, designated *khut* or *muqaddam*. These intermediaries collaborated with government functionaries to collect the land tax, but themselves enjoyed tax exemptions and several other socio-economic privileges.[34] During the thirteenth century, the sultans had left this class undisturbed because it (Delhi Sultanate) could not develop an efficient machinery to collect the land tax. It merely collected tribute or plunder from the dominant local elements represented by the rural aristocracy.

During the first of the fourteenth century, however, the Sultanate brought about fundamental changes in the system of agrarian taxation. The state share was determined on the basis of measurements of cultivated area, output, and prices. State-appointed revenue functionaries saw to the actual collection. The rural aristocracy was now superfluous and the village headmen were deprived of their traditional privileges. Since intermediaries were still indispensable, a new class of *chaudharis* was created from elements of both classes, aristocracy and village headmen, to collect the land tax from *parganas* or clusters of a hundred villages. The formerly dominant rural class suffered only a temporary setback, recovering much of its power in the second half of the fourteenth century. In the wake of political disintegration caused by Timur's invasions, the old rural aristocracy underwent a partial revival during the early fifteenth century.[35] It is in this context that the widespread rebellion of Jasrath Khokhar becomes understandable. This context is also relevant for us because the two protagonists in the legend of Hir and Ranjha belonged to the partially revived rural aristocracy.

The scale and intensity of Jasrath Khokhar's revolt constrains us to trace the history of his tribe from earlier times. Claiming a varying Rajput and Jat status, the Khokhars inhabited the valleys of the Jhelum and Chenab, particularly the districts of Jhang and Shahpur. In somewhat smaller numbers, they were found on the lower Indus and Sutlej.[36] In the beginning of the medieval period, the Khokhars joined hands with the local rulers in their struggle against the Turkish invaders. In 1009 they were a part of the Anandpal-led confederacy that fought Mahmud of Ghazni. In 1185, they assisted Khusro Malik (the last Ghaznavid ruler of Lahore) in besieging the fort of Sialkot, held by the Ghurids. Henceforth, the Khokhars aligned with the enemies of the Delhi Sultanate, invaders from the north-west and also disgruntled local officers. In 1205 they joined Rai Sal of the Salt Range in challenging the Ghaznavid occupation. They were suspected of having a hand in the assassination of Sultan Muizzuddin of Ghur. In 1221 Rai Khokhar Sankin gave his daughter in marriage to the fugitive Khwarazmian prince Jalaluddin Mangbarni and helped him against Nasiruddin Qabacha.[37] In 1245 a Khokhar chief Jaspal Sihra acted as guide for the Mangutah-led Mongols who had invaded Uch. The sultans in Delhi took serious note of the activities of the Khokhars and in 1247 Ghiasuddin Balban led a punitive expedition to the Salt Range. During the early years of his reign (1266–86), Balban undertook another expedition to the same region, which was subjected to complete devastation.

Three Khokhar chiefs—Sahij Rai, Gulchandra and Niju—played a significant role in the enthronement of Ghiasuddin Tughluq in Delhi.[38] In 1342 Gulchandra joined hands with Malik Halajun and killed Malik Tatar Khurd, Governor of Lahore. Taking advantage of the decline of the Sultanate in the wake of the death of Firuz Shah Tughluq, Shaikha Khokhar rose in revolt and even occupied (1394) Lahore. He adopted a submissive attitude towards Timur for a brief period. During his return journey through Lahore, Timur put Shaikha Khokhar to death and carried off his son, Jasrath Khokhar, as a prisoner to Samarqand.

On the death of Timur (1405), Jasrath Khokhar escaped to his native place and assumed the leadership of his tribe. A restless warrior and astute politician, he successfully intervened in a factional conflict in the ruling family of Kashmir, and grabbed some land belonging to the rulers of Jammu. Joining hands with the rebellious officer Tughan Rais, he overran territory up to the Sutlej.[39] It is not possible to record all his activities in chronological sequence, but one can discern the pattern of his objectives and moves. Time and again Jasrath Khokhar emerged from his stronghold at Tilhar,[40] 50 miles north of Sialkot, and carried out widespread depredations at various places in the fertile plains of Punjab: Jammu, Lahore, Dipalpur, Kalanaur, Gurdaspur, Jalandhar, Bajwara, Ropar, Ludhiana, and Sirhind. At each target, he expelled the officers appointed by Delhi and subjected the locality to plunder. Counter-insurgency measures—demolition of his fort at Tilhar (1422), reconstruction of the city of Lahore, the retreat of Shaikh Ali to Kabul and the frequent transfer of local officers—could prove only temporary setbacks for Jasrath Khokhar. Such was his resilience and determination that he managed to capture (1432) the Governor of Lahore, Malik Sikandar Tuhfa.[41] A myth about his invincibility came to be established in the minds of his contemporaries. Bahlol Lodi, deputed (1441) by Sultan Muhammad Shah as the Governor of Lahore and Dipalpur, preferred to befriend him instead of taking punitive action against him. Undoubtedly, Jasrath Khokhar dominated the political stage of Punjab at a time when the authority of the Delhi Sultanate was reduced to some isolated urban pockets. From 1420 to 1442, the Sultanate faced his resistance. Hir of the Siyal clan, who is said to have lived from 1425 to 1452 and fought against patriarchal repression, was a contemporary of Jasrath Khokhar. Though the contemporary chronicles are silent about this, the folk literature resounds with the social protest of Hir.

Islamic Fusion

The arrival of the Turks and establishment of the Sultanate in Delhi was a landmark in the social and cultural history of Punjab. With regard to conversion to Islam and its fusion in Punjab, four points need to be considered at this juncture.

First, conversion in the final analysis proved to be a kind of socio-cultural reciprocity between 'outsiders' and 'insiders'. What is being suggested is that conversion was neither hegemonic, nor religious in the strict sense. Initially, the conversion (if it can be termed so in the colonial sense) of the pastoral Jats of Punjab, who had been moving up from Sind into Multan between the seventh and eleventh centuries,[42] occurred in the second half of the thirteenth century. Before their conversion, these Jats had scarcely been integrated into the caste system, and were in the process of settling down as agriculturists.[43]

Second, unlike conversions to Christianity in the colonial period, medieval conversions to Islam were neither sudden nor imposed. There was a gradual process of spontaneous fusion of Islam. The shrine of Shaikh Farid, state patronage of the shrine, the charisma of the celebrated Chishti sufi, his *sajjada nishins* and their matrimonial alliances with the pastoral-cum-semi-agriculturist Jats, all played a significant role in converting the latter to a settled agrarian society, and in the process integrating them with Islam.[44] That the sufis/ pirs had a sacred status in Punjabi society is also evident from the folk literature such as *Hir Waris.*

Third, local sufis such as Shaikh Farid, Shah Husain, Bulleh Shah, and the sufi qissa-kars like Waris Shah, played a historic and non-antagonistic role in the diffusion and vernacularization of Islam among the masses rooted in a pastoral-cum-agrarian social structure. For a long span of time the immigrant military elite was the bearer of Islamic culture and had maintained a distance from the indigenous peasants.[45] Islam began to affect a large number of people only in the early modern era, the sixteenth to eighteenth centuries.

It may be argued that up to the rule of Khalsa Raj (1799–1839) under Ranjit Singh, the Muslims of the area were 'Punjabi' in culture, as is evident from an analysis of their social, religious, and cultural space. The qissa of *Hir* by Damodar Gulati and Waris Shah, the *kafis* of Shah Husain and Bulleh Shah, Shah Muhammad's *Jangnamah Hind-Punjab*, and Qadiryar's *Puran Bhagat*, all composed between 1600 to 1850, attest to a marked Punjabi disposition.

Fourth, at the subcontinental and the regional levels, there was a social fusion of settled agriculturists with pastoralists and shifting cultivators. The Delhi Sultanate, founded in the thirteenth century, encompassed a melting pot in which nomadic and sedentary societies fused. Generally speaking, nomadic pastoralists, committed to herding, have the military advantage over settled sedentary people. Extreme mobility was conferred by horse-riding. When circumstances required, a nomad could move to fresh pastures. Trade, which came naturally to nomads, also favoured, in the long run, exchanges with stable communities of peasants and artisans. Eaton illustrates this with the example of the pastoralists of the western Punjab who moved down to the plains in the hot dry months and returned to the *bar* and *thal* after the rains. This pattern created a symbiotic relationship between the pastoralists and cultivators in riverine area. The former, who would always need access to rivers to water their animals, could come into conflict with the latter. Nevertheless, for their grain pastoralists were obliged to depend upon the agriculture-based centres, apart from the rituals and belief structures of the riverine people.[46] Drawing a contrast between the steppe nomadism of Central Asia and settled agriculture in India, Andre Wink argues that these two modes of subsistence 'fused together in the eleventh to thirteenth centuries. . . . On the interface of frontier and settled society, at the very point where people, goods and precious metals were cut loose, in order to be mobilized, violence was endemic, and the transition between trading and raiding became fluid.'[47] However, in India the nomadism of Central Asia ceased to be true steppe nomadism. The Muslim Turks who entered India retained the military advantage of mounted archery, enhanced mobility, and a nomadic ancestry, but were 'already at one remove from nomadism'.[48] The confrontation and interaction between nomadic pastoralists and settled society was not a new phenomenon in the medieval period of Indian history, particularly its north-west frontier. We come across this phenomenon with the eruption of the Vedic Aryans in Punjab, then known as Sapt Sandhu.[49]

Turkish rule opened up Punjab to Iran and Central Asia, which at that time had come to share a place with Baghdad, Damascus, and Cairo as centres of Islamic culture and power. A new social composition began to be formed in Punjab because a large number of Persians, Turks, and Afghans began to settle here. But the higher administrative and command posts were the monopoly of the Turks, especially blood relatives of the Ghaznavid royalty.[50] The Turkish Muslims were steeped in Persian culture. The spirit of the Persian Renaissance had so prevailed upon their imagination that they recreated and revived as much Persian culture and tradition as possible. It is suggested that the period of the Turko-Persian empires (1000–1220) is to be regarded as the political expression of Persian ideals and includes the reigns of the Ghaznavid, Seljuq and Khwarazmian dynasties.[51] K.M. Ashraf states:

> At Ghazni—to which we may look for the source of political ideals of the sultans of Delhi—even the official titles of some of the departments were the same as those at the ancient Persian court; . . . in fact, the whole of the Ghaznavide monarchs and their character and function was in no way different from that of the ancient Persian Sassanians. In other respects this national Persian tradition found its best poetical expression in the celebrated epic of the *Shah-nama,* which was composed under the patronage of the Ghaznavide court. Herein the legendary heroes of ancient Persia live for ever in the immortal pages of a follower of Muhammad.[52]

Thus Turkish influence created a multi-faceted *Persian* scenario in Indian space, filtering down to the local levels of the multi-lingual population. But this was not one-way traffic. India's contribution to the Persian literature is considerable, and it is 'this Persian culture acclimatized to the Indian environment which came to be known as Indo-Persian culture'.[53] This culture, which reverberates even today in our day-to-day life, particularly in spoken language and in sufi-oriented music and songs, appeared in the eleventh and thirteenth centuries in Punjab and its vicinity.

In the evolving culture Central Asia too was conspicuous in many respects. Tribal values, a love of learning, commercial considerations, prospects of employment, and unsettled conditions, particularly caused by the Ghuzz and Mongol invasions, were factors that obliged people to move frequently between north-western India and Central Asia. Among them were some prominent families of Central Asian towns such as Bukhara, Samarqand, Nakhshab, and Muhmera. They not only supplied the personnel to the nascent Delhi Sultanate, but also planted the tradition of Muslim scholarship in India. Ghiasuddin Balban (1266–87), who was anxious to use the presence of these central Asian prominent families to augment his prestige in contemporary Asia, settled them in different localities and named their *muhallas* (exclusive residential localities) after their homes as Muhalla-i-Khwarazm Shahi, Muhalla-i-Atabeki, Muhalla- i-Samarqandi, and Muhalla-i-Khitai. The Central Asian immigrants soon acclimatized themselves to the Indian social milieu.[54] Many towns of Central Asia such as Aush, Jam, Suhraward, Gilan, Yasi, Bukhara, and Samarqand were the primordial space of mystic orders, and many important saints who introduced the sufi order in India migrated from Afghanistan, Central Asia, and Persia. Thus during the Sultanate period a new element with the most appeal among the rank and file was sufism. Sufis settled in numerous parts of India, and in Punjab they appeared in Uch, Multan, Dipalpur and other places. Among them, Muinuddin Chishti (Ajmer), Shaikh Farid (Ajodhan, Punjab), Bahauddin Zakariya (Multan, Punjab), Nizamuddin Auliya (Delhi), Sayyid Muhammad Gesudaraz (Gulbarga) and Shah Alam Bukhari (Gujarat), are the prominent names of the Sultanate period. Questioning the importance of formal rituals, prayer, and fasts, they placed emphasis on the true love of God.

The process of urbanization and the resultant social change that followed the establishment of Turkish political ascendancy helped transfigure the towns into cosmopolitan urban centres. The old towns underwent a significant demographic transformation due to the addition of Muslim colonies inhabited by immigrants from different Muslim lands. Obviously, a Muslim cultural mosaic appeared. Since these immigrants were urbanized, their contacts with the indigenous people enriched the urban culture. Lahore is a good example. It was the first city to diffuse its civilizing impact in the adjacent areas. The emergence of Lahore as a hub of culture, learning, and trade was facilitated by the flight of Khusrau Shah from Ghazni. He was one of the last descendants of Sultan Mahmud of Ghazni. Ghazni was seized by the Ghuzz Turks in AD 1153–4. Consequently, the elite (scholars, poets, artists, and rich merchants) of Ghazni and Khurasan took shelter in Lahore and the area around. Their arrival elevated the cultural stature of Lahore to that of Ghazni. The arrival of the Muslim elite in cities and towns facilitated the establishment of mosques, madrasahs, and khanqahs and the further progress of crafts and arts, because the slaves accompanying them were skilled artisans. The growth of urban centres in Punjab between Lahore, Uch, and Multan seems to have achieved international fame on account of the foreign trade. Many villages on the trade routes were transformed into towns. Merchants from Iran, Khurasan and Transoxiana facilitated the settlement and development of the entire region along the route from Multan. The villagers benefited by selling fodder and drinking water in pots to merchant caravans. Towns like Hansi, Hissar, and others expanded into cities.[55]

A brief account of language and literature will illuminate the socio-cultural milieu of the period in Punjab. The Turks contributed to birth and development of a new linguistic relationship between Iran and India, with the result that Punjabi 'gracefully accepted the impact of the Persian language and Persian poetry, and both the languages started acquiring a new status'.[56] It was in Punjab that contacts began between those who spoke Persian and those who spoke Hindawi (ancient Punjabi).[57] Masud, a court-poet of the Governor of Lahore, appointed by Sultan Mahmud of Ghazni, wrote extensively in Punjabi.[58] His poetry assumed the form of a *diwan* and three ancient genres of poetry, *baramaha* (the poet's calendar), *satvara* (the week), and *akhri* (the alphabet).[59] Masud is said to have been born in Lahore; and he is stated to have a tremendous affinity for his birth place. He writes: 'Lahore is my birth-place, I am far away from it. / Alas! Oh Lahore! no comfort or gaiety without you. / The memory of Lahore, of my friends and comrades haunts me, / God forbid that anyone should ever despise his friends and playmates and his home town.'[60]

Shaikh Farid and Guru Nanak were more cultural icons of Punjab than religious leaders. As cultural bearers, not as religious leaders as Grewal believes,[61] they contributed to the Punjabi language and literature. In the context of the reciprocity of languages, it is important to note that after the occupation of Delhi by Muhammad Ghori, a number of Muslims and Hindus from Lahore and other parts of north-western India, became acquainted with Persian and the admixture of Persian and Punjabi, and they began to move to Delhi in order to join the administration. The large-scale migration of the Indo-Afghans and Punjabis from Lahore to Delhi in the time of Qutbuddin Aibak, and more so in the reign of Iltutmish, influenced Khari Boli (the Hindi spoken in Delhi and its vicinities). With the passage of time Persian and Punjabi words and idioms became inextricably interwoven in the Hindi of Delhi and thus a new language, Urdu, came into being. Haryanvi also played a part in the process of formation of this new language.[62] It was during this period that the authors of love legend lived. A Muslim poet versified the romantic tragedy of Sassi-Punnun in Punjabi as early as AD 1123. The famous romance of Yusuf-Zulaikha was versified in Punjabi in the fifteenth century. These tragedies have been the favourite themes of Punjabi balladists and narrators since the rise of the Punjabi language.[63] Mohan Singh is of the view that Punjabi folk songs and folk poetry go back to the first period of the language, 850 to 1450, an era that partly covers the period of the Delhi Sultanate. He classifies Punjabi folk songs and folk poetry under nineteen heads.[64]

Thus the socio-cultural landscape of the Delhi Sultanate was dotted with jogis, sufis and bhaktas both of *nirguna* (without attributes, unconditioned) and *sarguna* traditions. There was mutual respect and harmony among them. They shared an ideology of non-conformism and were a counter-hegemonic force that defied existing divisions in the society. The earliest references to contacts between Hindus and Muslims are found in the medieval records pertaining to the khanqahs of the sufis. We hear of a Hindu being introduced to Shaikh Nizamuddin Auliya by a Muslim: 'This Hindu is my brother.'[65] The sufis had amicable relationship with the jogis, and both enjoyed the veneration and confidence of simple folk. The love legend of Hir–Ranjha testifies to this. In the popular imagination, sufi and jogi were identical. Both were detached, both practised renunciation of worldly possessions, both lived in a sort of trance or absorbed in the Supreme Reality, both observed service and submission to a pir or guru, both observed fasts and penance, both observed *zikr* or the recitation of the sacred word. Both adopted the use of the rosary, and believed in union with the supreme Being. Both believed in the toleration of other religions and advocated universal love and bhakti.[66]

The pir cult, that is prominent in *Hir Waris* was a significant feature of popular religion in the Sultanate period. Zahir Pir (or Gugga Pir) and Khwaja Khizar (or Zinda Pir) illustrate the typical Hindu-Muslim syncretic cult of pirs. When we look at their lives, we encounter the phenomenon of socio-cultural fusion typical of Sultanate times. Gugga Pir is said to have been converted to Islam by Khwaja Muinuddin Chishti. He is worshipped as a protector against snake bite. A number of tiny brick-mausoleums exist in almost each and every town and village of the eastern Punjab. R.C. Temple, writing in the last quarter of the nineteenth century, states that the story of Gugga is 'involved in the greatest obscurity. He is nowadays one of the chief Muhammadan saints or objects of worship of the lower classes of all sorts. . . . In life he appears to have been a Hindu and a leader of the Chauhan Rajputs against Mahmud of Ghazni. . . . His habitation was probably in Bikaner.'[67] Khwaja Khizar or Zinda Pir seems to have been originally a divinity of the river Indus. Fishermen and boatmen revere him as a god of rain in Sind and Punjab, and also in eastern Bengal. Ibbetson writes that the Pir is an 'extraordinary instance of a Musalman name being given to a Hindu deity'. In H.A. Rose's *A Glossary of the Tribes and Castes of the Punjab and North-West Frontier Province*, it is recorded that his original name was Ablia, the son of Mulkan, sixth in descent from Noah. He is said to have had a long white beard and was dressed in green. It is believed that wherever he sits or prays, the soil becomes green with verdure. As giver of the waters of immortality, he is called the Zinda Pir. The Khizri Gate of Lahore is so named because it was the river-gate when the Ravi flowed under the fort.[68] These pirs may not have existed as historical persons, but they survived in the popular cultural memory of the agrarian society of Punjab. They cured ailments and suffering and infused new energy into people. In the Hindu popular/folk religious domain, they might be minor deities who were the guardians of the people against evil spirits and calamities of nature, particularly of agrarian and pastoral society, but in the popular Muslim folk realm they assumed the status of pirs, as Islamic orthodoxy did not approve of deities but somehow tolerated the cult of pirs.

The Genre of Qissa (Narrative Poetry)

To understand the ethos of a particular age it is necessary to look into the interrelationship between history, society, and the dominant literary forms. A cultural study of the qissa *Hir* by Waris Shah, therefore, obliges us to understand qissa as a prominent and popular literary genre of medieval Punjab. Qissa, an Arabic word, means a story/tale narrated in poetic form. It is defined as a 'harmonious integration of well-knit plot, psychological analysis, fascinating narrative and perfect composition'.[69] Though Arabic in origin, Punjabi qissa-poetry is a prototype of the Persian poetic form of *masnavi* which is one of the three important Persian poetic forms (the other two being *ghazal*, a short lyric in which the themes of love predominate, and *qasida*, the ode).

The Persian masnavi deals only with two kinds of themes—love (*bazmia*) and war (*razmia*). These themes were illustrated by Amir Khusrau (1252–1325) in his *Miftah-ul-Futuh* and *Dawal Rani Khizr Khan*. In *Miftah-ul-Futuh*, he describes Jalaluddin Firuz Khalji's succession to the throne, and his victories against Malik Chhajju, the rebellious governor of Karra, the chiefs of Oudh, the Mongols, and the ruler of Jhain.[70] In spite of the rhyme and metre, the *Miftah-ul-Futuh* is an invaluable military history of India. Similarly, the *Dawal Rani Khizr Khan* is one of the best of Amir Khusrau's historical masnavis about love, specifically the pangs of

Khizr Khan, the eldest son of Sultan Alauddin Khalji, who was separated from Dawal Rani. The love or war-oriented poetic narrative called masnavi in Persian literature is in Punjabi a qissa (in case of love theme) or *jangnamah* (in case of the theme of war).

Prior to the emergence of qissa in the Indian literature, *kathakav* was prevalent. Much literature about Ram-Lakshman, Krishna, Hanuman, Sita, Janak and a host of mythical figures had been created in the form of *kathakav.* But long Turkish rule and the resultant dominance of Persian language and literature may be said to have influenced the creation of masnavi-style qissa poetry in Punjab. Wanjara Bedi, the Punjabi folklorist, is of the opinion that though the masnavi infused a new consciousness in Punjabi qissa, the latter is essentially born of the popular folk-poetic forms of *var* (ballads and lays), *kathakav* (narratives of love), *chitha,* and *swang.*[71] In the absence of the printing press before the nineteenth century, qissa constituted a rich tradition of oral literature, travelling from generation to generation of folk-singers called *bhands, bhattas,* and *mirasis.*

A qissa begins with propitiatory verses (*mangalacharana/hamad*) in praise of God. Then a certain amount of space is set aside for the mentor or guru/pir of a qissa-kar. Writes Waris Shah:

(a) I start with song in praise of the Lord / who made this world spring forth from love. / Prime lover of all is the Lord Himself, / and He gave His love to the Prophet-envoy. / Love is the sign of saint and sage / and the man of love will be solemn and shy. / And those who are fulfilled this wise / will find admittance to grace above.

(b) Then after the Lord I praise His Prophet – / all heavens and earths were made for him – / Who, made of dust, is raised so high, / purged of all evil of the world; / And who though chief of all the prophets, / made himself dust before the Lord, / Discarded joy, care-ridden to save / the faithful on the day of doom.

(c) Also I praise the friends of the Prophet / four gems indeed of the purest ray – Abu Bakar, Umar, Usman and Ali / each with an excellence all his own. . . .

(d) Next I must sing to the Pir Makhdum / whose goodness clothes his humblest ward. / We may seek a thousand other saints, / only he in the end befriends in truth. / And those to whom he lends his grace, /

enjoy all gifts of heaven and earth, / And on the judgment day they shall / wear robes of honour in reward.[72]

This pattern of the beginning of Punjabi qissa tallies with that of Amir Khusrau's masnavis. For example, the doxology of the *Dawal Rani*

contains the usual praises of God, 'the creator of all lovely things, who has attached the human heart to beauty and created the maidens of China and Khorasan for the excitement of love'. Next come praises of the Apostle, 'who, while Heaven had opened its nine doors wide for him, prided himself on a poor man's cottage'; of the Four Caliphs and of Shaikh Nizamuddin, 'whose heart is the treasury of divine love.' Sultan Alauddin, though he is mentioned after the poet's spiritual chief, nevertheless, occupies a prominent place.[73]

After the customary praises, the purpose of writing is stated in the qissa. Thereafter the entire story is presented, from the beginning to the logical end. Characters are described and depicted with the aid of metaphors and similes. Generally a garden or a place/house at the periphery of a village is the rendezvous; and the meeting of lovers is arranged by a female mediator. The lovers are destined to have the blessings of pir/faqir or guru. Nevertheless, the beloved is married off, against her wishes. The inherent tension in patriarchal society, ending generally in a tragedy, is the crux of the qissa. The hero does not lead a sedentary life, but roams from place to place. These characteristics signify a social situation ridden with conflict. For example, the garden at the periphery of a village is not simply a rendezvous for the lovers, but its marginalized location counters the patriarchal space that centralizes power and imposes restrictions on those who do not conform. Similarly, the female mediator from the social fringe, represents those forces that secretly help rebels against the patriarchs. The pir/faqir or guru (again the marginalized pro-people element) signifies forces that stand against the allies of the patriarchs, the orthodox priestly class. That a hero in the qissa does not lead a sedentary life means a constant struggle of the square peg in the vicious round hole of the patriarchy.

Unlike the blue-blooded lovers in the case of the Persian masnavi and Hindi *prem-katha*, the main characters of the Punjabi qissa belong to or represent the folk culture. Neither the love affair nor the chivalry of the feudal class inspires a Punjabi qissa-kar to construct his narrative. Kings and princes such as Rasalu and Puran become folk heroes only when they de-class themselves and stand in the camp of the subalterns. The hero/heroine of Punjabi qissa poetry does not accept the hegemony of patriarchal or feudal traditions, but defies them. In relation to the other genres of medieval Punjabi poetry (*dhora*, *saloka*, *kafi*, and *siharfi*), qissa constitutes a significant source of the past society of a locality or a regional society because it is essentially a social narrative. This particular feature of the qissa underlines that identity is not within us; it exists only as a narrative. Says a theorist, the only way to explain who we are is to 'tell our own story, to select key events which characterize us and organize them according to the formal principles of narrative—to externalize ourselves as if talking to someone else, and for the purpose of self-representation. . . .'[74]

Another noteworthy characteristic of qissa is that it presents a multi-layered social reality in an adequate context because in its narration incident, characters, and social milieu are all interrelated. The plot presents the numerous stresses and strains which create a dramatic situation; thus social reality emerges more clearly and boldly before a reader or an audience. Unlike *dhora*, *saloka*, *kafi* and *siharfi*, the qissa does not remain confined to the aesthetic use of language and poetic meter. By revealing a multi-faceted social reality, it is a richer source. Its value for a historian thus does not lie in the story but in the multiple contexts of social reality—contexts that are revealed by the different characters when they come into conflict and compromise with each other. These social beings do not simply reveal what happens in a story but what a story means or the sense it makes. Qissa not only acquaints us with the pluralistic and contending discourses of social life, but also with the social life of discourses: how and when divergent discourses come into conflict and compromise. Heterogeneous voices collectively form an ideological vision and the message of the qissa-kar. However, the ideology and vision cannot be identified with the reading of a single voice or speech separated from the others.

The characters in a qissa and their interpersonal relationship are the constituents of a qissa-text. The author does not simply record or imitate social reality, but produces it textually in the context of specific time and space. He makes his text a semiotic being in terms of its meaningfulness. The text of *Hir*, as constructed by Waris Shah, is not simply a *record* of the legend, which is said to have been popular among Punjabi folk since the fifteenth century. Waris *produces* the legend within a particular, historically evolved, society and culture. As Hir and Ranjha do not simply *denote* themselves as lovers, the qazi and the parents of Hir (Chuchak Siyal and his wife, Malki) are not just the elders of the society. Hir, Ranjha and the five pirs connote social forces who struggled against hegemony and violence of a patriarchal system represented by the qazi and the parents of Hir. The characters in qissas are not only the producers of history, but also products of history. The qissa of Hir, therefore, assumes a tremendous significance as source of social history. It is an inter-text: a social and cultural text of Punjab is present in the legend.

During the rule of Maharaja Ranjit Singh in the early nineteenth-century qissa flourished in Punjab. The birth of an indigenous polity had activated and inspired Punjabi qissa-kars like Hasham (1735–1843), Ahmed Yar (1768–1848), Imam Bakhsh (1778–1863), and Qadiryar (1805–92). They enriched the genre and were mainly inspired by sufi and bhakti thought. The vast mass of Punjabi literature was based on folklore told in simple Punjabi dialect and presented in local metaphors and similes.[75] The open-ended nature of the native state had a bearing on the poets, as is evident from the types of sources the qissa-kars tapped for their literary plots. They laid their hands on three kinds of sources: (a) local Punjabi romances of Puran Bhagat, Raja Rasalu, Sohni–Mahiwal, Raj Bibi, Roda–Jalali and Keema–Malki; (b) non-Punjabi romances of Sassi–Punnu, Gopi Chand, Nal–Damyanti and Chander–Badan; and (c) the non-Indian romances of Islamic origin such as Yusuf–Zulaikha from the holy Quran, Laila–Majnu, and Shirin– Farhad.[76] Now the opening verses (*mangalacharana*) were dedicated to Guru Gobind Singh. Vir Singh, a baptized poet (an *amritdhari* qissa-kar), introduced his qissa of Hir with such propitiatory verses in 1812.[77] In typical sufi style, he presented Guru Gobind Singh as his lover, himself as the beloved.[78] Similarly, Joga Singh, another qissa-kar of the period, characterizes Krishna as a lover (Ranjha) and Radha as the beloved (Hir). The flute of Ranjha is the flute (*bansri* or *murli*) of Krishna.[79]

A question may be raised here: why did qissa and *var/jangnamah* remain dominant as literary genres in Punjab for a century (1750–1850)? As a matter of fact, the qissa and *var* (ballad) was a protest against the socio-religious hegemony. Creative writers like Waris Shah, Qadiryar and Shah Muhammad represented the people's problems and aspirations, and narrated them in their vernacular. That is why they succeeded in developing a rapport between their own voice and that of the people, and hence, elevated their creation to the level of popular literature and themselves to that of poets of the Punjabi people. Their work takes one from the world of simple 'facts' (or apparent reality, called empiricism) to the world of underlying reality or the message they intended to convey. The poetry and the poets of this period were non-conformist. The aim was to bring about a socially accepted change in the society of Punjab. Hir and Ranjha do not simply confront the qazi, mullah and jogi, but attempt to establish a new social praxis. Ranjha succeeded in reuniting with Hir as per the orders of Raja Adli. Nevertheless, he was not ready to adopt her as his wife without social approval.[80] His stand is similar to that of the Khalsa, who were not mere rebels engaged in armed confrontation but sought to bring about a change by establishing a native rule in Punjab, accepted and approved by the people of the region.

Thus the rise of qissa-poetry or var as a dominant literary form reflects eighteenth-century Punjab, particularly its western and central regions. The former region was the hub of sufism, and the latter was the central axis of Sikhism and the Khalsa. During this century the exploitation and violence of the ruling class and its feudal allies, and associated patriarchal and ecclesiastical institutions, were countered at two levels: in poetry and in armed struggle under the leadership of the Khalsa. Both the trends had assumed the character of a movement in the west and central parts of Punjab. It was for this reason that qissa, with its rebellious discourse against the patriarchs, could not attain royal patronage. However, with the establishment of the *Sarkar-i-Khalsa*, which did not encourage the hegemony of any religious group, the open-ended cultural ethos of qissa-poetry or var found a congenial atmosphere, and flourished.

With the annexation of the Lahore kingdom by the British in 1849, and the resultant rise of communal consciousness among the new Punjabi Hindu, Sikh and Muslim middle class, literary protest against patriarchy and religious fundamentalism subsided. Middle-class Punjabis turned to 'communal' ethnography and launched a programme of 'reforming' the people. As a result, the genre of qissa and jangnamah or var came down on the literary graph of the region, and we witness the rise of 'communal' tracts of Hindus, Muslims and Sikhs reaching the people through the advanced print industry. The protest movement of the qissa was hijacked by the socio-religious reform movements, Arya Samaj, Singh Sabha, and Anjumans; and, as Jones states, each 'possessed missionaries, tract societies, parochial schools, centres of worship, systems of fund-raising, bureaucracy, and central associations'. Further, 'Lines dividing one religion from another and one socio-religious movement from all others were defined, and aggressively defended. By the end of the nineteenth century, religious identity was in the process of expressing itself in combinations of symbols based on language, script and religion.'[81] British imperialism, its education system and its printing industry disintegrated the historic bloc of the sufis, bhaktas and Sikh gurus; and the holistic religious protest movement with khanqahs and gurdwaras as the common religious spaces of the people of Punjab also received a severe setback. Punjabi middle classes caused cleavages in the cultural legacy of Punjab: Mardana, the 'Muslim' bard was separated from the 'Sikh' Guru Nanak, and Dhido Ranjha, a 'Muslim', could now no longer be heard singing the devotional songs of Vishnu. The middle-class reform movements became the harbingers of political activism. Lahore and Amritsar, once enriched in the ambience of holistic religiosity, became centres of the printing of propaganda tracts of different religious communities. Very soon the print network took Islam, Hinduism, and Sikhism into its fold.

It is significant that *Hir Waris* was published for the first time in the British Punjab in the Shahmukhi script of Punjabi around 1851, by the Chashma Noor Press and the Afghani Press Amritsar, and in the Gurmukhi script in 1861.[82] This development may be characterized as the beginning of the complex linguistic and cultural polysystem of nineteenth-century Punjab. It may be interpreted as the first sign of a schism leading to a conflict between the Shahmukhi and Gurmukhi scripts. It may be regarded as the beginning of the 'market' cultural relations and of the advent of professional poets sponsored by the state or patronized by the Arya Samaj, Singh Sabhas, and Anjumans. In other words, if the medieval state patronized the priests, the modern state patronized poets, poetry, languages, and scripts. Now the purpose of patronage was not confined to an individual monarch or his nobility. Instead the object was to protect and support the religious communities in an atmosphere charged with the cut-throat competition of power politics. The game was being played through language and literature. 'The promotion of Urdu', Shackle states, 'in Punjab after its conquest by the British and their destruction of Mughal Delhi in 1857 combined to give Lahore a new significance as a centre for Urdu.'[83] Colonel W.R.M. Holroyd, Director of Public Instruction addressed a meeting of the Anjuman on 9 May 1874. He stressed the need to find ways and means for the development of Urdu poetry, which, according to him, was in a state of decadence. He suggested the foundation of a new *mushaira* and proposed to hold monthly meetings.[84]

In response a Punjabi *mushaira* also began to be held in Lahore, at the house of Nawab Gulab Mahboob Subhani near Matti Chowk and Mochi Darwaza, and at Amritsar in the house of Sant Ram Sapra and near Talaab Durgiana, Ram Talai, and Mizar Fatehshah. Similarly, Batala and Gujranwala also became centres of Punjabi *mushairas.* Since 1920 the holding of *kavi darbars* on the occasions of Sikh festivals (*gurpurbs*) became a significant feature. Similar poetic recitations were held on the occasions of the annual functions of the Singh Sabhas. On these occasions poets were honoured.[85] In such a sectarian socio-political milieu, the Punjabi qissa began to sink.

NOTES

1. Peter Gottschalk, 'Mapping Muslims: Categories of Evolutionary Difference and Interaction in South Asia', in Imtiaz Ahmad and Helmut Reifeld, eds., *Lived Islam in South Asia: Adaptation, Accommodation and Conflict*, Delhi, 2004, pp. 12–13.
2. Claude Lévi-Strauss, *Structural Anthropology*, vol. 2, 1973, p. 328.
3. The land of seven rivers, namely the Indus (Sindhu), the Vitasta (Jhelum), the Akesines (Chenab), the Parushni (Ravi), the Vipas (Beas), the Sutdra (Sutlej), and the Saraswati.
4. 'Penta' derived from Greek 'Pente' means five and 'potamas' means rivers. The Greeks named these rivers the Hypasis (Jhelum), Akesines (Chenab), Hydrotes (Ravi), Hypeasis (Beas), and Zaradvos (Sutlej).
5. A.C. Cunningham identifies the geographical boundaries of the province of Taki that 'comprised the plains of Punjab lying between the Indus and Beas, to the north of Multan District, or the whole of Chaj Doab, together with the upper portions of the three Doabs of Sindh-Sagar, Rachna and Bari.' Cunningham, *The Ancient Geography of India*, ed. Surendranath Majumdar Sastri, Calcutta, 1924, p. 176. The vast plains of Punjab are divided into five intra-fluvial tracts or Doabs, a Persian word that means 'two waters' or land between two rivers. The Doabs are still known by the names given to them by Akbar: from east to west they are: (1) the Bist Jullundar Doab between the Sutlej and the Beas with important towns of Jullundar and Hoshiarpur; (2) the Bari Doab between the Beas and the Ravi, with Lahore and Amritsar located on it. It is also known as Majha or the middle tract; (3) the Rachna Doab enclosed by the Ravi and Chenab, with the notable towns of Gujranwala and Sheikhupura, (4) the Chaj Doab between the Chenab and the Jhelum, Gujrat, Bhera and Shahpur being its important towns; and (5) the Sindh-Sagar Doab between the Jhelum and the Indus, with Jhelum, Rawalpindi, Attock and Mianwali.
6. J.S. Grewal, *The Sikhs of Punjab* (The New Cambridge History of India, II.3), New Delhi, first paperback Indian edition, 1994, p. 1.
7. While defining the territorial organization of the kingdom of Punjab under Maharaja Ranjit Singh, Fauja Singh identifies the three broad territorial zones from the viewpoint of the actual exercise of power. The first zone is the core or heartland of Punjab, which extended from the Sutlej to the Jhelum. The intermediate zone constituted the area between the Indus and the Jhelum. It included the subas of

Multan and Kashmir. The peripheral zone comprised the territories on the borders of the kingdom, such as Peshawar, Hazara, Dera Ismail Khan, Dera Ghazi Khan, and Bannu Tank. Fauja Singh, 'Territorial Organization: Concept of State Role and Distribution of Power', in J.S. Grewal and Indu Banga, eds., *Maharaja Ranjit Singh and His Times*, Amritsar, 1980, pp. 88–102.

8. Lachman M. Khubchandani acquaints us with the term *kshetra* (or cultural zone):

   The composition of the population of the entire Punjab region, ranging from the southern parts of NWFP to Delhi, and from Jammu valley and Bilaspur (in Himachal Pradesh) to the Ganganagar district (in Rajasthan), shows it is a composite sociolinguistic region, a kshetra in the traditional Indian framework. There are many groups, belonging to different religions (Muslims, Sikhs, Hindus) and affiliated to different socio-cultural identities (such as Pathans, Multanis, Dogras, Gujars, Paharis, Jats) who have over the years been sharing a common cultural ethos, though on the surface, the diversity of speech (styles, dialects, languages) around these identities is quite apparent. This plural mosaic comprises not only the rich Panjabi language and literature written in Punjabi script, the Sikh holy scriptures, the mystic Sufi poetry written in Arabic and Devanagari letters, but it is also manifested through the common folk heritage, folk arts, dances, songs, and the tonal rhythm when speaking Panjabi, Dogri, Kangri, Bagru, Hindi or Urdu, and the new idiom developed in recent years around Delhi, called 'Milijhuli' (Panjabized Hindustani).

   Khubchandani, *Language, Culture and Nation-Building: Challenge of Modernization*, Shimla and New Delhi, 1991, p. 74.

9. Buddha Prakash, *Political and Social Movements in Ancient Panjab*, p. 240.
10. L.M. Joshi, 'Invasions and their Impact', in L.M. Joshi, ed., *History and Culture of Punjab*, pt. I, Patiala, 1989, p. 72.
11. Prakash, 'Presidential Address', *Proceedings of Punjab History Conference*, Patiala, 1965.
12. Prakash, *Political and Social Movements in Ancient Panjab*, pp. 217-61; idem, 'Presidential Address', *Proceedings of Punjab History Conference*, 1965.
13. Ibid.
14. For details see Romila Thapar, *A History of India: From the Discovery*

of India to 1526, Delhi, 1992, *Interpreting Early India*, Delhi, 1995; D.N. Jha, *Ancient India: An Introductory Outline*, New Delhi, 1977; D.D. Kosambi, *The Culture and Civilization of Ancient India in Historical Outline*, Delhi, 1970; Prakash, *Glimpses of Ancient Panjab*, Patiala, 1983, *Political and Social Movements in Ancient Panjab*, 'Ancient Panjab—A Panoramic View', in Harbans Singh and N. Gerald Barrier, eds., *Essays in Honour of Dr. Ganda Singh*, Patiala, 1976; Nurul Zaman Ahmad Auj, *Harappan Heritage*, Multan, 1998; K.C. Chakravarti, *Ancient Indian Culture and Civilization*, Bombay, 1961; Bhaskar Chattopadhay, *The Kushanas—A Numismatic Study*, Calcutta, 1967; Nalinee M. Chapekar, *Ancient India and Greece: A Study of Their Cultural Contacts*, Delhi, 1977; K. Krishna Murthy, *Mirrors of Indian Culture*, Delhi, 1982 and L.M. Joshi, ed., *History and Culture of Punjab*, pt. I, Patiala, 1989. R.S. Sharma, *India's Ancient Past*, New Delhi, 2005.

15. Hugh Kennedy Trevaskis, *Punjab of To-Day: An Economic Survey of Punjab in Recent Years 1890–1925*, Lahore, 1931, pp. 5–6.
16. As quoted in Hari Ram Gupta, 'Chandragupta Maurya: A Native of Panjab' in Singh and Barrier, eds., *Essays in Honour of Dr Ganda Singh*, Patiala, 1976, p. 31.
17. Prakash, 'Ancient Punjab: A Panoramic View', in ibid., p. 24.
18. For an account of Sultan Mahmud's Indian invasions, which is based on contemporary sources, see Muhammad Nazim, *The Life and Times of Sultan Mahmud of Ghazna*, New Delhi, rpt., 1971, pp. 86–121.
19. Edward Thomas, *The Chronicles of Pathan Kings of Delhi*, New Delhi, 1967, p. 47.
20. Muhammad Qasim Farishta, *Tarikh-i-Farishta*, tr., *History of the Rise of the Mohomedan Power in India*, vol. I, New Delhi, 1990, pp. 70–1.
21. Mohammad Habib, *Sultan Mahmud of Ghaznin*, New Delhi, 1967, p. 77, perceived that Mahmud looked at Lahore and Multan simply as robber's perches, from where he could plunge into Hindustan and Gujrat at will.
22. Thapar, *The Penguin History of Early India: From the Origins to AD 1300*, New Delhi, 2003, p. 432.
23. For the nature of the Ghurid occupation of northern India, with reference to its political, social, economic and religious aspects, see Khaliq Ahmad Nizami, *Religion and Politics in India during the Thirteenth Century*, New Delhi, 2002, pp. 83–94.

24. Mohammad Habib and Khaliq Ahmad Nizami, ed., *A Comprehensive History of India,* vol. V: *The Delhi Sultanate,* AD *1206–1526,* New Delhi, 1970, pp. 213–17 (henceforth cited as Habib and Nizami, ed., *A Comprehensive History of India,* vol. V).
25. A.B.M. Habibullah, *The Foundation of Muslim Rule in India,* Allahabad, 1976, pp. 176–81.
26. For insightful analysis of the Mongol polity, its internal conflicts, and the evidence of Mongol sources in addition to conventional chronicles, see Peter Jackson, *The Delhi Sultanate: A Political and Military History,* Cambridge, 1999, pp. 101–22.
27. S.B.P. Nigam, *Nobility under the Sultans of Delhi,* AD *1206–1398,* New Delhi, 1968, pp. 51–67.
28. Habib and Nizami, ed., *A Comprehensive History of India,* vol. V, pp. 497, 560–5.
29. For a translation and interpretation of Alauddin Khalji's agrarian regulations, recorded in Ziauddin Barani's *Tarikh-i-Firuz Shahi,* see Irfan Habib, 'The Price Regulations of Alauddin Khalji: A Defence of Zia Barani', in Sanjay Subrahmanyam, ed., *Money and the Market in India 1000–1700,* New Delhi, 1998, pp. 85–111.
30. Habib and Nizami, ed., *A Comprehensive History of India,* vol. V, pp. 587–9.
31. Ainul Mulk Mahru, who had been appointed the governor of Multan, provides valuable evidence on the state initiative for digging canals in his jurisdiction. Surinder Singh, 'Dynamics of Statecraft in the Delhi Sultanate: A Reconstruction from the Letters of Ainul Mulk Mahru', *Proceedings of the Indian History Congress,* Kolkata, 2001, pp. 285–93.
32. Habib and Nizami, ed., *A Comprehensive History of India,* vol. V, pp. 119–24.
33. Khwaja Nizamuddin Ahmad, *Tabqat-i-Akbari,* vol. I, tr. B. De, Calcutta, 1973, p. 289.
34. In a detailed conversation with Qazi Mughisuddin of Biana, recorded by Ziauddin Barani in *Tarikh-i-Firuz Shahi,* Alauddin Khalji highlighted the privileges and arrogance of *khuts* and *muqaddams.* Khaliq Ahmad Nizami, ed., *Politics and Society during the Early Medieval Period: Collected Works of Professor Mohammad Habib,* vol. I, New Delhi, 1974, p. 86.
35. This portion is based on Irfan Habib's insightful analysis of the relative position of the various rural classes and the changes experienced by them. Tapan Ray Chaudhury and Irfan Habib,

eds., *The Cambridge Economic History of India,* vol. I, *c. 1200–c. 1750,* Hyderabad, pp. 55–9.

36. H.A. Rose, *A Glossary of the Tribes and Castes of Punjab and North West Frontier Province,* vol. I, Patiala, 1970, p. 539; Denzil Ibbetson, *Punjab Castes,* Patiala, 1970, p. 172.
37. A.B.M. Habibullah, *The Foundation of Muslim Rule in India,* p. 173.
38. Habib and Nizami, ed., *A Comprehensive History of India,* vol. V, pp. 452–4.
39. Fauja Singh, ed., *History of Punjab, AD 1000–1526,* vol. III, Patiala, 1972, pp. 189–90.
40. Kishori Saran Lal, *Twilight of the Sultanate,* New Delhi, 1980, p. 88.
41. The military exploits and plundering raids of Jasrath Khokhar have occurred frequently in Persian chronicles. Yahya Ahmad Sirhindi, *Tarikh-i-Mubarak Shahi,* tr. H. Beveridge, New Delhi, 1990, pp. 200–34; Khwaja Nizamuddin Ahmad, *Tabqat-i-Abbari,* vol. I, pp. 300–5, 315–16, 328; Farishta, *Tarikh-i-Farishta,* vol. I, pp. 298–330, 303, 306–7, 311, 318.
42. Irfan Habib, 'Jats of Punjab and Sind', in Singh and Barrier, eds., *Punjab Past and Present: Essays in Honour of Dr. Ganda Singh,* p. 94.
43. Richard M. Eaton, *Essays on Islam and Indian History,* New Delhi, 2000, pp. 35–7.
44. For details, see ibid., pp. 203–46.
45. Andre Wink, *Al-Hind: The Making of the Indo-Islamic World,* vol. II, New Delhi, 1999, p. 5.
46. Eaton, *Essays on Islam and Indian History,* p. 211.
47. Wink, *Al-Hind,* vol. II, pp. 43–4.
48. Ibid., pp. 381–4.
49. For details see Vinayak Purohit, 'The Pastoralist Class Society in Indian History and Historiography', Presented at the 41st Session of *The Indian History Congress,* Bombay, December 1980.
50. Wink, *Al-Hind,* vol. II, p. 113.
51. Mohammad Habib, *Sultan Mahmud of Ghaznin,* p. 63.
52. K.M. Ashraf, *Life and Conditions of the People Hindustan,* New Delhi, 1988, p. 30.
53. Muzaffar Alam, Francoise 'Nalini' Delvoye and Marc Gaborieau, 'Introduction', in *The Making of Indo-Persian Culture: Indian and French Studies,* New Delhi, 2000, p. 23.

54. Khaliq Ahmad Nizami, 'India's Relation with Central Asia During the Medieval Period', in Amalendu Guha, ed., *Central Asia: Movement of Peoples and Ideas from Times Prehistoric to Modern*, New York, 1971, pp. 157–66.
55. I.H. Siddiqui, 'The Process of Urbanization and Social Change in Pre-Mughal India', *Islamic Culture*, vol. LXXVII, no. 2, 2003.
56. Jit Singh Sital, 'Language and Literature during the Sultanate Period', in Fauja Singh, ed., *History of Punjab, AD 1000–1526*, vol. III, p. 373.
57. Ibid.
58. See Sunil Sharma, *Persian Poetry at the Indian Frontier: Masud Sad Salman of Lahore*, Delhi, 2000.
59. Mohan Singh, *An Introduction to Panjabi Literature*, Amritsar, 1951, p. 45. *Week*: Some Indian poets have composed poem-cycles on seven days of the week, in the manner of poem-cycles on the twelve months of the year, called *baramaha*. In the 'week' genre the seeker (a poet) waits anxiously for the Beloved. Then when the last hope is fading he/she finds himself/herself in the divine embrace on the eighth day. *Akhri: akhri* is an acrostic on the alphabet. The oldest verse of this kind is found in the Adi Granth. Later on it appears to have become a popular verse-form of the sufis.
60. Sital, 'Language and Literature during the Sultanate Period', p. 375.
61. J.S. Grewal, 'Historical Geography of the Punjab', *Journal of Punjab Studies*, vol. 11, no. 1, 2004, pp. 11–12.
62. Yusuf Husain, *Indo-Muslim Polity (Turko-Afghan Period)*, Shimla, 1971, pp. 66–7.
63. Mohan Singh, *An Introduction to Panjabi Literature*, pp. 45–6.
64. These comprise nursery rhymes and lullabies and nonsensical verses (*thal and lori*); ditties of outdoor sport and labour, and of indoor games (*gaun*); festival songs (*maho mahi, holi*); songs for ceremonies connected with birth, marriage, death (*mumarakh, gharoli, ghori, suhag-doli, vain-alahnian*); love-carols (*tappe, mahia*); brother-sister dialogue songs; songs connected with mythical or semi-historical native heroes; songs of divine love; dance ditties and swing-songs; songs of the seasons; topical, political songs; songs to accompany daily labour with the spinning wheel, the hand grindstone, and the plough (*charkha, chakki,* and *hall*); riddles in verse (*bujharat*); songs about agriculture, the weather, astronomy, and professional-

occupational wisdom; hagiolatrous poetry; lascivious sex catches and outpours (*jhok*); songs to familiarize children with numbers, names of objects, relationships, etc.; verses witty, satirical, and parodistical; songs relating to historical heroes and popular contemporary lovers, leaders, even oppressors. Ibid., pp. 47–8.

65. Nizami, *Religion and Politics in India during the Thirteenth Century*, p. 340.
66. A.M.A. Shushtery, *Outlines of Islamic Culture: Historical and Cultural Aspects*, Bangalore, 1954, p. 365.
67. R.C. Temple, *The Legends of the Punjab*, vol. I, Patiala, 1962, p. 121.
68. H.A. Rose, *A Glossary of the Tribes and Castes of the Punjab and North-West Frontier Province*, vol. I, Patiala, 1990, pp. 562–3.
69. Khanna al-Fahuri, *History of Arab Literature*, Moscow, 1961, vol. 2, p. 190 as quoted in I. Serebryakov, *Punjabi Literature: A Brief Outline*, Chandigarh, 2000, pp. 42–3.
70. Mohammad Wahid Mirza, *The Life and Works of Amir Khusrau*, Delhi, 1974, pp. 176–7.
71. Sohinder Singh Wanjara Bedi, *Panjabi Lokedhara Vishav Kosh*, Delhi, 1991, vol. 5, pp. 1132–5.
72. Sital, ed., *Hir Waris*, Delhi, 1973, stanza nos. 1–4. Henceforth referred to as *Hir Waris*.
73. Mirza, *The Life and Works of Amir Khusrau*, op. cit., pp. 176–9.
74. Mark Currie, *Postmodern Narrative Theory*, London, 1998, p. 17.
75. Bikrama Jit Hasrat, *Life and Times of Ranjit Singh: A Saga of Benevolent Despotism*, Nabha, 1977, pp. 416–17.
76. Attar Singh, 'Political Change and Punjabi Literature in the Nineteenth Century', in Indu Banga, ed., *Five Punjabi Centuries: Polity, Economy, Society and Culture, c. 1500–1900*, Delhi, 1997, pp. 535–47.
77. For the Punjabi verses see Ajmer Singh, *Maharaja Ranjit Singh Ate Punjabi Sahit*, Patiala, 1982, p. 73.
78. Ibid., pp. 77–8.
79. Ibid.
80. Attar Singh, *Darishtikon*, Chandigarh, 1991, pp. 107–8.
81. Kenneth W. Jones, *Socio-Religious Reform Movements in British India*, New Delhi, 1999, p. 121.
82. Sital, ed., *Hir Waris*, p. 13. Also see Mohan Singh, *Hir Waris*, Lahore, 1947, p. 10.

83. Christopher Shackle, 'Making Punjabi Literary History', in Christopher Shackle, Gurharpal Singh and Arvindpal Singh Mandair, eds., *Sikh Religion, Culture and Ethnicity*, Richmond, 2001, p. 98.
84. As quoted by Shackle, ibid.
85. Moula Bakhsh Kushta, *Punjab De Heerey*, ed., Gurmukh Singh, Sirhind, 1996, pp. 28–9.

CHAPTER 4

The Age of Waris Shah

> O Bullah! If in the heart dwells the lord,
> One would renounce both Hindu and Muslim.
> I am neither a Hindu, nor a Muslim
>
> BULLEH SHAH (1680–1758)

The eighteenth century is a watershed in the history of Punjab. The century reverberates with multiple sounds: the clink of the swords of the Khalsa-Singhs, the clatter of their horses' hooves, and the bold literary voices of Waris Shah and Bulleh Shah. From the 1730s invasions from Persia and Afghanistan offered opportunities to Punjabis to see themselves as a historically evolved ethnic community.[1] They confronted the oppression of the Mughal state and the invasions of Nadir Shah and Ahmad Shah Abdali. Under the leadership of the Khalsa, they expressed their political will for their own state. During these days of struggle, their concern for preserving the sanctity of their socio-cultural space was reflected audaciously in their vernacular literature.

THE HISTORIOGRAPHIC PERSPECTIVE

It is, however, curious that the eighteenth century in Punjab is generally looked upon and studied in the religious and communitarian perspective. The century is emplotted and characterized as a century of the 'Sikh struggle' against the 'Muslim oppression' and vice versa.

It was Joseph Davey Cunningham (1812–51), the popular historian of 'the Sikhs', who introduced a partisan and communitarian discourse in Punjab historiography during the period between 1846 and 1848 when he completed his *A History of the Sikhs*.[2] Cunningham's skill in emplotting Punjab history and his narrative language tend to marginalize the role of the people in defending and expanding the geographical and political horizons of Punjab under the leadership of the Khalsa. The colonial policy had humoured Punjabi Jat Sikhs in order to mobilize them as allies in perpetuating the political, military, and economic interests of the imperialist power.[3] Thus Cunningham began his *History* with the following statement: 'During the sixteenth and seventeenth centuries of the Christian era, Nanak and Gobind, of the Kshattriya *race*, obtained a few converts to their doctrines of religious reform and social emancipation among the Jat peasants of Lahore and southern banks of the Sutlej'[4] (emphasis added). After identifying the Sikhs with Jats and implicitly associating the martial Kshatriyas with Sikh Jats, Cunningham assigned the latter the status of a 'nation'[5] and acknowledged the Jat-dominated areas as the 'country' of the Sikhs. He stated that the land of the Sikhs lay 'around Lahore, Amritsar, and even Gujrat to the north of the Sutlej, and around Bhatinda and Sunam to the south of that river. The one tract is pre-eminently called Manjha or the middle land, and the other is known as Malwa. . . .'[6] Thus Sikhism, part of an historically evolved Punjab cultural fusion (the other significant addition being sufism and bhakti) and the Jats were placed in the category of 'country and nation'. The undercurrents of the colonial craft, which tended to cause cleavages among the people and form a strategic friendship between imperialist and 'Sikhs', can be appreciated in the following language of narration used by Cunningham:

> Thus, at the end of two centuries, the Sikh faith had become established as a prevailing sentiment and guiding principle to work its way in the world. Nanak *disengaged* his little society of worshippers from Hindu idolatry and Muhammadan superstition, and placed them free on a broad basis of religious and moral purity; Amar Das preserved the infant community from declining into a sect of quietists or ascetics; Arjun gave his increasing followers a written rule of conduct and civil organization; Har Gobind added the use of arms and military system; and Gobind Singh bestowed upon them a distinct political existence, and inspired them with the desire of being socially free and nationally independent. No further legislation was required; a firm persuasion had been elaborated, and a vague feeling had acquired consistence as an active principle. The operation of this faith become a fact, is only

now in progress, and the fruit it may yet bear cannot be foreseen. Sikhism arose where fallen and corrupt Brahmanical doctrines were mostly acted by the vital and spreading Muhammadan belief. *It has now come into contact with the civilization and Christianity of Europe, and the result can only be known to a distant prosperity*[7] (emphasis added).

Cunningham did not only 'disengage' the Sikhs from the rest of the Punjabis, he also laid the foundation of the discourse of Khalsa martiality and of Khalsa martyrdom by implicitly 'disengaging' Guru Nanak from Guru Gobind Singh. With the intention to place the Khalsa Singhs at the top among the Sikhs and to present them and the tenth Guru as a political-cum-military force to be reckoned with, Cunningham replaces *Guru* Gobind Singh with *king* Gobind Singh. In a footnote to the above-quoted paragraph, Cunningham with the skill of an imperialist states: 'Nevertheless, the peaceful Sikhs of the first teacher are still to be everywhere met within the cities of India, although the warlike Singhs of the tenth king [Guru Gobind Singh] have become predominant in Punjab, and have scattered themselves as soldiers from Kabul to the south of India.'[8] Banda Bahadur, who gathered a huge following in the Punjab irrespective of caste, creed, or community[9] under the banner of the Khalsa against state oppression, and who carried on the 'Sikh' tradition of martyrdom, is for Cunningham a 'sectarian Hindu'.[10] The simple reason may be that he was not a Jat-Sikh, a newly constructed ethnographic identity which was a central figure of the imperialist discourse of the Khalsa during the colonial era in India and particularly in Punjab.

The imperialist communitarian approach to Punjab history may also be assessed from the character of Ranjit Singh's kingdom as seen by the British. Bal observes that the British looked upon Ranjit Singh's state as a Sikh state based on 'close Hindu–Sikh alliance and basically opposed to the Muslims'. Of the opinion that the Khalsa Raj entertained strong anti-Afghan feelings, they (the British) believed that the 'Sikh' State suited them as a 'good buffer state between the Afghans and the British'. It was a 'stable state' and 'strong enough to resist the Afghans'.[11]

The imperialist emplotment of the history of 'the 'Sikhs'

subsequently influenced both the writing of history (particularly of the eighteenth century) and people's perceptions. Sikh-Muslim conflict is the dominant, indeed single, narrative of the eighteenth century.[12] The political narrative gives great importance to Sikh-Mughal conflicts. The Sikh rebellion is either characterized as a national movement or a national as well as a religious struggle. Overall, the unrest in medieval Punjab is understood as a confrontation 'between the Mughal rulers and the Sikh community'.[13] Hence, the lack of ethnic-community perspectives tends to exclude or marginalize Punjabis as a historically evolved cultural and linguistic community.

For instance, a Ganda Singh states that a 'new era' began in the Panjab with the beginning of the eighteenth century. 'A will to resist tyranny—social, religious and political—had been created in the Sikhs, and a new life had been infused in them. The tenth and last Guru, Gobind Singh, was still living, preparing his people, through precept and example, for *dharma-yudh* that seemed to him inevitable in the years to come.'[14] Hari Ram Gupta also views the eighteenth century as one of the most important chapters of Sikh history. To him during this century the Sikhs evolved by the strength of their own arms, into one of the best military people of the world. They 'developed the germs of a worthier political existence' and 'played the most important part in the politics of Northern India, during the whirlwind incursions of foreign hordes from 1739 to 1799'. The Sikhs 'rendered the most invaluable services to the cause of our country by putting a deep stop to all foreign invasions from the North-West'.[15]

A similar communitarian perspective is prevalent in the historiography of Pakistan. I.H. Qureshi states:

> The Sikhs rose into a formidable military power in East Panjab during the eighteenth century. Up to the time of the fifth Guru Arjan, the Sikhs were a 'small and obscure sect of no wealth or importance'. Guru Arjan was the first to organize his following into a homogeneous and well-organized community. His political support to Prince Khusrau during the latter's rebellion against his father Jahangir, brought upon him the wrath of the Emperor. This made the Sikhs hostile to Islam, and a religion which had hoped to serve the cause of better understanding

between the two, turned totally against the religion from which its main inspiration had come. . . . From this time onward the Sikh Gurus became suspects in the eyes of the Mughal emperors because the religious spirit in the Sikh community was entirely eclipsed by military aggressiveness.[16]

Similarly, Syed Abdul Quddus is of the view that in Ahmad Shah Abdali's campaigns against the Sikhs and Marathas 'the newly converted Muslims of Punjab, who were never recruited in the Mughal armies and remained mostly unarmed, were the main targets of Sikh marauding *jathas* [bands] and the Maratha advance guards'.[17] Quddus is of the opinion that Punjabi Muslims who had flourished during Mughal rule were 'harried and harassed', but 'emerged stronger [and] more zealous' during the confrontation between Muslims and Sikhs.[18] The tendency to perceive animosity between the two religious groups has led some scholars to argue that Aurangzeb's suppression of the Sikh movement had backfired, giving the Sikhs a militant identity that was later to become a form of nationalism.[19]

A number of historical facts falsify these presentations. For instance, many Sikh *sardars* were sympathetic to the Durranis, 'even joined hand with them in fighting against the other Sikh Sardars'.[20] There was, besides, the episode of Ghani Khan and Nabhi Khan, two Pathan brothers who called Guru Gobind Singh the Pir of Uch and arranged his escape when he was being followed by imperial troops. Single-thread discourses of Khalsa or Islam or 'Sikh-Muslim' conflict tend to deprive the century of the wider cultural character that Waris Shah and Bulleh Shah delineate in their verses. Thus we must not exaggerate the importance of military conflict.[21]

A history of the uprising represented by the Khalsa would be empty of historical substance if the Khalsa leadership is not explained with reference to its support base and the response it elicited from Punjabi people of diverse castes, classes, and communities. It is obligatory to ask who they were. A historian must mediate between leaders and participants and supporters, if the latter are to be made part and parcel of a historical struggle. Depriving the marginalized section of Punjabi society of their historic role in the mass-insurrection under the leadership of Banda

Bahadur, a historian is of the view that the persons who had previously been associated with Guru Gobind Singh fought with devotion and sacrifice, but the majority of Banda's followers were plunderers who 'would go home to unburden themselves of the booty and join again whenever they felt like doing so. Whenever they found a situation fraught with danger they would slowly melt away.'[22]

Such a narrative leaves the text of history unconnected with the genuine context. In this connection three pertinent questions demand our attention. (1) How do historians proceed in order to know the past? (2) What is correct, true and virtuous in their practice? (3) What, ultimately, legitimizes history as a discipline?[23] From the time of Cunningham's *History* to the contemporary discourse of 'Sikh/Muslim' historians, the ethnic-community perspective has suffered a good deal. The Khalsa emerged so boldly in the eighteenth century Punjab that it became a dominant historical perspective and paradigm for historians so as to *separate* the Sikhs culturally, socially, and biologically from their (Punjabi) cultural matrix.

The martial image of the Khalsa-Singhs, for instance, is generalized by Hari Ram Gupta for all 'Sikhs' of the eighteenth century, 'accustomed from infancy to the most laborious outdoor life and hardest fare', 'tall, muscular and healthy' with a 'martial bearing and dignified appearance'. A very ambivalent image of the Sikhs emerges from the narration of Hari Ram Gupta because the general characteristics of the people of Punjab have been specified as those of just the Sikhs. Sometimes the specific characteristics of the Khalsa-Singhs have been applied to all Sikhs. Some florid details follow: the Sikhs had 'the elasticity of character, the power to adapt themselves to all circumstances' and the 'vigour of body and mind to withstand the challenges of climate. The burning sun, heavy rains, freezing winter and rough weather exercised no deterring influence on them'. An ample turban of coarse cloth of white or blue cotton, and drawers (*kachha*), generally blue, were their dress. They were 'manly, robust and vigorous and were passionately devoted to sports. The boys generally played *gulli-danda, pitaudi* or *kabaddi*', and so on. As for the women, they were generally 'fine-looking, tall and graceful'.[24]

Hari Ram Gupta's account is not different from Bingley's *Sikhs* written on the eve of the First World War. As the British needed more Jat Sikhs in the army Bingley's narrative eulogized the Sikhs. He betrays his own intentions in his introductory remarks:

> 'Sikh' is the name given to the members of a military order of Hindu dissenters and puritans, and not, as is sometimes supposed, to any particular race. Owing, however, to the social and political preponderance of the Jats throughout Punjab, and to the fact that considerably more than two-thirds of the Sikh population belonged to this tribe, the history of Sikhism must necessarily be prefaced by an account of the Jats, and of the circumstances which caused this race of peaceful cultivators to be transformed into a fraternity of warriors.'. . . Sturdy independence and patient vigorous labour are perhaps the strongest characteristics of the Jat Sikhs. . . . In agriculture the Jat Sikh is a pre-eminent. No one can rival him as a landowner and yeoman cultivator. . . . The typical Jat Sikh is faithful and true to his employer, seldom shows insubordination, and with a good deal of self-esteem has a higher standard of honour than is common among the most Orient lists. . . . The Sikh is essentially a fighting man and his fine qualities are best shown in the army. . . . The Jat Sikhs have always been famous for their fine physique and are surpassed by no race in India for high-bred looks, smartness, and soldierly bearing. Their length of limb makes them excellent marchers, and their physical activity is developed by active habits. They are fond of running, jumping, wielding enormous wooden clubs called *mugdars,* and lifting and tossing heavy weights. The younger men are fond of wrestling, and quoit-throwing. . . .[25]

This kind of characterization tends to construct a parochial social and cultural image of the Sikhs, separate from the rest of the people of Punjab.

Historic Bloc from Below

Punjabi literature of the eighteenth century, discussed in this chapter, reveals that on the social and literary fronts sufi poets like Bulleh Shah, Ali Haider, and Waris Shah were representing the voice of Punjabi ethnicity; on the political front, the Khalsa-Singhs took the lead. For assessing the historically evolved character and nature of Punjabi ethnicity, one also needs to appreciate the forms it assumed from time to time, i.e. the sufi khanqahs, Harmandir Sahib, Adi Granth, sufi poetry, Gurmukhi and Shahmukhi scripts of Punjabi *zuban*, the leadership of the Khalsa-Singhs, the *misls* and their administration, and the establishment of the Khalsa Raj. These expressions of Punjabi identity were devoid of communal connotation and crisis.

Throughout Punjab's eighteenth-century struggle, the leadership of the Khalsa never faced opposition from below on account of caste or religion, not even from Muslims who happened to be the co-religionists of those against whom the Khalsa was waging a deadly war. It needs to be understood that if the Muslim sufis could elicit the devotion of the non-Muslim people of Punjab, the Khalsa-Singhs could secure a response of the Muslim people of Punjab, as the latter were also victims of the same oppression. Transcending religious boundaries, in the first two decades of the eighteenth century the people of Punjab constituted their own resistence under the leadership of Banda Bahadur. The peasantry and the lower 'polluted' castes and communities like scavengers and leather-dressers and also the Gosains, the Udasi *sadhus* and the *vanjaras* (the Sikh trading class),[27] rallied round Banda Bahadur and in the process, created what in Gramsci's term is the 'popular collective will'.[28] The Hindus and Muslims of Punjab too did not remain aloof. The uprising under Banda Bahadur furnishes an impression that it was anti-Muslim because the state beneficiaries against whom it stood were Muslims. Mosques, seminaries, mansions, and mausoleums were targets as they figured prominently among state beneficiaries. It is stated in the context of the egalitarian character of the social structure of the Sikh religion that the *madad-i-maash* holders suffered 'heavily at the hands of the Sikhs. In almost all the towns, which fell into their possession, the Muslim *shurafa* and their mosques and the graveyards were the chief targets of Sikh raids'. At Thanesar, for instance, scholars (*fuzala*) and gentry (*shurafa*) were 'reported to have been specially affected by Sikh depredations'.[29]

However, in this uprising, which was like a class struggle, the deprived Muslims were on the side of Banda Bahadur who was fighting under the banner of the Khalsa. Contemporary records such as the *Akhbarat-i-Darbar-i-Mualla* confirm that five thousand Muslims rallied round him. Not only were they given daily allowances, they were 'specifically permitted by Banda Bahadur to say their daily prayers and even *azan*'.[30] Bhagwati' Das harkarah, through Hidayatullah Khan, presented to His Majesty Bahadur Shah a news-sheet (28 April 1711) reporting that Banda had promised he would not oppress the Muslims. As a result, 'any Muslim who approaches him, he fixes a daily allowance and wages, and looks after him'. Further, Banda Bahadur permitted Muslims to 'read *khutba* and *namaz*'.[31] The Punjabi Khatri association with the Mughal ruling class must not be generalized into a proposition that they as a class and caste were pro-Mughal, and aloof from the struggle waged under the leadership of the Khalsa. There is no denying that a large number of the Khatris were merchants and their fortunes were closely linked with political stability in Punjab, a factor that 'created a gap between them and the Sikhs of Banda'.[32] Nevertheless, the Khatris helped Banda Bahadur at a critical juncture.[33] A contemporary Persian chronicler informs us that among the large number of Khatri officials at the court there could have been followers of Banda.[34]

After the execution of Banda and his followers in 1716, the Mughal state pursued a series of repressive measures against the Khalsa-Singh rebels, now without a leader. They took shelter in the hills, deserts, and forest and had to pursue the lifestyles of free-booters. Gradually, a number of people joined them. Apart from the deplorable economic state of the people of Punjab, which served as a 'necessary' condition to inspire them to join the order of the Khalsa, longstanding kinship relationships too played a role of 'sufficient' cause, creating the primary politico-military bands of the Khalsa which later came to be known as *misls*.[35] The leaders were designated *jathedars*. There were sixty-five of them as identified by Hari Ram Gupta.[36] Since the kinship involved in the Khalsa leadership was based on clan, *got*, or occupation, the various jathedars were autonomous. Each had his own programme of advancement, which would materialize on small-scale predatory excursions on his own account. Thus there was no longer a unity of command. The jathedars hardly formed a united front, though following the tradition of social fraternity (*bhaichara*) they would readily offer their aid to a brother jathedar whenever the latter sought it. They agreed to pool resources for the service of the Panth and consented to fight under the common flag of the Khalsa. During the phase from 1754 to 1765 the different units combined to take united action. It was during this period that *Dal Khalsa, Misls, Gurmatta* and *Rakhi*—the four institutions—constituted a significant chapter of the Khalsa-Singh struggle. During this period, Sikh rule was established over a large part of Punjab; and 'the bearing of these institutions on the acquisition of power and acquisition of territories was quite close'.[37] The year 1765, just about two years before the versification of *Hir* by Waris, marks a watershed in the history of the Khalsa-Singhs. They brought their fifty-year resistance against the Mughals and Afghans to a successful conclusion and embarked upon conquest and the consolidation of their power. In a few years they became 'masters of Punjab'.[38]

Literary Renaissance

The eighteenth century was an age not only of political awakening but also of literary renaissance in Punjab.[39] 'It is small wonder', observes Annemarie Schimmel, 'that during the hopeless situation of the floundering Mughal Empire after Aurangzeb's death (1707) in the turmoil of incessant internal and external attacks and continuous destruction, Persian literature somewhat stagnated. Truly great poetry needed a new medium, which proved to be Urdu; yet Sindhi, Panjabi, and Pashto also developed an impressive literature of their own.'[40] Men of literary talent communicated the spirit of their age, often characterized as 'dark and barbarous'. The eighteenth-century poets of Punjab made a historic and ideological contribution to the realm of Punjabi literature. Sufi and bhakti traditions, the rebel wings of Islam and Hinduism, inspired them. They debunked religious conservatism and formalism in the face of theocratic taunts. Like Guru Nanak, for instance, Bulleh Shah (1680–1758) in his *kafis* spoke of the empty performance of both traditional Muslim and Hindu rituals: 'Mecca shall not end thy tale of woe / If thy mind be not purged of filth. / Going to Gaya shall not save thy soul, / Even by thou offering sacrificial feast.'[41] In another *kafi*: he says, 'If they call thee a heretic / And spurn thee away, / Say, 'yes' to what they declare, / And reckon not their slander.' As for Ali Haider (1690–1785), in his *siharfi* he expressed his anguish over the failure of the Mughal state during the invasion of Nadir Shah:

> They should die by eating poison, / These Hindustanis have no sense of shame. / The Turanis are so devoid of honour. / The fools have opened their treasures, / to Persians and Khurasanis. / They should dip their noses in the water of pitchers, / if they don't find a pool to drown in, / What should be said of these, / the elephantine Afghans?

After Guru Nanak, Ali Haider was the second (Punjabi Muslim) poet who used the word Hindustan/Hindustani to express his concern for his homeland.[42] Bulleh Shah and Waris Shah for their part worried about the safety of Punjab and their native places. Anguished to see the deplorable condition of Punjab, Bulleh Shah spoke: 'The gate of Doom's torments has opened, / Punjab is in a very bad state.' Waris in his *Hir* expressed his anxiety about the safety of Jandiala and Qasur where he had received his education. Prominent qissa-kars of the age, Muqbil, Waris, and Hamid, penned the popular love-tale of Hir–Ranjha in 1748, 1767 and 1783 respectively. The non-sectarian and non-conformist vernacular literature emerged concomitantly with political awakening represented by the Khalsa-Singhs. This signifies that vernacular regional literature did not decline *in tandem* with the Mughal empire. The qissa of Hir–Ranjha reconstructed by the aforesaid poets instead reveals a spirit of 'struggle and strife' in Punjab. The people of Punjab were not only waging a war on the political front, but also against the hegemony of the patriarchy and the priestly classes.

The vars also reflect the valour and vitality of eighteenth-century Punjab. The prominent lays of this period written on Guru Gobind Singh, Lav and Kush (the sons of Lord Rama) are: *Guru Gobind Singh Ji Di Var, Var Patshahi Dasvin Ki* by Gurdas Singh, *Var* by Gurdas III, and *Var Lav Kush* by Devi Das. A *var* based on the *Mahabharata* is available; it concerns the battle between Krishna and Kansa and is written by Tej Bhan. These lays, besides representing the interaction between the Great and the Little Traditions, constitute a major source-material of the history of the Punjabi spirit of collectivity and cooperation, which elite traditions tend to see as Hindu-Sikh-Muslim *unity*, not through the prism of cultural fusion. In the ballad-literature, *Chathian Di Var* (Lay of the Chathas) by Pir Mohammad, a resident of Gujrat, *Var Nadir Shah* (Lay of Nadir Shah) by Najabat, and *Var Haqiqat Rai* (Lay of Haqiqat Rai) by Agra deserve mention.[43] Pir Mohammad in his *Chathian Di Var* does not hesitate to pay Maha Singh, the father of Ranjit Singh, his due even when he praises the Muslim Chatha chief in the scene of battle.

> The horses of Maha Singh roar in the field, / His soldiers are arrayed in coats of arms, / He has not spared any one who defied him, / He obtains victory through Divine ordinance, wherever he goes, / Nobody is born who could turn the tables on him, / But blessed are you, O Chatha's mother, not many are born like him.[44]

Similarly, Najabat condemns the treachery of the Mughal nobles during Nadir Shah's invasion.[45] Najabat particularly condemns Nizamul Mulk, who invited Nadir Shah to invade Delhi: 'May damn Nizamul Mulk, be pulled out from his roots, / Who lit a spark to show the inside of the house to the thief'.[46] *Var Haqiqat Rai* by Agra, a resident of Lahore and Sethi by caste,[47] is a spirited account (versified in 1784) of the martyrdom of Haqiqat, a young Hindu boy of Lahore. He was put to death under the orders of the Governor of Lahore in 1734.

Muslim religious poetry of the eighteenth century included Muqbil's *Jangnamah of Imam Hussain.* In it the poet describes the battle of Karbala in which Imam Hussain, son of Ali and grandson of the Prophet Muhammad, was slain by a rival claimant to the caliphate of Yazid. The *Jangnamah* begins with the praise of the Almighty who, to Muqbil, is worshipped both by the Hindus and the Muslims.[48] It is written in a typical Punjabi dialect, but Arabic and Persian words are used liberally because for a mixed population.

The rising in the later half of the eighteenth century under the leadership of the Khalsa evoked the interest of Sikh poets in the gurus, particularly the tenth. In the 1750s Kesar Singh Chhiber composed his *Bansawali Nama Dasam Padshah Ka.* Chhiber claimed that he was basing the account of the Tenth Master on a *bahi*, or a record book of his time, the possession of his ancestors. Two decades later, in 1776, Sarup Das Bhalla wrote an account of the Tenth Master in poetry, and Kirpal Singh wrote his prose *Mahima Prakash.*[49] A characteristic feature, but lesser known, of the age of Waris Shah was poetry about Rama and Krishna in short folk-metres and folk-stanzas.[50] The prominent poets are Bhavan Das, Gual Das, Chand Sakhi, Nauna, Keval Ram, Keval Das, Bhagvan, Bal Krishan, Rasak Lal, Anant Das, Manhar and Madho. No scholarly work has been done so far on these poets or their devotional poetry. Recognizing the contribution of the Punjabi poets to Krishanaite and Ramaite poetry, Mohan Singh states,'No single love story . . . aroused so much genuine emotion . . . as that of Sri Krishna and Radha . . . Punjabi poets have not lagged behind their Braj brethren . . . in making real an ideal, spiritual passion.'[51] In his verses Rasak Lal, one of these poets, communicates his devotion:

> Whenever at daybreak I proceed to the riverside / To fill my pitcher, / The ever-smiling Mohan / Aims a sure aim at it / And casts a pebble. / So charming, so clever, so sweetly mischievous! / Nanda is a simple-minded Ahir, / You, Yashoda, are just a simple-minded lady. / Sure Kanhaya's father is someone else, / So too his mother. / But who else except you can I complain to? / O revered Yashoda, do rebuke him, / For the queen of Braj are you, / So wise, / But your Krishna! / He never scruples to resort to force, /Depending ever on your backing. / He has, indeed, forced the doors of my mind / So that in freedom he can strangely come and go. / As I enter my home, I seem to see Mohan, / As I come out, the same Mohan I behold. / Dark is his face, / Darker are his eyes. / He seems to have wrenched away my heart from me.[52]

During this period Qasur, Lahore, Batala and Multan became the chief centres that imparted education in Punjabi. Maulvi Mohammad Murtaza of the Qasur School was a protagonist of Punjabi language and literature. He translated the famous *Gulistan* of Sheikh Saadi into Punjabi. Both Waris Shah and Bulleh Shah were his disciples.[53] The period beginning with the illustrious

Maulvi and ending with the death of Maharaja Ranjit Singh may be safely characterized as the Augustan Age of Punjabi literature.[54]

During the age of Waris Shah the people of Punjab had begun to project themselves as a historically evolved ethnic community not only in their struggle for political power but also in their language and literature. Their cultural ethos crystallized in different poetic genres. Vernacular poetry played a crucial role in defining Punjabi community as a historical reality. It was a period so fertile in so many aspects that the concept and practice of Punjabi identity surfaced spontaneously, instead of being 'invented' from above. The poetry communicated the free expression and self-assertion of the Punjabis, and also their will for freedom from the authority of a wilful and tyrannical monarchy and its feudal and priestly allies. In an atmosphere of war and struggle, literary texts about revolt, dissent and heroism were being composed.

The socio-cultural and political emergence of the Punjabi community was likely to cause anxiety among the orthodox Muslim intellectuals in Delhi, the seat of political power. It has been observed: that so long as the political domination of the Muslims was assured, Muslims did not require a separate organisation. Most of the leaders of the eighteenth century were concerned with doctrinal matters and the reform of Muslims whose manners and custom were Hindu. 'It was only when there came the awareness of the loss of political power and its repercussions on the economic life of the Musalmans that a more activist or comprehensive religious reformist movement was organized.'[55] This movement was spear-headed by Shah Waliullah (1703–62) of Delhi. His father Shah Abdur Rahim had participated in the compilation of *Fatawa-i-Alamgir*, a code of Islamic law, at the court of Aurangzeb. Shah Waliullah received his early education from his father and later joined the staff of the Madrasah-i-Rahimiyah. After having spent twelve years at the *madrasah*, he moved to Arabia. There he came into contact with a great scholar of *hadis*, named Shaikh Abu Tahir bin Ibrahim. Shah Waliullah returned with a mission to establish a new order. The root of the entire problem, he perceived, was the deviation of the Muslims from Islam. The remedy lay, writes Waheed-uz Zaman, in 'making concerted efforts to bring them closer to the true spirit of Islam. The fundamentals of the faith could be strengthened and the teachings of Islam made intelligible to the common man only if the message of the Holy Quran reached the votaries of Islam in word and spirit.'[56] For that purpose Shah Waliullah rendered the Quran into Persian, which was generally understood by the educated people. Not only that, he attempted to unite Shias and Sunnis. He perceived himself as an agent of the amelioration of the Muslim condition. He invited Ahmad Shah Abdali to invade India for the sake of Islam, though historians differ on the interpretation of his deed.[57] In 1759 he wrote to Abdali pleading with him to take up arms for the protection of Muslims of India: 'Certainly it is incumbent upon you to march to India, destroy Maratha domination and rescue weak and old Muslims from the clutches of non-Muslims.' If not, Muslims would forget their religion and 'become such a nation that there will be nothing left to distinguish them from non-Muslims'.[58]

In sum, in this chapter I have shown that histories written from the slanted perspective of sectarian orthodoxy undermine the historical character of a people's struggle and deny the spirit of Punjabi identity.

NOTES

1. I have used the concept of ethnicity in the context of the language, religious belief, heritage, and political institutions shared by the people of Punjab, i.e. a primordial ethnicity. This concept is now employed in a broader sense to signify self-consciousness of a group of people. Otherwise the concept is very elusive: 'Whether an ethnic group should be called an ethnic group at all, or rather a nation, nationality, a minority, a tribe, a community, a culture, a society, or a people, or be denied any of these labels, has become more of a political issue than a simple procedure of scientific inquiry.' A.S. Narang, *Ethnic Identities and Federalism*, Shimla, 1995, p. 1. Besides the primordial concept of ethnicity, there is a concept of situational or contextual ethnicity. Here ethnicity is multi-dimensional and consists of several ingredients—skin colour, religion, language, and

so on. Which of them is relevant depends on the requirements of the situation. Ishtiaq Ahmed, *State, Nation and Ethnicity in Contemporary South Asia*, London, 1996, p. 20. Those who subscribe to the primordial concept are E. Shils, 'Primordial, Personal, Sacred and Civil Ties', *British Journal of Sociology*, vol. 7, 1957; C. Geertz, 'The Integrative Revolution', in C. Geertz, ed., *Old Societies and New State,* New York, 1963. Those who subscribe to the situational or con-textual notion of ethnicity are: H. Alavi, 'Politics of Ethnicity in India and Pakistan', in H. Alavi and J. Harris, eds., *Sociology of Developing Societies: South Asia*, London, 1989; U. Phadnis, *Ethnicity and Nation-Building in South Asia,* New Delhi, 1989; C. Young, *The Politics of Cultural Pluralism*, Madison, 1976.

2. On the life and work of J.D. Cunningham see S.S. Bal, 'Joseph Davey Cunningham', in Fauja Singh, ed., *Historians and Historiography of the Sikhs*, New Delhi, 1978, pp. 85–133.
3. 'The Lions [Sikhs] of Punjab', writes Richard G. Fox, after the British successfully subdued them, 'became, oddly enough, braver under British upkeep, as the imperial masters tried to turn the Singhs into guardians of the Raj. The British hoped to keep these new domesticates of colonialism on a short leash by having Sikhism's religious institutions and functionaries discipline them to obedience. . . . After annexing Punjab, British administrators developed two separate methods of bringing their former opponents, the Singhs, to heel. One method aimed at securing the loyalty of Sikh temple functionaries to British rule; the other hoped to recruit a cheap but dependable and, above all, obedient soldiery for the Raj by promoting Sikhism as a separate religion and Singh as a separate social identity based on that religion.' Richard G. Fox, *Lions of Punjab: Culture in the Making*, Delhi, 1990, pp. 141–2.
4. J.D. Cunningham, *A History of the Sikhs*, New Delhi, 1985, p. 1.
5. Ibid. p. 1.
6. Ibid. p. 7.
7. Ibid. pp. 80–1.
8. Ibid. p. 81n.
9. Muzaffar Alam, *The Crisis of Empire in Mughal North India: Awadh and Punjab,1707–48*, New Delhi, 1986, pp. 134–75. M.L. Ahluwalia, *Landmarks in Sikh History: A Fully Researched and Document History 1699–1947*, New Delhi, 1996, pp. 19–20.
10. Cunningham, *A History of the Sikhs*, p. 79.
11. S.S. Bal, 'Character of Ranjit Singh's Kingdom as seen by the British',

The Panjab Past and Present, vol. XXII-I, April 1988, sr. no. 43, p. 5.

12. Jadunath Sarkar, *Fall of the Mughal Empire*, vol. 1, *1739–1754*, Hyderabad, 1997; Ganda Singh, *A Brief History of the Sikh People*, Delhi, 1971; Hari Ram Gupta, *History of the Sikhs*, vol. II, *Evolution of the Sikh Confederacies (1708–1769)*, New Delhi, 1978; S.S. Arshi, *Atharvin Sadi Da Sikh Itihas*, Chandigarh; Sohan Singh Sital, *Sikh Raj Kiven Baniya*, Ludhiana, 2000. One may read the critique of the discourse in Chetan Singh, *Region and Empire: Punjab in the Seventeenth Century*, Delhi, 1991, pp. 1–11.
13. Chetan Singh, *Region And Empire: Panjab in the Seventeenth Century*, p. 2.
14. Ganda Singh, 'History in Panjabi', *The Panjab Past and Present.* vol. V, pt. I, April 1971, sr. no. 9.
15. Hari Ram Gupta, *History of The Sikhs*, vol. II, p. xiii.
16. I.H. Qureshi, *A Short History of Pakistan*, Karachi, 2000, p. 571.
17. Syed Abdul Quddus, *Punjab: The Land of Beauty, Love and Mysticism*, Karachi, 1992, p. 19.
18. Ibid.
19. Mohammed Yunus and Aradhana Parmar, *South Asia: A Historical Narrative*, Karachi, 2003, p. 166.
20. J.C. Dua, *British Historiography on the Eighteenth Century Punjab*, New Delhi, 1992, p. 16.
21. See George D. Bearce, 'Intellectual and Cultural Characteristics of India in a Changing Era, 1740–1800', *The Journal of Asian Studies*, vol. XXIV, nos. 1–4, 1965–6, p. 3.
22. Bhagat Singh, *Sikh Polity: In the Eighteenth and Nineteenth Centuries*, New Delhi, 1978, p. 46. Ganda Singh, *Life of Banda Singh Bahadur*, Amritsar, 1935, pp. 60–1.
23. 'History and Postmodernism', in Keith Jenkins, *The Postmodern History Reader*, London, 1997, p. 261.
24. Gupta, *History of the Sikhs*, vol. II, pp. 261–76; Shamsher Singh Ashok, *Madhkalin Panjab*, Amritsar, n.d., pp. 235–7.
25. A.H. Bingley, *Sikhs*, Patiala, 1970, pp. 1 and 121–42.
26. The confrontation is attributed to numerous reasons. See Seema Alavi, ed., *The Eighteenth Century in India*, New Delhi, 2002, pp. 17–18.
27. Alam, *The Crisis of Empire*, pp. 134–75. Ahluwalia states that in the reign of Farruk Siyar 'frequent reports came that Gosains and Udasi sadhus as far as Banaras and Prayag were helping Banda by

keeping him informed of the movements of the Mughal armies sent from that side against him. . . . To add to them Banjaras, who were Sikhs . . . and mostly carried trade in Rajasthan, Delhi, Saharanpur area had come in large numbers in order to ensure supplies of grain and fodder besides taking part in fighting at a few places.' *Landmarks in Sikh History*, pp. 19–20. Banda's earlier career as a *bairagi sadhu* might have been helpful in eliciting response from *fakirs, jogis, sanyasis*, and *bairagis* who carried the news as unpaid *harkaras* from the camps of the Mughals.' Ibid., p. 20.

28. Characterizing the insurrection 'from below' under Banda, Chetan Singh states: 'Whatever else may have been, the rebellions of the early eighteenth century were also very obviously an expression of the wrath of the lower classes. In so far as the Sikhs were concerned, the rejection of caste differentiation by the Gurus had attracted a very large number of low-caste followers. In their challenge to the established social hierarchy, the Sikhs under Banda apparently welcomed in their ranks any and every section of society that chose to join them, though these invariably belonged to the lower social orders.' As quoted in Harjot Oberoi, *The Construction of Religious Boundaries: Culture, Identity and Diversity in the Sikh Traditions*, New Delhi, 1997, p. 72.
29. Alam, *The Crisis of Empire*, p. 146.
30. Ahluwalia, *Landmarks in Sikh History*, p. 19.
31. As quoted in Ganda Singh, 'Punjab News in the Akhbar-i-Darbar-i-Mulla', *Punjab Past and Present*, vol. IV, pt. II, 1970, sr. no. 8.
32. Alam, *The Crisis of Empire*, p. 150.
33. Ibid., p. 149. Also see Hari Ram Gupta, *History of the Sikhs*, vol. II, p. 20.
34. Alam, *The Crisis of Empire*, p. 149.
35. Sita Ram Kohli, 'Foreword', in Lala Sohan Lal Suri, *Umdat-ut-Tawarikh*, Daftar III, pts. I-V, 1831–1839, Eng. tr. V.S. Suri, Chandigarh, 1974, p. vi.
36. Gupta, *History of the Sikhs*, vol. II, p. 90.
37. J.S. Grewal, *Sikh Ideology, Polity and Social Order*, New Delhi, 1996, p. 95.
38. Fauja Singh, 'The Misaldari Period of Sikh History', *The Panjab Past and Present*, vol. XI, pt. I, 1977, sr. no. 21.
39. Attar Singh, 'The Medieval Panjabi Literature', *Panjab Past and Present*, vol. II, pt. I, 1968, sr. no. 3.

40. Annemarie Schimmel, *Islamic Literature of India*, Wiesbaden, 1973, p. 48.
41. For details see Robin Rineheart, 'Interpretations of the Poetry of Bulleh Shah', *International Journal of Punjab Studies*, vol. 3, no. 1, 1996.
42. Jit Singh Sital and Gulwant Singh, eds., *Punjabi Sahit Vich Pramukh Jhakau*, Patiala, 1976, p. 57.
43. See Jit Singh Sital, ed., *Punjabi Bir Sahit*, Patiala, 1970.
44. As translated by Sant Singh Sekhon, *A History of Panjabi Literature*, Patiala, 1996, vol. II, p. 119. A complete text of the lay of the Chatha chief is given in Piyara Singh Padam, *Punjabi Varan*, Ludhiana, 1951, pp. 245–70. Opinions vary among scholars about the year in which this lay was written. Rattan Singh Jaggi is of the opinion that it was written immediately after the two wars between the two chiefs that took place between 1780 and 1790. *Punjabi Sahit Da Itihas, 1701–1850*, Patiala, 1976, vol. II, p. 47. But Sant Singh Sekhon, quoting Sita Ram Kohli, writes that it was composed some fifty years after the battle, *A History of Panjabi Literature*, vol. II, p. 117.
45. Sant Singh Sekhon, *A History of Panjabi Literature*, vol. II, p. 121.
46. Ibid., Piyara Singh Padam, *Punjabi Varan*, pp. 271–311. Also see S.S. Bal, 'Presidential Address', *Proceedings of Punjab History Conference*, Twenty-Sixth Session, 1994, Patiala.
47. Rattan Singh Jaggi, *Punjabi Sahit Da Itihas 1701–1850*, p. 49.
48. Ibid., p. 54.
49. S.S. Bal, 'Presidential Address'.
50. Mohan Singh, *Introduction to Panjabi Literature*, Amritsar, n.d., p. 116.
51. Ibid., pp. 117–18.
52. As quoted in ibid., p. 134.
53. K.K. Mukerji, *Rose-Garden of the Punjab*, ed. Gurbachan Singh Talib, Patiala, n.d., pp. 40–1.
54. Ibid., p. 42.
55. Shaikh Abdur Rashid, 'Decline of Mughal Power', in Ahmad Hasan Dani, ed., *Proceedings of the First Congress of Pakistan History and Culture*, vol. I, Islamabad, 1975.
56. Waheed-uz-Zaman, 'Shah Wali Ullah and His Times', in Ahmad Hasan Dani, ed., *Proceedings of the First Congress of Pakistan History and Culture*, vol. I.

57. See Muhammad al-Faruque, 'Some Aspects of Muslim Revivalist Movements in India During the 18th Century: The Activities of Shah Wali Allah of Delhi', *Islamic Culture*, vol. LXIII, no. 3, 1989.
58. Khaliq Ahmad Nizami, ed., *Shah Wali Ullah Ke Siyasi Maktubat*, Delhi, 1969, letter no. 2, pp. 83–98, as quoted in Muhammad Al-Faruque, 'Some Aspects of Muslim Revivalist Movements in India During the 18th Century: The Activities of Shah Wali-Allah of Delhi', p. 106.

CHAPTER 5

Waris Shah and the Qissa of Hir

> Speak thou O Waris Shah, / from the portals of thy grave, / and turn over a page / of the Book of Love again! / A daughter of the fabled Punjab / Once wept in pain and woe, / And thou, O great bard of yore / gave tongue to her long lament! / A million daughters, ravished, / now howl in silent rage, / O that your wing'd song may / rise to their epic pain today! / O thou succourer of the distressed, / Wake and see thy Punjab! / See, how her lush pastures / are laid waste with carrion flesh, / How the waters of the sacred Chenab / are turned red with spilled blood! / See, how an evil hand has poured / poison into the rivers of Punjab, / and how a poison'd harvest / springs dark and wild in her fair fields!
>
> AMRITA PRITAM, *Aj Akhan Waris Shah Nun*

This popular Punjabi poem (rendered into English)[1] was penned by Amrita Pritam in the wake of the bloodshed of Partition in 1947. The wide readership of the poem during a cataclysm certifies the perennial popularity of Waris Shah's *Hir* two hundred years after it was composed (1766–7).[2] *Hir Waris* is considered as a central text of Punjabi literature and culture[3] and the Punjabi psyche has not cast it off despite the fact that the world around has got so much sophisticated.[4] *Hir Waris* is a prominent component of the historical and cultural commonalities shared by Punjabis that obliterate their geographic and national separatrion and difference. The image of the Punjabi Muslim in this piece of folk literature is realistic and speaks of the vernacular identity that history has conferred on him/her. During the eighteenth century, when Punjab was undergoing a tremendous crisis of political and religious bigotry, Waris Shah looked back to the cultural roots of Punjab and protected them from being devoured and contaminated by sectarian and conservative forces, even though he may not have welcomed the rise of the lowly peasants under the leadership of the Khalsa-Singhs.

Romance and Rebellion in Punjabi Literature

A large number of qissa-kars from the time of Akbar to the present day have versified the folk legend of Hir–Ranjha. Damodar Gulati, an Arora Hindu of Jhang (now in the west Punjab), is said to have been the pioneer who introduced the folk tale of Hir in the genre of Punjabi qissa around AD 1605.[5] In Punjabi sufi poetry, Shah Husain (1538–1601) was the first poet who used the motif of Hir–Ranjha in his *kafis* to communicate his mystic or sufic experience of divine love (*ishq*). However, Damodar is accredited with emplotting Punjab's social life through the narration of the love legend of Hir–Ranjha.[6] He made Punjabi qissa a social document and associated himself with human beings, their struggles, their aspirations and dreams. In its qissa-form Punjabi poetry thus transcended the old traditions and themes of mysticism and spirituality.

The earliest reference to Damodar is made by R.C. Temple in 1885 in his *The Legends of Punjab*. But Temple could not trace the manuscript of Damodar's *Hir* and recorded only some segments from bards (*mirasis*) and other folk singers such as *bhatts* and *bhands*. It was in 1927 that Bawa Ganga Singh Bedi offered us in print the love story of Hir and Ranjha versified by Damodar.[7] The qissa-kar (Damodar) is popularly believed to have been a *patwari* of a zamindar of Jhang, probably a descendant of Hir's father, Chuchak.[8] Since Bawa Ganga Singh Bedi himself belonged to Jhang proper,[9] he seems to have been motivated to trace the manuscript. In the preface Bedi mentions that a good deal of labour resulted in the discovery of two old manuscripts: one from Bhai Hari Singh of Shah Jivana, district Jhang (Pakistan), and the second from Bhai Mehtab Singh of village Ballon in the same district. In fact, it was Bawa Ganga Singh Bedi who introduced the unknown Damodar to early twentieth-century readers of Punjabi literature. Even so, no Punjabi poet who composed the qissa of Hir after Damodar, has mentioned his name, not even Muqbil and Waris Shah.[10] That Damodar Gulati, a Punjabi 'Hindu' composed the qissa of Hir, a Punjabi 'Muslim' girl, and that he created sometimes in his *Hir* an aura of bhakti and the Krishna–Radha cult, reveals a degree of cultural syncretism surviving in the Punjabi qissa since inception.

The legend of Hir has been narrated in the Punjabi (Shahmukhi and Gurmukhi scripts), Hindi, Rajasthani, and Persian languages and dialects by more than sixty qissa-kars. Nevertheless, in the assemblage of idioms, customs, taunts, and gibes, and proper names of persons, places, and professions, Waris Shah made an improvement upon his predecessors Damodar Gulati, Ahmad Gujjar and Muqbil who all had reconstructed on the same romance. It has been rightly observed that Waris Shah was unique among the qissa-writers for the realism in his narratives. His weavery strikes true with its monologues, dialogues and descriptions of the countryside landscape, vivid scenes of grassy grazing grounds and other countryside views. There are group-meetings, discussions, vituperative arguments, exchanges of sentiments, soliloquies that recreate live scenes of the life of rural Punjab belonging to the times of Waris Shah.[11]

Moreover, Waris Shah fused together the Multani and Majhi dialects while versifying the legend. The synthesis would have appealed to the people of Punjab in general.[12] There was . . . from the very start of Panjabi literature a desire among the wandering singers and popular balladists . . . to appeal to men of other faiths and beliefs; to appeal to all tastes, vocations and avocations; all levels and strata. Catering to the emotional needs of the people is as important a function of literature as ministering to their intellectual needs.'[13] Waris Shah's, predecessor, Damodar, composed *Hir* in the Jhangi dialect, a sub-variety of Multani. Since Multani did not make much progress as a literary language, Damodar's *Hir* could not rise to a literary status equal to that of Waris Shah, despite the fact the Shaikh Farid in the thirteenth century and Ghulam Farid (1849–1901) in the nineteenth century had used the Multani dialect.[14] Waris Shah made *Hir* a classic of Punjabi literature. He offered it to the Punjabi world in 1180 Hijri/1823 Samvat corresponding to AD 1767.

Before we proceed to present the biographical sketch of Waris Shah, it seems necessary to talk about Ahmad Gujjar from whom Waris Shah borrowed the literary plot and the poetic metre. Damodar Gulati winds up his qissa on a happy note with Hir and her lover Ranjha setting out for Mecca, where they lived as *fakirs* till their death. However, it was Ahmad Gujjar who first rendered the legend a tragic one. Hir is poisoned to death by the members of her family. But Ahmad Gujjar shows Hir and Ranjha repairing to Mecca only after death.

Hajjis (pilgrims) saw on the road to the Mecca / Ranjha and Hir with a brown buffalo. / Ranjha showed the path to the pilgrims / and Hir distributed *churi* in *langar*.[15]

Ahmad Gujjar composed the qissa of *Hir-Ranjha* in AD 1693 during the reign of Emperor Aurangzeb. This was the first romance written in the verse form called *bait*, which means in Arabic and Persian a line of verse of any length. Waris Shah too used the same metre. He puts a sufic slant (*ishq-i-haqiqi*) on the love legend. He characterizes Hir as the soul (*ruh*) and Ranjha as the body (*kalbut*), whereas his predecessor Damodar, in the same mystical tone but following the typical bhakti tradition, compares Hir's love for Ranjha with that of Radha's for Krishna.[16] The popularity of the legend of Hir, thus wrapped in both the bhakti and sufi flavour and fragrance, alludes to the harmonious prevalence or fusion of these traditions at the popular level in Punjabi society. Being non-conformist in nature, the bhakti and sufi traditions played a significant role in maintaining and consolidating non-sectarian views in Punjabi society and culture. Thus these traditions/movements offset the communitarian impact produced by the theological discourses of the priestly classes of Hinduism and Islam.

In 1885, R.C. Temple recorded the 'sacred' popularity of Hir–Ranjha under the title of 'The Legend of Abdullah Shah of Samin'. Originally taken down in the Balochi language from the narrative of Ghulam Muhammad, the story was rendered into English by M. Longworth Dames. Temple saw the story as remarkable for the introduction of the heroes of the tale of Hir and Ranjha in the after-world. Ranjha is represented as still following his occupation, a buffalo-herdsman, now as supplying milk to the Prophet. The story recorded by Temple runs as follows:

Abdullah Shah Sayyid lived at Samin [a village some miles south of Dera Ghazi Khan]. He started on a pilgrimage [to Mecca] and went on board a ship. Going on he proceeded, when the ship stopped. The crew exerted themselves, but the ship did not move. A flock of birds were sitting on the seashore. The ship's master said: 'Is there any such man here, who, for the sake of God, will risk his life and alight from the ship, and go and make those birds fly away? If these birds fly away the wind will reach the ship, and the ship will go on.' Abdullah Shah said, 'I will risk my life for God's sake.' He alighted from the ship, and went and made the birds fly away, the wind reached the ship and the ship went on. Abdullah Shah (left alone) on the edge of the sea started off along the land. He came to a certain place, and there he saw tracks of buffaloes. He took up these tracks, and following and following them he went on and saw a smoke rising. There was a buffaloes' grazing station (*jhok*) there. A red-headed woman was seated there. When Abdullah Shah approached, the woman rose and said, 'In the name of God, Abdullah Shah of Samin, you are welcome!' He asked her, saying, 'Mother, who art thou?' The woman said, 'I am Hir; Mian Ranjha is with his buffaloes. For the present sit down and rest. In the evening Mian Ranjha will also come.' In the evening the buffaloes returned to the station, and a red-bearded man came with them. Abdullah Shah asked (of Hir) 'Who is this man that is coming in the track of the buffaloes?' Hir replied, 'This is Mian Ranjha.' When he came Abdullah Shah rose. The man said, 'In the name of God, Abdullah Shah, you are welcome!' Abdullah Shah said, 'All is well, Mian Ranjha.' Ranjha asked him for his news. Abdullah Shah told him all that happened to him. Ranjha said, 'Thy pilgrimage is accepted at the (divine) threshold. In the evening I shall take some milk, and bring you into the presence (of the Prophet).' Then having filled an earthen pot with milk and lifted it on to his head, he took Abdullah Shah by the hand, and said, 'Shut yours eyes.' When he opened his eyes he saw the Apostle of God sitting on his throne. The Prophet saluted him, and his pilgrimage was accepted.[17]

This story may be decoded at many levels. First, the grazing-station of Hir–Ranjha signifies the peripheral social location of the social rebels, who did not conform to the ideas and ideals of the social and religious patriarchs. Second, the grazing station stands for the sufi monasteries (khanqahs) where the dejected and inflicted people like Abdullah Shah Sayyid of Samin got solace and received amulets (*tawiz*) to get rid of their problems. Waris Shah begins his qissa with a reference to such blessings that Shaikh Farid bestowed on Punjab: 'The arrival of the Sufi saint, Baba Farid Ganj Shakkar dispels all the sorrows of Punjab.'[18]

Biographical Note

Like Mir Muhammad Taqi 'Mir' (1723–1810) the great Mughal author of *ghazals* in the eighteenth century,[19] Waris Shah was an outstanding writer of Punjabi qissa-poetry in the same period. During medieval times, the poet would approach his audience personally and sing. Jogis and bhaktas were roving singers. During his odysseys Guru Nanak himself sang his devotional verses, while his companion, Mardana, played on the *rabab*. Waris Shah too did this. The creation of *Hir* carried the name of Waris Shah far and wide, as he is said to have left the audience spellbound with the skill of his recitation.[20] Nevertheless, he is a poet of obscure origin. Scant biographical information is available about him, except some oral matter collected by scholars from his native village, and from the customary introduction given by Waris Shah himself in his *Hir*.

His year of birth is still a moot point. Assessing the literary skill evident in his *Hir*, scholars have surmised that Waris Shah was in his fifties when he versified it, in 1767,[21] at Hansa Malik, a little to the north-west of Pakpattan (Ajodhan). Since Waris Shah had observed and endured the turbulent currents of the age and was familiar with the ethos of medieval Punjabi society, he could draw a true social, religious and political picture of the land. Waris Shah is believed to have been born in 1720 in a Sayyid family[22] of the village Jandiala in western Punjab.[23] The genealogy of the Saiyyids, available with the descendants of Waris Shah at Jandiala, refers to the poet as the thirty-fourth descendant of Sayyid Imam Husain.[24] 'Jandiala' is believed to be the corrupt form of 'Janda Wala', which means a place infested with wild plants and bushes like *jand* and *karir.*[25] During the time of Humayun in the middle of the sixteenth century a feudal sardar, Sher Khan had the bushy tract cleared and settled.[26] It is also said that since the troops of Sher Khan (founder of the second Afghan empire) once encamped in this area, the place came to be called Jandiala Sher Khan.[27] The village still treasures the traces of the Mughal legacy—building having twelve doors (*baradari*), a large step-well (*baoli*) and tombs (*mazars*) including that of Waris Shah. He is worshipped as a pir. Offerings are made at his mazar. Food prepared in common kitchen collectively (*degs*) is distributed, and a fair is celebrated every year in the memory of this great poet of Punjab.[28]

The youngest and most loved son of Sayyid Gulsher Shah, Waris Shah, lost his parents during his childhood.[29] He attended the native elementary school (*maktab*) in the mosque at Jandiala. At that time those who were keen to acquire higher education had to join the *madrasas* where reputed scholars (*ulama*) imparted knowledge on language, grammar, literature, rhetoric, commentaries on the Quran, hadis, jurisprudence, logic, philosophy and mathematics.[30] For this purpose Qasur, Lahore, and Multan were known for their madrasas.[31] Seekers of knowledge had to travel from place to place because reputed teachers of various disciplines were available in different places.[32] Waris Shah too had to go to Qasur. His scholarly pursuits began here under Ghulam Muhiuddin Makhdum and Maulavi Ghulam Murtaza.[33] In *Hir*, Waris Shah says he was a disciple of 'Makhdum', meaning one who is served or worshipped. Qasur was not only reputed for its madrasas but also for the abode of the celebrated *dervishes* Saiyyid Jalaluddin Bhukhari (also known as Makhdum Jahaniyan), Maulvi Ghulam Murtaza, and Inayat Shah Qadiri.[34] At Qasur, Waris Shah took lessons in the higher Persian and Arabic language and literature, and in Muslim law (*shariat*), traditions of Prophet Muhammad (*hadis*), the Quran and system of medicine (*ilm tib*). Having spent a long span of his life in Qasur, with its ambience of scholarship, Waris Shah was infatuated with the town. In *Hir* he laments its destruction by Ahmed Shah Abdali.

Eighteenth-century Punjab witnessed the resurgence of the Chishti silsilah. It is interesting to observe that the revival of this silsilah should have come about at a time when the Naqshbandi divines of Sirhind were making claims to widespread influence, popularity, and predominance.[35] Waris Shah's inordinate thirst for mysticism (*ruhani talim*) inspired him to visit the shrine of the Chishti sufi saint Baba Farid at Pakpattan.[36] Here he took *bai'at* (adopting someone as his mentor) with Diwan Mohammad Yar, who succeeded to Baba Farid's spiritual seat (*gaddi*). Waris Shah was initiated into the Chishti silsilah and adopted the lifestyle of a sufi. At Pakpattan he studied philosophy and sufi mysticism. Since Qasur and Pakpattan were the main sufi centres, and many people visited them for spells, charms, hex and amulets, Waris Shah too acquired some magico-religious skills.[37] Thereafter he could not afford to be sedentary. He left Pakpattan and reached Malika Hans. On the outskirts of the town he made a mosque (*masit*) his abode. It is said that here he fell in a love with a lady named Bhag Bhari, though this information does not hold good among the majority of the scholars.[38] At Malika Hans in 1767 Waris Shah wrote his classic.[39] Since he remained in exile and almost led the life of a nomad, the idea of 'country' (*vatan* or *desh*) haunted him throughout his life.[40]

A Literary Artist

The legend of Hir–Ranjha in the qissa, *Hir* presents Waris Shah as (i) the architect of the genre, (ii) an ethnographer and also (iii) a historian.[41] He was capable of associating the Little Traditions of Punjab with sufism, Islam, the eroticism of bhakti, and the epics of the Great Tradition. As we shall see, his *Hir* is a *history* of Punjabi society and culture in general, and of Punjabi Muslims in particular. True, his is not the historian's narrative that breathes in *facts*, which we are generally accustomed to consider authentic and true. But does the narrative of history always breathe out facts? The way Waris Shah unfolds Punjabi society reminds us of the dictum that history is the art of narrative. Waris Shah goes ahead as a story-teller with his 'material', the folk love legend that he handles sagaciously. He infuses life into it with the help of situations, contending dialogues and discourses, resuscitating and creating characters, and with landscapes. His narrative reflects his ability to 'write' the cultural profile of Punjabi Muslims, their great civilizational traditions, their hybrid culture, their inner social conflicts, and their lifestyle in general. He seeks to say something 'real' and 'historical' through 'fiction'. He produces eventually and successfully a cultural text of Punjab.

Waris Shah is a master of narration. In less words he portrays more. He creates situations that give the reader a feeling of what goes on in his story. Detailed and delineated scenes pull the reader spontaneously into the story and involve him/her in the immediacy of experience. Waris Shah imparts the mood of a story through a language and style of his own. History, folklore, and literature combine in a 'text' that provokes the historian and sociologist, and suggests multiple meanings through images, objects, myths, and actions. In *Hir*, Ranjha, Hir, Jogi Balnath, Chuchak, Kaido, qazi, mosque, flute (*vanjhli*) of Ranjha, collective spinning (*trinjan*), the Chenab, the pastures (*bela*), and water games constitute the symbols and imageries, which need to be decoded.

Waris Shah was ahead of his contemporary Bulleh Shah. This was not a difference of ideology as both were non-conformist and non-sectarian, and both were 'Punjabi' Muslims. The difference lies in the genres they adopted to present the reality of their age. *Kafi*, the poetic genre which Bulleh Shah chose and for which he is known, could reveal the social and cultural facets of Punjab only at the level of symbols and motifs. Bulleh Shah's kafis, like the verses of other sufi and bhakti saints, were mystic and devoid of the socio-cultural 'emplotment' of Punjabi society. This vacuum was filled by Waris Shah in qissa. Neither sufi-centric nor Islam-centric, he was a poet-narrator. As a poet-narrator, Waris Shah seems to be less bothered about versification and prosody and more concerned with what is called 'poetics of the text', the 'meaning potentials'[42] of the legend of Hir–Ranjha. Instead of beautifying the text of *Hir* with skilled 'versification', Waris Shah is, as the genre obliges him, committed to the creation of meanings and hence the cultural text of Punjab. Whatever he chose to touch upon, he gave ample details, for instance, music, astronomy, mythology, history, the system of medicine, social rites, clothing, jewellery, sweets, delicacies, horses, snakes, or buffaloes. Conscious literary artist as he was, Waris Shah composed *Hir* in a dramatic style, encyclopaedic in scope and coverage, and popular in treatment. He adopted the *baint* metre and made his production a delightful collage of passionate love, emotion, humour, satire, social violence, jealousy, fire, anger, lust, avarice, resistance, struggle, ethics, spiritual contentment, and worldly wisdom. Thus he maintains a flow of socio-cultural information in such a manner that from beginning to end it enables a historian to comprehend the nature of medieval Punjabi society. In view of the political and religious environment of north-western Punjab and the way Waris Shah narrates the love legend, it becomes easy to understand his message and from which camp he was speaking: social rebels or patriarchs and priests. *Hir Waris* also enables us to appreciate the cultural fusion that diluted the dominant Great Traditions of the Hindus, Muslims, and Sikhs. Aryans, Indo-Greeks, Parthians, Scythians or Shakas, Kushanas, Arabs, Turks, Afghans, and Mughals had migrated into this region, and during the course of time had mingled with the mainstream. As a consequence, Punjab acquired specific cultural contours, remarkably devoid of any pronounced sectarian characteristics.

Waris Shah was blessed with linguistic virtuosity. His *Hir* makes us familiar with the power and drama of each word that he picks up. The synthesis of Persian, Hindi, and Punjabi rendered in idiomatic flavour charms the reader. In the realm of secular poetry there was perhaps none before Waris Shah who could use the Punjabi language so 'felicitously and soulfully'.[43] His 'pen manipulated the rugged Punjabi idiom into forceful expression with a magic touch'.[44] Waris Shah had a knack of adapting and situating words into their local flavour. For example, he gives the following Persian and Arabic words the touch of a local dialect: *makhmali* (velvet) as *makhbali*, *sawar* (rider) as *aswar*, *madad* (help) as *madat*, *farishtey* (angels) as *farestey*, *diwar* (wall) as *dwar*, *waqat* (time) as *wakhat*, *tadbir* (plan) as *tatbir*, etc.[45] He pruned and trimmed his words and made them lyrical.[46] There is a kind of rhythm in the narration of *Hir*. To make his *Hir* popular, he does not make frequent use of symbols, signs, far-fetched metaphors, or similes beyond the appreciation of common people.[47] On the contrary, *Hir* is flecked with the adages and proverbs, and the smells and sights of medieval towns.

(a) 'Ah, Waris, the smell of asafoetida will out! / even if with camphor it is alloyed.'
(b) 'It is a universal truth: / there is no grace like the grace of God. / No art like lying, no magic like Kamrup's, / no bow like one made in Lahore. / And no disgrace like jilted love, / no scandal like in Dipalpur. / There is nothing to match the beauty of Yusuf, / no turban like that of Bijwara, / no tissue like that of Kasur. / There is no light like that of sun, / no country beautiful as Kashmir. / The beloved is fairest by one's side, / great is the charm of a distant drum.'[48]

The didactic nature of *Hir Waris* has led some scholars to characterize it as the 'Bible of the rural Punjabis'.[49] Perhaps Waris Shah is the only Punjabi qissa-kar whose language and variegated vocabulary illumines the Punjabi socio-cultural and religious milieu. The first meeting between Hir and Ranjha on the banks of the Chenab, the verbal encounters of Hir with her mother and the qazi of her village, and the long debate of Ranjha with jogi Balnath, all speak of Waris Shah's skilled creation of dramatic effects and transfiguring the qissa into an ideological vehicle. The main characters, Hir and Ranjha, have dramatic attributes such as action, adventure, expression, imitation, and impersonation. Waris Shah was adept in adapting language to the needs of varying situations and characters of different nature, castes, professions and places. While narrating the legend of Hir and Ranjha, Waris Shah himself emerges as an iconographer who has tremendous knowledge of history and mythology, of objects and places, of metaphors and similes, and of life itself. He paints artistically and in minute detail the scene of dawn descending on a village, for instance:

With the chirp of the sparrow and the swirl of the churn, / when the traveler set out on his track; / When the genuine dawn has broken at last, / and reds and pinks began to glow; / And ploughmen put their beasts to the yoke, / who have to break the earth to sow; / And wives at the handmill grind the corn, / for oven full of loaves to bake; / And maidens sit at the spinning-wheel, / and the world resumes its daily chores; / While those who enjoyed their wives' embraces, / run for a bath to pond or well.[50]

Waris Shah begins with the chirping of a sparrow. It is sparrow's loud cry, not the *bang* (call for Islamic prayer) of the *mulla* (whom Waris Shah calls a 'sack of quarrels') which begins the schedule of the day. Peasants are taking their oxen out to plough, girls are bringing their milking stools and cleaning their milk cans, peasants' wives are grinding corn and kneading flour, and their daughters are spinning. The noise of the grinding-stone is heard in every courtyard. With equal skill Waris Shah portrays the physiognomy of Hir:

Followed by her sixty maids, she comes / full of youth's pride and beauty's charm. / Bunches of pearls hanging from her ears,/ she looks a hourie of heavenly birth./ The bright red bodice over her breasts, / makes one forget both heaven and earth. / Her nose-ring like the pole-star dares /the fury of the summer's storm./ O reckless one, relent, for here / so many have pitched their tents and gone! / The squire's daughter sweeps all before, / so arrogant she, so proud and vain! / What praise may one bestow on Hir! / A full moon shines indeed in her brow,/ With serpentine tresses spread round like night: / her eyes are wild like those of a fawn. / Her cheeks pulsate like petals of rose, / and the red in them is the colour of wine. / Like arches of Lahore her brows / are arched, no end of beauty there! / And as she marches at the head / of her fair host, she sways in the air / like eagle's wing – a majesty / that queens may well be proud to show. / Inebriate, elephant-like she rocks / as ever she walks before her maids. / Ineffable should be the state of those / who dare to have a glimpse of her./ The winsome make-up of her face / reminds of a beautiful calligraphy;/ To see her would be a pilgrimage / indeed, to the Prophet's cenotaph! / Her lips are brilliant red like rubies, / and chin a pear-fruit from Iran. / Her teeth a string of lilies, pearls / (for swans!) or seeds of pomegranate. / Tall like a cypress brought from heaven / and fair as a Chinese marionette, / Her neck is as a swan's and shoulders / marble of the purest vein. / Her arms are rolls of kneaded butter, / thighs round and slender and camphor-white, / On her bosom heaving like a wave, / two silken spheroids rise and fall, / And the naval like a musk-pod floats / on the crystal of a heavenly pool! / Her loins are velvet-soft, while shins / are slim like shafts of a minaret. / A fairy from the garden of Lanka, / or the court of Indra, or the circle of the moon, / Hir would outshine a thousand beauties, / far lovelier than the loveliest queen. / All like a row of forest deer, / the amazons come with Hir at their head, / Who rolls like a wave or skims the skies / as a crane that flies ahead of the flock, / And shines like a sword that is just unsheathed / to fall upon the fatal block. / And gallants coming across her path / will surely fall upon its blade. / Throbs passion in every inch of her, like music trembling in a guitar, / Her peasant step falls all on her feet, / Or like a Qazilbash [a tribe of Afghans] horseman who / has run amuck . . . / Or is it swords that clang afar / as the host advances from Qandhar / Her lips are red with chewing bark, / she has slain all merchants of the town.[51]

This sketch makes one feel as if Hir was Waris Shah's beloved.[52] As a scholar puts it, beauty resides in art, but without art beauty is not illumined.[53]

It is futile to attempt either purely mystical or purely profane, purely aesthetic or purely Islamic/Persian sufic interpretations of this long poem. Yet I will talk presently of some imagery used by Waris Shah in the context of Islam and sufism. Typically, his images turn into symbols of purely aesthetic character. Defining the characteristics of Persian sufi poetry, Ernst says that, love poetry primarily describes the physiognomy of the beloved.

Most important are the moonlike face and the black tresses, which reflect the twin attributes of grace and wrath, Islam and infidelity. . . . Many of the attributes . . . are based on the ideal of youthful manly beauty that arose in the Turco-Iranian courts of Central Asia: a moonlike face, skill at polo, long locks of hair, the beginnings of a mustache, a tall and slender stature and cruel indifference to the sufferings of the lover. It was a male homoerotic model of love, typified by the tales of Sultan Mahmud of Ghazna and his devoted slave Ayaz, that formed the basis for both courtly and mystical love poetry in the Persian tradition.[54]

The motif of the (red)rose occurs five times in the text. History tells us that Ruzbihan Baqli, a mystic of Iran (d. 1209) illuminated the prophetic tradition according to which Muhammad pronounced and presented a rose as the manifestation of God's glory. He gave the rose a sanction of religious experience. Baqli's vision of God is a 'cloud of roses, the divine presence fulgent as a marvellous red rose. Since this flower reveals divine beauty and glory most perfectly, the nightingale, symbol of the longing soul, is once and forever bound to love it'—hence the roses and nightingales of Persian and Turkish poetry.[55]

Mystical love is one of the most fascinating facets of sufism. In fact, in the realm of sufism love has its own autonomy. Annemarie Schimmel observes that 'the spiritual life becomes so highly intensified, so delicately differentiated, that it almost develops into an art of its own' with love at its centre. 'Sometimes', she further observes, 'such a refined and deepened love would find its object in a human being, in which the fullness of divine beauty and radiant glory seemed to be reflected, and out of this attitude the hybrid Persian mystical-erotic poetry developed'.[56] Waris Shah, who was a follower of the Chishti silsila, contemplates in the body and beauty of Hir the perfect manifestation of divine beauty. He depicts a beautiful Hir as she is the beloved. Beauty is meaningless in Punjabi qissa poetry when there is no love to contemplate. It is love that makes the qissa a conflict-ridden social narrative ending in the death of lovers. Hir, in her first meeting with Ranjha, reveals her aspiration to be a martyr. She tells him: 'On the dice of love I stake my head/ to lose it and to see you win.' In sufism the term *shahid* (martyr) which literally means 'witness', is used for the beautiful beloved, for the latter is the true witness of divine beauty.[57] In the above cited long verse, Waris Shah makes a reference to the calligraphy: 'The winsome make-up of her face/reminds of a beautiful calligraphy;/ To look at her would be the vision of the Night of Nights.'[58] It is Islam that places a premium on the aesthetic experience, says al Faruqi,

> the culture of Islam regards beauty as the value on which hangs the whole validity of Islam itself. . . . The aesthetic experience must therefore be extremely important and extraordinarily powerful for it to constitute the base for divine revelation and authority.

The Quran, as perfect and unique embodiment of the literary sublime, has affected the aesthetic consciousness of all Muslims. The literary effect of the Quran spilled into visual, first affecting the art of calligraphy, and through it, the arts of decoration, whether in the illuminated page, bookbinding, bookstand decoration, prayer rugs, mosque pulpits, walls and lamps, or of the house and its utensils and the garden with its horticulture and aquaculture. . . . The life of the Muslim, whether Arabic speaking or otherwise, thus became totally infused with aesthetic values stemming from the Quran.[59]

Acquainted with the Great Traditions of Islam and Hinduism, and also with the process of their spontaneous assimilation in Punjabi society, Waris Shah was capable of presenting the form and content of Punjabi life in his qissa. He combined the crowd-pleasing traditionalism (involved in the genre of qissa) with the narration of the cultural character of the society. *Hir* is full of situations and scenes which apparently seem to be simple, but contain a rich history of Punjab, otherwise unspoken in the text. Waris Shah was himself aware of the literary stature of his *Hir*:

Other poets have wasted their efforts in writing on petty themes. I have composed a grand poem. Oh wise man, you should note that there is a secret under the guise of my words. I have written this Hir with care and meditation. Young people read it with pleasure. I have planted a flower to give a sweet savour. Thank God my purpose is achieved. I have worked at it anxiously day and night.[60]

An Ideological Poet

Waris Shah was a pungent critic of the patriarchs who dominated medieval Punjabi society. He gives ample space in his qissa to the rebellious Punjabi voice against these dominant forces. In the beginning, Waris Shah gives us a clue about his counter-hegemonic predilections:

Friends came one day and made request / that the tale of Hir be told anew; / And bowing to the friends' command /did I this wondrous tale compose / In phrases elegant and demure / fresh as rose petals on the stalk. / This bouquet is of the choicest flowers, / with a perfume nobler than that of rose.[61]

The 'request' signifies the popular urge in the eighteenth-century Punjab people for the revival of the legend in which a passionate, sensitive, and resourceful Punjabi girl defied the hegemony of the feudal patriarchs and religious bigots of her own Muslim community. It may also be pointed out that the popular urge under reference to resuscitate the non-conformist heritage of resistance also arose when the people of Punjab, under the leadership of the Khalsa, were resisting Mughal oppression and the invasions of Ahmad Shah Abdali. A social and political resistance against several forces of oppression coalesced together in the eighteenth century. A similar popular demand was made in the middle of the nineteenth century to the poet Shah Muhammad when the Khalsa Raj was facing turbulence and the Khalsa army had confronted the British in the First Anglo–Sikh War. In his *Jangnama*, Shah Muhammad alludes to such an urge or desire.

> One day as I sat in Wadala; wholly lost, / The Feringhee [the British] became the subject of our talk. / Hira Lal and Nur Khan, two of my bosom friends, / Suddenly did they accost me, asking: / How in the midst of Musalmans and Hindus, / living happily together, / Had a scourge of sorts descended from nowhere? / For, O Shah Mohammed! never in Punjab, / Was a third caste ever known to have come?[62]

In view of the 'request' made to Waris Shah by his friends to versify the legend of Hir, I wish to make four suggestions. First, the request signifies why and how Waris Shah transformed a folk legend into a *text.* He used the legend to narrate the life pattern of Punjabi Muslims, and hence he may be said to have come into conflict with those of his contemporaries who were presenting a patriarchal and monolithic view of the Muslims irrespective of their indigenous roots.[63] Second, the request and the construction of *Hir* by Waris Shah reveal that the legend of Hir is rooted in popular cutlure. Third, the fact that I view *Hir Waris* from the view point of Punjabi Muslims also indicates that texts are not pre-determined, neither do contexts exist readymade but take shape according to the circumstances. They are not guaranteed in advance but are the site for conflicting discourses. Besides, *Hir Waris* is full of meaning potentials. Fourth, and this is of crucial importance, the revival of a folk tale or people's literature in pre-colonial times was different from 'revivals' of traditions made by the middle classes in the colonial period. Thus one may draw a distinction between Waris Shah and his *Hir* and the 'modern' revivalists and their religious tracts of the mid-nineteenth century with a view to appreciate the communal harmony and the syncretic character of medieval Punjabi culture.

Waris Shah presents Hir as a martyr who laid down her life battling social and religious patriarchy. Hir, as a lover-martyr, has carved a niche in Punjab society and its literature. Nevertheless, her martyrdom has not yet been allotted due space in history. Waris Shah's narrative of the hazardous game of love played by Hir was not less adventurous than that of those martyrs who are said to have fought with religious zeal or with caste, community, and class consciousness. The martyrdom of Hir assumes considerable significance in the history of Punjab culture when one finds her conducting debates (as constructed by Waris Shah) with the patriarchs. The latter believed only in their own monologue and would not grant the 'other' a prerogative to speak or dialogue. Thus the struggle of Hir, as narrated by Waris Shah, throws ample light on the domineering patriarchs and their tyranny. Therefore, the anti-patriarchal adventure of Hir, Waris Shah seems to suggest, should not be understood by a historian as just a romantic or sufic exercise, but as a person who encountered the patriarchs and refused to follow their normative codes of conduct. 'History' looks down upon such counter-hegemonic lovers surviving in popular literature as fictitious characters. In his *Hir*, Waris Shah implicitly defines a lover-martyr who witnessesd to his/her faith in love by the sacrifice of his/her life. Hir relishes sacrifice, revels in risks, disregards danger, disdains death, and values nobility. She is boisterous and ebullient, has an enthusiasm and lust for life, and shuns renunciation or withdrawal. She directs her energy and courage towards her pursuits. She dies a heroic death before oppressors and unjust magistrates. Hir is a Punjabi rebel girl who fights the social and religious patriarchs of her own community. Therefore, Waris Shah suggests that one needs to decentralize the monolithic religion-centric notion imposed on the concept and praxis of martyrdom.

It is Waris Shah who immortalized Jhang, the village of Hir, and transformed it into a 'site' for struggle against the patriarchs. This site may be identified as a space of the marginalized characters of society and history. It is not bound to political, administrative, temporal, or geographical boundaries. It is not sacrosanct in the conventional meaning of the word. It has its own membership, different from the citizenship, nation, and nationality. Hir is revered as a martyr. Jhang throbs and reverberates with the memories of Hir, her love, her struggle, and her sacrifices. Waris Shah has not only culturalized and historicized Jhang, but also transformed the flute of Ranjha into an icon.

THE ISLAMICATE CHARACTER OF THE QISSA-KAR

Waris Shah starts his qissa with a sufic note:

> I start with song in praise of the Lord / who made this word spring forth from love. / Prime lover of all is the Lord himself, / and He gave His love to the Prophet-envoy. / Love is the sign of saint and sage / and the man of love will be solemn and shy.[64]

He concludes the qissa in a similar vein. A sufic quest for mystical union with Allah is reflected in the last stanza of *Hir*. Waris Shah characterizes Hir as the Spirit (*ruh*) and Ranjha as the physical frame or body (*kalbut*) that enshrines the Spirit. It was the sufi in Waris Shah that deconstructed the traditional discourse of love (*ishq*).[65] His entire text is steeped in the non-conformist ambience of sufism and the bhakti traditions that confronted religious patriarchs such as the qazi and the mullah. The *pir–murid* relationship and the praxis of martyrdom on the part of murid can be read into the dialogue during Hir's first meeting with Ranjha on the banks of the Chenab. The dialogue underscores two significant features of sufism: submission to and sacrifice for a pir (Ranjha) The following lines extracted from the conversation illustrate my point.

> 'How fortunate I did not swear at you or give you offence!' 'I would live like a beggar at your feet.' 'I will roll like a carpet on your path.' 'Along with all my spinster friends, / Your bond-slave ever I shall stay.' 'My life is dedicated to you.' 'On the dice of love I stake my head, / to lose it and see you win.[66]

Hir was the daughter of a *sardar*, a feudal lord of five villages, and her submission to Ranjha implies many things. Waris Shah sets their relationship within the sufic ambience from the start. The first sight of Ranjha (pir) makes Hir a slave (murid). Punjabi qissas, based on the folk love legends, bring sufi mysticism to the fore. The boat of Hir on which Ranjha (pir) is resting is transformed onto the threshold of his khanqah. For Ranjha, all worldly possessions have lost their lustre, as he has left his village and renounced his patrimony in search for love. If Hir needs to be blessed with the 'love' of a pir or a murshid, she has to be 'poor' and humble. Spiritual poverty (*faqr*) demands complete submission to the pir and humility in his presence. In the realm of sufism, the term *faqir* signifies spiritual poverty, being poor in relation to God, and hence being dependent upon Him. Poverty for the sufis was a sign of turning away from the world and concentrating on divine reality. 'Poverty is my Pride', the Prophet Muhammad is reported to have uttered.[67] Waris Shah must have been acquainted with the episode of Akbar's submission to Salimuddin Chishti when he versified the said debut meeting between Hir and Ranjha. If not aware of the episode, certainly Waris Shah understood the meaning of the relationship that exists between a pir and his murid. Let me recall the episode which is current at the popular level so as to illuminate the humility of Hir. Akbar went to the abode of Salimuddin Chishti in the hope of being blessed with a son. The barefoot emperor, having left behind his palace and entourage, walked on burning desert sand in order to petition the mystic. One aspect of the meeting of Hir–Ranjha and Hir's submission to the latter, and of Akbar's visit to Salimuddin Chishti's abode, underlines that sufis look askance at the powerful and belittle anybody who pay homage to them.[68] Waris Shah is also well acquainted with the Great Traditions of Islam. Time and again he quotes the Quran. But he never lets his text to be wholly swayed by Islamic injunctions. He is not just a 'Muslim', but also a 'Punjabi': he journeys in his own text for some time as a *Muslim* but by and large, like other Punjabis, is more inclined to respond to bhakti and sufi traditions.[69] We come across three references from the Quran when Ranjha is thrown out of employment by Chuchak, as he is annoyed with the affair between his herdsman and his daughter. Chuchak tells his wife, 'we did not want him [Ranjha] for a bull / to lead our daughters to pasture-haunts'. Now Ranjha has been deprived of bread. On this situation, Waris Shah gives his own comments and substantiates them with partial references drawn from the Quran. Only the italicized passages are given in the text of *Hir*, but I cite the complete *Ayat* (verse):

(i) 'And He listens to / Those who believe and / Do deeds of righteousness, / *And gives them increase / Of His Bounty*: but / For the unbelievers there is / A terrible Chastisement.' (S. 42, A. 26, p. 1483)[70]

(ii) 'And remember Moses prayed / For water for his people; / We said: "Strike the rock / with thy staff". Then gushed forth / There from twelve springs. / Each group knew its own place / For water. *So eat and drink* / Of the sustenance provided by Allah, / And do no evil nor mischief / On the (face of the) earth.' (S. 2, A. 60, p. 24)[71]

(iii) '*There is no moving creature / On earth but its sustenance / Dependeth on Allah*: He knoweth / Its resting place and its / Temporary deposit: / All is in a clear Record.' (S. 11, A. 7, p. 582)[72]

Hir is about to be married to Saida Khera, a lad of the Khera clan of village Rangpur Khera. Ranjha is agonized, helpless. Waris Shah makes him say that all ills must be borne with patience. If God is good, then Khera and Hir would never mate together. Ranjha utters a verse from the Quran:

'*The Day the heaven shall be / Rent asunder with clouds*, / And angels shall be sent down, / Descending (in ranks).' (S. 25 A. 25, p. 1039)[73]

'*One day the Earth will be / Changed to a different Earth, / And so will be the Heavens*, / And (men) will be marshaled / Forth, before Allah, the One, / The Irresistible.' (S.14 A. 48, p. 707)[74]

During her conversation with the qazi on the occasion of her nikah, Hir pleads her case and justifies her love for Ranjha: 'All things I have created in pairs,/ does He not say in the holy Quran'. She quotes the following verse:

'*And of everything / We have created pairs*: / That ye may reflect.' (S. 51 A. 49)[75]

One comes across many such references in *Hir Waris*.[76] But an overall reading and analysis of *Hir* present Waris Shah as the protagonist of inter-cultural dialogue, who implicitly conveys that no culture or religion is a system totally closed within itself, or an independent reality. He is not comfortable with degenerate persons who are at the helm of religious affairs, as is evident from the encounters with mullah, qazi and jogi Balnath. At the beginning of the qissa, Ranjha debunks the corrupt character of the mullah of a village mosque.

Ranjha leaves his village Takht Hazara, for Jhang Siyal, the village of Hir. During the journey he wonders at the life pattern of the mullah of the village mosque. Then from Jhang he proceeds to the hillock (*tilla*) of jogi Balnath, who too does not escape scathing remarks about corrupt and homosexual jogis. The motif of encounters with the religious representatives of a society reminds one of Guru Nanak, who during his odysseys in the fifteenth-sixteenth centuries, discoursed with the mullahs and brahmans and in the process critiqued their orthodoxy, conservatism, and superstitions. If one reads the margins of the text of *Hir*, one may discern the collective conscious and subconscious Punjabi mind and ethos represented by the qissa-kar. Let me add here that the motif of a *pardesi* (one who makes adventurous journeys) is prominent in Punjabi literature and is mainly illustrated by Raja Rasalu, the legendary old Punjabi hero, and by Guru Nanak. Ranjha stands in the same category. Generally, a pardesi who survives in Punjab literature is non-sectarian, adventurous, critic, argumentative and logical. Waris Shah too was one, as has been observed.

It is interesting to read how the three facets of Waris Shah, Muslim, qissa-kar and sufi, combine together in the beginning of the narration of his *Hir*. Waris Shah illustrates this blend through Ranjha. After having quarrelled with his sisters-in-law, Ranjha leaves Takht Hazara for Jhang Siyal. Before crossing the Chenab, Ranjha reached a local mosque after much travelling. The grandeur of the mosque inspired him to transpose it to the Rock Mosque in Jerusalem (*bait al-muqaddas*), also known as the 'Distant Mosque' (*masjid al-aqsa*). Such a transposition has a deeper meaning. The special veneration for the Dome of the Rock in the twelfth century was derived from a belief that it was the site to which Muhammad was transported from Mecca before he ascended to heaven.[77] Now Waris Shah's Ranjha is to be transported to the world of *ishq*. For that matter he has to cross the river Chenab. Obviously, Waris Shah, 'the Muslim' transforms the local mosque, where Ranjha is to stay for a night, into masjid al-aqsa. Interestingly, Waris Shah, the 'sufi' makes Ranjha set out for the river-bank in the morning not with the *bang* of a mullah but with the chirp of the sparrow. The open mind of Waris Shah is characterized by historian Mujeeb: 'His work transcends all barriers. It is not Muslim or Hindu or Sikh. It is the most perfect image of Punjab, an image such as even the sufi could not create anywhere else in India.'[78] In his *Hir* Waris Shah suggests that Punjabi Muslims cannot be historically understood purely in terms of a religious category, because of the cultural reciprocity between Islam and the 'other' non-Islamic elements and the resultant cultural fusion. The phenomenon of cultural reciprocity is central to any analysis.[79]

NOTES

1. Darshan Singh Maini, *Studies in Punjabi Poetry*, New Delhi, 1979, p. 113
2. Denis Matringe, '*Hir* Waris Shah', in M. Waseem, ed., *On Becoming an Indian Muslim: French Essays on Aspects of Syncretism*, New Delhi, 2003, p. 209.
3. Sutinder Singh Noor, 'Waris Di Talash Kardian', in Sutinder Singh Noor, ed., *Heer Waris: Jagat Te Jugat*, New Delhi, 1999, p. 56. In his introduction to *Hir Waris* Jit Singh Sital stated in 1963: 'Every year in the united Punjab more than 50,000 printed copies of *Hir* sell.' *Hir Waris*, Delhi, 1973, p. 11. Shafqat Tanveer Mirza informs us: 'After the Holy Quran the next bestseller is the Heer [Hir] written by Waris Shah.' *Resistance Themes in Punjabi Literature*, Lahore, n.d., p. 211 Waris Shah fired the imagination of the subsequent qissa-kars writing about the same love-legend to the extent that the 650 *band* and 4,500 *baint* (a meter in prosody) constituting the original text of *Hir* rose to the number of 1,200 and 12,000 respectively. Jit Singh Sital, *Hir Waris*, pp. 13–15. Also see Mohan Singh Diwana, ed., *Hir Waris*, Lahore, 1947, pp. 9–15.

4. Sant Singh Sekhon, *A History of Panjabi Literature*, Patiala, 1993, vol. I, p. 4.
5. Jagtar Singh, ed., *Heer Damodar*, Patiala, 2000, pp. 3–9.
6. The first qissa of Hir–Ranjha, written in a non-Punjabi language, is said to have been versified in Balochi by Baki Kolabi in AD 1575. He is said to have come from Bukhara to India and was killed in Jaunpur in 1579 during the time of Akbar. Rattan Singh Jaggi, *Punjabi Sahit Da Srot Moolak Itihas*, pt. III, Patiala, 1999, pp. 242–3.
7. Jagtar Singh, ed., *Heer Damodar*, p. 1.
8. Sant Singh Sekhon, *A History of Panjabi Literature*, Patiala, 1996, vol. II, p. 60
9. Rattan Singh Jaggi, *Punjabi Sahit Da Srot Moolak Itihas*, pt. III, p. 236.
10. Sekhon, *A History of Panjabi Literature*, vol. II, p. 65.
11. Gurcharan Singh, *Studies in Punjab History and Culture*, New Delhi, 1990, p. 201.
12. Gurdit Singh Premi, *Waris Shah: Ik Pariche*, Patiala, 1999, pp. 101–8. Prem Prakash Singh is of the view that Multani and the other dialects of West Punjab like Pathohari, Hindko, Jhangi, and others are collectively known as Lahendi. Prem Prakash Singh, *Punjabi Bhasha Da Srot Te Bantar*, Patiala, 1996, pp. 350–2.
13. Mohan Singh, *An Introduction to Panjabi Literature*, Amritsar, n.d., p. 114.
14. Sekhon, *A History of Panjabi Literature*, vol. II, p. 69.
15. *Churi* means loaves crumpled into balls and sweetened with sugar. For Punjabi version see S.S. Padam, ed., *Hir Ahmad*, Barnala, 1960, p. 295.
16. For Punjabi version see Jagtar Singh, ed., *Heer Damodar*, Delhi, stanza 642.
17. R.C. Temple, *The Legends of Punjab*, Patiala, 1963, vol. II, pp. 180–1.
18. Jit Singh Sital, ed., *Hir Waris*, Delhi, 1973, stanza no. 5 (henceforth cited as *Hir Waris*).
19. For details see C.M. Naim, *Zikr-i-Mir: The Autobiography of the Eighteenth Century Poet: Mir Muhammad Taqi 'Mir'*, Delhi, 2002.
20. Gurdit Singh Premi, *Waris Shah: Ik Pariche*, p. 6
21. Jit Singh Sital, ed., *Hir Waris*, Patiala, n.d., p. 37.
22. Sayyids (the noble ones) wore, as a sign of distinction, a green turban. They were descendants of Ali, who married Fatima, the

daughter of Prophet Muhammad. Ibbetson is of the view that Sayyids 'for the most part came in with the Mohammedan conquerors or under their dynasties, and were granted land or revenue which their descendants still hold and enjoy'. Denzil Ibbetson, *Punjab Castes*, Delhi, 1993, pp. 222–3.

23. *Hir Waris*, stanza no. 608.
24. Gurdit Singh Premi, *Waris Shah: Ik Pariche*, p. 3.
25. Tanvir Bukhari, 'Waris Shah Da Pind', in Jit Singh Sital, ed., *Waris Shah: Jivan Te Rachana*, Patiala, 1970.
26. S.S. Amol, ed., *Hir Sayad Waris Shah*, Amritsar, 1949, p. 11.
27. Gurdit Singh Premi, *Waris Shah: Ik Pariche*, p. 3.
28. Tanvir Bukhari, 'Waris Shah Da Pind', and Gurdit Singh Premi, *Waris Shah: Ik Pariche*, p. 3.
29. Avtar Singh Azad, *Satt Sitarey*, New Delhi, 1957, pp. 103–4; S.S. Amol, ed., *Hir Sayad Waris Shah*, p. 12. According to Moula Bakhsh Kushta, Waris Shah's father's name was Sayad Qutab Shah. *Punjab De Heere*, ed. Gurmukh Singh, Sirhind, 1996.
30. Muhammad Umar, *Islam in Northern India during the Eighteenth Century*, New Delhi, 1993, p. 259.
31. Moula Bakhsh Kushta, *Punjab De Heere*, p. 155.
32. Muhammad Umar, *Islam in Northern India during the Eighteenth Century*, p. 259.
33. Gurdit Singh Premi, *Waris Shah: Ik Pariche*, p. 8.
34. Amrit Lal Pal, *Sufi Kissa Ate Bir Kav*, Patiala, 1999, p. 2.
35. M. Zameeruddin Siddiqi, 'The Resurgence of the Chishti Silsilah in Punjab during the Eighteenth Century', *Indian History Congress Proceedings*, 1970.
36. In *Hir*, Waris Shah pays tribute to Baba Farid. See stanza no. 5.
37. Amrit Lal Pal, *Sufi Kissa Ate Bir Kav*, p. 3.
38. *Hir Waris*, pp. 40–1. Moula Bakhsh Kushta, *Punjab De Heere*, p. 155.
39. *Hir Waris*, stanza no. 607.
40. In this connection Surjit Hans states that 'Waris Shah and Charat Singh (grandfather of Maharaja Ranjit Singh) were born in 1722. Charat Singh was carving a territory around Gujranwala. Jandiala, the birth place of Waris Shah, was in the jurisdiction of Gujranwala. It is very likely that the rise of Charat Singh was responsible for Waris Shah's exile in Qasur. The town was under a constant threat from the Sikh chiefs after 1765 when Ahmad Shah Abdali was finally driven out of Punjab. Waris Shah composed his *Hir* in

Malika Hans in 1766 after his second exile from Qasur. Even Malika Hans fell to the Sikhs before his death in 1798. It was his (third) exile into the next world. Waris Shah, the exile, was unconsciously pre-occupied with the "country".' 'The Idea of Country in *Hir* By Waris Shah', *Punjab Journal of Sikh Studies*, vol. XX, no. 2, 1996.

41. Some scholars consider *Hir* to be the first and the last literary production of Waris Shah but Moula Bakhsh Kushta and others refer to other works of his: *Kissa Burad, Chuheri Nama, Siharfi Lahore, Sassi Waris Shah,* and *Dohrey Waris Shah.*
42. Mikko Lehtonen, *The Cultural Analysis of Texts*, tr. Aija-Leena Ahonen and Kris Clarke, New Delhi, 2000, pp. 78 and 123–7.
43. Darshan Singh Maini, *Studies in Punjabi Poetry*, New Delhi, 1979, p. 52.
44. Bikrama Jit Hasrat, *Life and Times of Ranjit Singh: A Saga of Benevolent Despotism*, Nabha, 1977, p. 418.
45. Jit Singh Sital, 'Waris Shah Di Boli', in Jit Singh Sital, ed., *Waris Shah: Jivan Te Rachana.*
46. K.S. Kang, *Sukhan Da Waris (Sayad Waris Shah)*, Amritsar, 1990, p. 99.
47. Mohan Singh Diwana, ed., *Hir Waris Shah,* Lahore, 1947, p. 30.
48. *Hir Waris*, stanza nos. 35, 339 and 340.
49. Mohan Singh Diwana, ed., *Hir Waris Shah*, p. 28.
50. *Hir Waris*, stanza no. 42.
51. Ibid., stanza no. 53.
52. Mohan Singh Diwana, ed., *Hir Waris Shah*, p. 31.
53. Surjit Hans, 'Hir Waris Shah Ate Atharvin Sadi Da Punjab', in Bikram Singh Ghuman, ed., *Punjabi Qissa Ate Bir Kav*, Amritsar, 1998, p. 119.
54. Carl W. Ernst, *The Shambhala Guide to Sufism*, New Delhi, 2000, pp. 159–60.
55. Annemarie Schimmel, *Mystical Dimensions of Islam*, Lahore, rpt. 2003, p. 299.
56. Ibid, p. 289.
57. Ibid., p. 291.
58. *Hir Waris*, stanza no. 54.
59. Ismail al-Faruqi, 'Islam as Culture and Civilization', in Salem Azzam, ed., *Islam and Contemporary Society*, London, 1982, pp. 167, 171–2.
60. *Hir Waris*, stanza nos. 607–10.

61. *Hir Waris*, stanza nos. 6 and 7.
62. For the English rendering of the *Jangnamah* see P.K. Nijhawan, *The First Punjab War: Shah Mohammed's Jangnamah*, Amritsar, 2001.
63. In this connection the following statement issued at the International Punjabi conference Lahore in 1986, needs to be read carefully:

    We, the Punjabi writers of progressive culture have found our identity afresh in the living and vibrant part of our cultural heritage, as well as in the literature of progress and resistance . . . we reject what is decadent in our past heritage; we adopt what is full-blooded and alive in it. To accept all past is a tragic blunder. It stokes the fires of chauvinism. We subscribe to the scientific world-view; we reject fundamentalism in all its forms. We declare that the real Punjabi literature is synthesis of reason and emotion.

    Fateh Mohammad Malik, *Punjabi Identity*, Lahore, 1989, p. 15.
64. *Hir Waris*, stanza no. 1.
65. A reader may study Jagbir Singh, 'Qissa *Hir Waris* Da Virchnatamik Adhiyan' (A Deconstructive Study of the Qissa *Hir Waris*), in Sutinder Singh Noor, ed., *Heer Waris: Jagat Te Jugat*, pp. 119–31.
66. *Hir Waris*, stanza nos. 64–5.
67. Carl W. Ernst, *The Shambhala Guide to Sufism*, p. 4.
68. I have borrowed this episode and argument from Syed Akbar Hyder, *Reliving Karbala: Martyrdom in South Asian Memory*, New Delhi, 2006, pp. 105–35.
69. Critics of Punjabi literature have two opinions on Waris Shah's *Hir*. Tejwant Singh Gill is of the view that Waris Shah never aimed at constructing an 'Islamic' narrative of the legend. But Hirdejit Singh premises that Waris Shah did have such an objective. See Tejwant Singh Gill, 'Hir Waris Shah: Ideology and Narrative'; Hirdejit Singh, 'Narrative of Hir Waris Shah' (in Punjabi) in Bikram Singh Ghuman, ed., *Punjabi Kissa Kav Da Birtant Shashtar*, Amritsar, 2001.
70. To highlight the Quranic element in *Hir Waris*, I have consulted the text edited by Sant Singh Sekhon titled *Hir Waris Shah*, published by Sahitya Akademi, New Delhi, p. 66.
71. Ibid.
72. Ibid.
73. Ibid., p. 98.

74. Ibid.
75. Ibid., p. 109.
76. Ibid., pp. 245, 249, 255, 258, 276, 322.
77. Sunil Kumar, 'Assertions of Authority: A Study of Discursive Statements of Two Sultanates of Delhi', in Muzaffar Alam, Françoise 'Nalini' Delvoye and Marc Gaborieau, eds., *The Making of Indo-Persian Culture: Indian and French Studies*, New Delhi, 2000, p. 58.
78. M. Mujeeb, *The Indian Muslims*, London, 1967, p. 327.
79. M. Athar Ali, *Mughal India: Studies in Polity, Ideas, Society, and Culture*, New Delhi, 2006, p. 4.

CHAPTER 6

Social Landscape

> The coming of the Arabs, the Tuks and the Afghans introduced further layers on the palimpsest of Indian ethnic identities. Today we speak of them as a collective entity, labeling them 'the Muslims', and label the hosts also collectively 'the Hindus'. But . . . it is historically more accurate to use the labels and terms that were current in those times. . . . Even if defined by religious beliefs and practices, the sense of community was diverse within each category. People were more frequently identified by caste, occupation, language, religion and religious sects, than by the religious labels we use today.
>
> ROMILA THAPAR, *The Penguin History of Early India: From the Origins to* AD *1300*

Unlike the standardized routes mapped by the protagonists of grand narratives, *Hir Waris* apprises us of the local lanes of Islamic life and the indigenous culture of Punjabi Muslims. The major focus of this chapter is to illumine what it meant to be a Muslim in the medieval Punjab. A 'Punjabi Muslim' community, as it is portrayed by Waris Shah, when deprived of a reference to its indigenous geographical site and socio-cultural space, gets reduced to the level of simply an imagined one, not a concrete historical reality. It is observed that often Muslims 'do not form a community by themselves; they come from diverse social, cultural, and ethnic backgrounds, and essentially remain members of such "communities" though they may share a common objective: that of "purifying" the Faith'.[1]

LOCALES

It needs to be underscored that tribal organization was the chief characteristic of society in medieval Punjab, the pivot on which administration and policies revolved. The tribe (*qaum* or *jat*), the clan (*qabila*), and smaller groups of kin dominated social relations and also materially influenced the relationships of production. Besides, even where agriculture and trade were highly developed, society retained many pastoral characteristics.[2] A reading of *Hir Waris* reveals that its entire canvas has been set on three villages and three dominant Muslim Jat (agriculturist) communities: Siyals, Ranjhas, and Kheras. Except for one implicit reference,[3] Waris does not furnish information regarding the Rajput ancestry of these communities. The internal evidence in *Hir Waris*, however, indicates that they were Jats, and proud to be so.[4] But later evidence produced by Steedman, Denzil Ibbetson, and Lepel Griffin describes them as Rajput Muslims with agriculture as the basis of their economy and social structure. Initially the Jats were nomadic pastoralists.[5] How they sedentarized as agriculturists and acquired the status of Rajput before being converted to Islam is a complex phenomenon. I have briefly discussed their transformation from nomadic pastoralists to a settled agrarian society in Chapter 3. It is said that India's early medieval nobility arose in the newly expanding agrarian economies of the time. It represented a small segment of a vast peasant society in the making. This emerging nobility fabricated, through bardic tradition, the status of what is known as 'fire-born' Rajputs. For instance, Andre Wink cites the royal Pratiharas, established at Kanauj in the early ninth century, originating mostly from groups of pastoral Gujjars. It is most likely that the Rajput clans were of a similar pastoral origin. Projecting themselves as the descendants of ancient Kshatriyas, these new Rajput aristocracies 'obliterated their obscure, often pastoral, origins in the expanding agricultural society of early medieval North India'. When genealogical claims were made, especially in the eighth to twelfth centuries, 'the early Rajput tradition was in practice a rather open and flexible one, able to accommodate newcomers from the frontier areas beyond the pale of a settled Hindu society. . . . By the eleventh and twelfth centuries, ideals of chivalry and heroism were widespread in Indian society.'[6]

Two significant points, which may be cited here as argument, deserve our attention. First, these Muslim converts among the Jat Rajput clans of Siyals, Ranjhas and Kheras (which we come across in *Hir Waris*), unlike the Rajput Hindus, did not make an attempt to enter caste society, because of the fact that the Muslims were the ruling class and being Muslim provided them a religious identity and status by association. Second, originally, nomadic tribes as they were, they would have made efforts to claim Rajput lineage for status and power. While their endeavours to enter caste society were in the process, the Muslims established their political supremacy in northern India. Having acquired a Rajput lineage, they were not prepared to renounce it.

The protagonist Hir is the daughter of Chuchak, a Muslim Rajput of the Siyal clan who is a sardar of five villages. The Siyals are supposed to be descendants of one Rai Shanker, a Punwar Rajput, whose original home was in Daranagar or Dharanagari between Allahabad and Fattapur. A branch of the Punwars had previously emigrated to Jaunpur, and it was there that Rai Shanker was born. Later, when he died, dissensions arose among the members of the family, and his son Siyal emigrated during the reign of Sultan Muizzuddin of Ghor (1178–1206) to Punjab, where he is said to have been converted to Islam by Shaikh Farid.[7] One Mal Khan, a descendant in the ninth generation of Siyals, founded the town of Jhang in 1462. Mal Khan was the first among the Siyals to attain political importance. He exercised extensive sway over the territory around Jhang. Later on, the Mughal government recognized the Siyal chiefs as the zamindars of the Jhang *ilaqa*, to collect the land revenue and transmit it to the provincial headquarters.[8] Thus by the middle of the fifteenth century, the Siyals had established their feudal status. In the early eighteenth century Walidad Khan was the representative chief of the Siyals. He served the Mughal government and was granted the pargana of Chiniot. On the decline of the Mughal power in the eighteenth century, the Siyals, under the leadership of Inyatullah Khan, the successor of Walidad Khan, became independent. Writing about the correlation between the phenomenon of the decline of central authority and that of the rise of the zamindar class, S. Nurul Hasan states that the zamindars

> sought to build up hereditary territorial rights and, whenever the occasion arose, tried to become chieftains. As the Mughal empire became weak and the crisis of the jagirdari system was intensified, these intermediaries

enhanced their power and frequently arose in rebellion along with other intermediary zamindars of their own clan or joined hands with some of the chieftains who were in revolt against the imperial authority. . . . While the imperial authorities strove to subjugate the recalcitrant zamindars and attempted to force them to conform to the imperial land-revenue regulations, they could not afford to suppress this class as a whole. Under strong administrators the intermediaries generally performed their duties in accordance with imperial regulations and exercised their rights within specified limits. But under weak administrators the situation frequently got out of hand.[9]

Thus the Siyals appear to have reached the height of their power shortly after Ahmed Shah Abdali's first invasion of Punjab (1754–5).[10] But in 1760, just seven years before Waris Shah composed *Hir* and when the Sikh *misls* were acquiring political dominance, Hari Singh Bhangi (with Karam Singh Dulu as his collaborator) invaded Jhang and Chiniot. Jhang was given to Karam Singh. And the domination of the Siyals in Jhang was eventually done away with when Maharaja Ranjit Singh conquered it in 1816.[11]

Another significant locale in the qissa is a village named Takht Hazara. It is situated on the other side of the river Chenab.[12] The Muslim Jats of the Ranjha clan lived here. Prior to their conversion to Islam, they subsisted chiefly on agriculture.[13] Takht Hazara was once one of the big towns of Punjab, spreading over an area of a thousand acres.[14] Dhido Ranjha belonged to this village. Mauju, his father, was its headman (*chaudhari*).[15] The third territory referred to in *Hir Waris* is Rangpur Khera, a village of the Khera clan of a Muslim Rajput lineage. Its boundaries touch the district of Jhang. The chief of the village was Ajju, whose son Saida was married to Hir.

Clan-chiefs such as Mauju, Chuchak, and Ajju, who were recognized as *chaudharis*, *khuts*, and *muqaddams* in the sultanate period, were designated as zamindars in the Mughal period. In the political, social, economic and cultural life of medieval India/Punjab, this zamindar class played a vital role. The state administration had to rely on them as 'sub-contractors', in the sense that the state derived its power largely because it could secure their collaboration. It was this class of zamindars who had local roots, that provided patronage to separatist, localist, and parochial elements. They were the autonomous rulers of their territories.[16] Waris Shah characterizes the pelf and power of this class:

In Takht Hazara, a wondrous place, / the Ranjhas live in joy and mirth; / Of where the youth are gallant and brave, / with handsome faces and broad chests; / Rings on their fingers and on their ears, / and *lungis* flowing round their waists; / How can you, Waris, describe Hazara, / a paradise, verily on this earth.[17]

Mauju, the head, with a say in the village, / accepted chief among his peers; / a man of wealth and numerous issue, / two daughters and sons as many as eight; / Held in full trust by all his tribe, / and competent to arbitrate. . . .[18]

Proud of her [Hir] youth and her father's [Chuchak] power, / what does she care for man or God.[19]

Persons, Places and Metaphors

In Punjabi literature Ranjha and his village, Takht Hazara, are metaphors for love and devotion. The poets and people of Punjab call Takht Hazara a pilgrimage centre of lovers, and Ranjha the lord of Takht Hazara. Shah Husain, the sufi-poet of the sixteenth century, wrote:

Ever calling upon Ranjhan, /I have become Ranjhan myself. / Call me Ranjhan, everybody, / Nobody should call me Hir, / The lord whom I ever looked for, / I have found the very same.[20]

The lord of Takht Hazara (Ranjha) is conceived as charismatic and alleviates all pains and agonies. Shah Husain sings:

Centuries old ailments should go, / If Ranjha looks for one. / The sharp prick of Ranjha's love has pierced, / Only the intimate one can draw it out. / Lakhs of needles and nail clippers, / Lakhs of pliers and wrenches have broken./ Lakhs of mullahs and qazis / Have tired with reading charms, / If Ranjha shows his face for a moment, / Hir would be delivered of her pain.[21]

Similarly, in the kafis of Bulleh Shah, the eighteenth-century sufi-poet, the sanctity of Takht Hazara is commensurate with that of Mecca and the Kaba, the supreme religious spaces of Islam all over the world:

'Why should I go to Kaba? / My heart pines for the throne of Hazara' 'The *hajis* go to Mecca, my Mecca is dear Ranjha; / My friends, I am crazy! / Betrothed, I belonged to Ranjha, my father is being stubborn. / The *hajis* go to Mecca; / my house [Takht Hazara] with my bride-groom is my Mecca.'[22]

Thus the motif of 'Ranjha' and 'Takht Hazara' that occurs and reoccurs in the poetry underscores the vernacular character of Punjabi Islam. The vernacularization of Islam in Punjabi sufi poetry enables us to understand the phenomenon of adoption and adaptation of 'the other'.

Takht Hazara, Jhang, and Rangpur Khera are also referred to in *Hir Waris* as the *vatan* or *des.*[23] In medieval times, the concept of a vatan was framed by a kinship network and an ancestral land. Thus the 'social' identity of a country was prominent and dominant among the folk. A country was closely associated with the 'rule' of a zamindar. In the *Qissa Hir* the extent of the zamindari of Hir's father is explicitly stated. It covers five villages. At the local level, a zamindar was called raja. Hir addresses her father as 'Raja'. Ranjha's father is equally a chaudhari of his kin group and a 'state'. Hir explicitly connects a country with chaudhari when making enquiries about Ranjha, the jogi. Thus, the kinship network and zamindari constituted the idea of country (vatan or des) in medieval Punjab.[24] Irfan Habib is of the opinion that the zamindari right could arise when a village was settled by a person who brought its untilled land under cultivation. 'We must suppose, therefore, that there were well-marked blocks of territory, each consisting of a single pargana or group of parganas, under the zamindari of members of the same caste.'[25] How passionate love for a vatan resides in the self of a native may be assessed from an episode in *Hir Waris.* A Jat girl of her (Hir) in-laws' village, Rangpur Khera, goes to Jhang, the native village of Hir. The latter entreats her to offer her salutation (*salaam*) to her des, Jhang, with 'folded hands and in the garments of humility'.[26] Hir speaks of her vatan with love and reverence and this is a motif that occurs and recurs in *Hir Waris.* Again, while passing by the outskirts of Jhang along with Ranjha after having been permitted to marry him, Hir, reminiscing about the past, says: 'This is the valley where we met. This is where we beat Kaidon, bound him with ropes and dragged him along the ground. This is where we used to talk together. . . .'[27]

The 'countries' of the Ranjha, Siyal, and Khera clans were tracts of varying size which derived their names from the tribes. A reading of 'The Elements of Punjab People' in H.A. Rose's *A Glossary of the Tribes and Castes of Punjab and North-West Frontier Province* furnishes valuable information regarding the local roots of many groups. For example, we find a Ranjha des in the Chaj Doab. In the Rachna Doab there was a Chima des. In Sialkot lay Bajwat or the territory of the Baju Rajputs. The Manj or Manjki tract includes the western part of the Phillaur tahsil and a large part of Nakodar. Possibly Manj or Manjki is named after the tribe which held it. In Hoshiarpur, the Khokhars hold the Khokharian, a tract on the Kapurthala border. In Hisar the Punwars held Punwarwati. The system under which a tract was named after the tribe that held it or was dominant in it must have been one of great antiquity. Primitive men rarely, perhaps never, conceived of a great country, Punjab for instance, as a whole; they named a tract after the people who inhabited it or they gave it a descriptive title.[28] In this connection the following observation of S. Nurul Hasan is significant: 'The fact that in the majority of the parganas the zamindari belonged to a single caste and also that persons of the same caste were the zamindars of many contiguous parganas suggests that certain families or clans held zamindari rights over large tracts.'[29] While introducing Takht Hazara, the village of Ranjha clan, Waris Shah describes:

> In Takht Hazara, a wondrous place, /the Ranjhas live in joy and mirth; / Of where the youth are gallant and brave, / with handsome faces and broad chests; Rings on their fingers and on their ears, / and *lungis* round their waists; / How can you, Waris, describe Hazara, / a paradise, on this earth?'

Waris offers us a comprehensive picture of a country ruled by a sardar or chaudhari who is equivalent to a king of his kingdom/

domain comprising a village or cluster of villages, as Chuchak is a sardar of five villages and Mauju of one. The range of the 'local country' defined by the network of kinship and other social ties can be assessed from the social composition of the marriage party of Saida Khera, the son of Ajju, the sardar of Rangpur Khera. Apart from the relatives, musicians, bards and buffoons, the marriage party was attended by men and women of twelve castes (*jatis*) and seven service classes (*sanat*). Though Waris Shah does not provide us the details of the twelve jatis and seven sanats, Jit Singh Sital, the editor of *Hir Waris*, in the endnotes names them: Arain,[30] Awan,[31] Syed,[32] Shaikh,[33] Kamboh,[34] Gakhar,[35] Jat,[36] Dogar,[37] Pathan,[38] Rajput[39] and Mughal.[40] The seven service classes were cobbler (*mochi*), oilman (*teli*), barber (*nai*), water-carrier (*jhiaur*), blacksmith (*luhar*), carpenter (*tarkhan*) and potter (*ghumiar*). That the des/vatan refers to an ancestral village or home can be further illustrated with a list of the names of Punjab villages revealing the dominance of Gujjars, Ahirs, and Gakhkhars, and the presence of Turks, Sayyids, Mughals and Miyas. Mohan Singh Diwana informs that

> along the highway from Peshawar to Delhi one sees the following: Gujjarkhan (tahsil and town), Gujrat (district and town), Gujjarval (town in Ludhiana district). There is Gojra (town in Layallpur district). Gujjar is found in Gujjar Mal, a proper name; Gujral, a sub-caste of Khatris. Still more remarkable are the names of Muslim villages clustering round a very ancient village Gujjarkhan tahsil, Devi, within a radius of 7 miles. Here they are: Gorsia, Panjgrai, Sayyada, Turkvala, Mughla, Jhangi, Madvai, Macchia, Sarja, Hir di Dhok, Miyania di Dhok, and Jattli Thatta. Here are some personal names: Laurasap Khan, Jahandad Khan, Mamu Kasbi, Mir Ghulam, Sikandar Shah, Mathra Singh (or Mathru) Qandhari (sub-caste), Hukam Singh (or Hukku), Gopi Singh, Kauda Singh.[41]

Tribe and Kinship

Punjabi Muslims did not disconnect themselves from their primordial Rajput or Jat moorings and were proud of their legacy.[42] With regard to the general status of the Ranjhas, Siyals, and Kheras, there was not so much difference as could lead to conflict. The chiefs of the three clans, Mauju, Chuchak and Ajju, constituted the higher class of the feudal chaudharis and sardars. They enjoyed a status higher than the peasants and artisans. Nevertheless, in terms of the traditions of the social hierarchy, the Ranjhas of Takht Hazara were considered inferior to the Siyals of Jhang. The former, though economically well off, as is evident from the economic status of Mauju in the *Qissa Hir*, were looked down upon as Jat or agriculturists, not Rajputs. As early as in 1885, Temple listed Dhido as Ranjha Jat, 'known almost exclusively by his caste name'. He further records that 'the Siyals are of Rajput origin, and claim higher rank than the surrounding Jat tribes, to whom they will not give their daughters in marriage, although they may marry Jat women. Thus, though Hir and Ranjha were both Mohammedans, their love was illicit'.[43]

Muslim society in the medieval Punjab was structurally based on customary, not Islamic, laws.[44] The collective decisions of a clan fraternity (*biradari*) prevailed to such an extent that a chief, even if he had economic power, could not implement his will without the consent of the biradari. The chief's power, in other words, was circumscribed by the collective tradition of the fraternity. Violation of such traditions could endanger the legitimacy of a sardar. It was thus to a clan as a whole, not its nominal leader, that the individual owed allegiance, and it was from the clan as a whole that he obtained protection for his interests. To a clan as a whole belonged the power to determine the standard by which its members were expected to lead a social life. A clan brotherhood was conceived as a historical-cultural entity embracing past, present, and future generations.[45] And this notion was the rationale of customary law. The clan was bound by a body of unwritten laws and rules which evolved along with its own historical growth in terms of structure and character. When Hir's father Chuchak became inclined to marry her to Dhido Ranjha, his proposal was rejected by his kinsmen:

Chuchak tells a council of his kin, / his daughter should be married away. / 'We may give her to Ranjha if you approve, / or she may be wedded to someone else. / 'We should so plan it that the coin / of our clan's honour ring not false.'/ 'To be sure, O Chuchak, let us call / some man of the law,' the kinsmen say. / 'We never allied ourselves with the Ranjhas, / their sons could never marry our girls. / 'To add to it, he is servant, / and she the daughter of the best of us. / 'Let us give her to a youth of the Kheras, / with whom our clan has age-old ties.'[46]

Control over marriage was considered a major factor in maintaining the cohesion of biradaris and the authority of biradari panchayats.[47] The Jat Dhido Ranjha, was not a proper match for the daughter of the Siyals. He was only a servant of Chuchak, the father of Hir. 'How could a master give the hand of his daughter in marriage to a slave?'[48] The Siyal biradari suggested a matrimonial alliance with the Kheras with whom they had a longstanding relationship. The Siyals did not tend to break the continuity and sanctity of traditions despite their religious (Islamic) identity with the Ranjhas also. Being exogamous, the Siyals sought a spouse for Hir from the clan of the Kheras but of the same Rajput lineage, an index of social prestige.

Ibbetson's ethnographic study helps us understand the reason why the Siyals did not permit the marriage of Hir with a youth of the Ranjha clan. The chief of the Ranjhas is Mauju who, the text informs us, is the chaudhari of one village, Takht Hazara; whereas Chuchak Siyal, the father of Hir is the sardar of five villages, and whose ancestors, as pointed out in the beginning, had enjoyed political power and high status. Both families are Rajput, agriculturist Muslim, but the matrimonial issue between them does not get resolved. Thus the longstanding political and economic power of the Siyals cannot be ignored. Punjab and north-west frontier regions were open societies where to be a 'Rajput' was not a matter of 'blood' or fixed pedigree but a fluid representation of status as claimed by men of power. It is difficult to draw a distinction between a Jat and a Rajput. Ibbetson maintains that the two were of a common stock, the distinction being social rather than ethnic. He believes that those who rose in the political arena thereby became Rajput.[49] If a Rajput family lost status it became Jat even if it did not part with its tribal name.[50] This point can be illustrated further in the words of Ibbetson:

Setting aside the priests and traders on the one hand and artisans and menials on the other, we have left the great body of agriculturalists who constitute by far the larger portion of the population. This great body of people subsists by husbandry and cattle-farming, and so far their occupation is one and the same. But they are also the owners and occupiers of the land, the holders of more or less compact tribal territories; they are overlords as well as villein; and hence springs the cardinal distinction between the occupation of ruling and occupation of being ruled. Where the actual calling of every-day life is the same, social standing . . . depends very largely upon political importance, whether present or belonging to the recent past. There is the widest distinction between the dominant and the subject tribes; and a tribe which has acquired political independence in one part of the country, will there enjoy a position in the ranks of caste which is denied to it in tracts where it occupies a subordinate position.[51]

Thus, this is the reason why Hir, the daughter of Chuchak Siyal, is curious to know the origin of Dhido Ranjha: 'I will roll like a carpet on your path, / O tell me from which side you come, / What is your tribe, your father' home, / and after what clan are you known?'[52]

The daughter of a sardar, Hir is conditioned to think in terms of socio-economic status. Dhido Ranjha too is introduced to Chuchak as a son of the chaudhari whose caste is Ranjha. 'Son of the squire of Takht Hazara, / he is of the noble Ranjha clan.'[53]

The Ranjhas' 'Rajput' status had come down to the level of the Jat agriculturalists. The Rajput status is not assigned to the Ranjhas by the fraternity of the Siyals. Sociologically speaking, one of the reasons for not assigning it may be that the higher castes, such as Rajputs, Brahmans, Charans, and Baniyas, would not touch the plough. A Rajput considered it degrading to follow the plough.[54]

Hir presents a picture of Punjab Muslim society which is neither monolithic, strictly following the commands of a single religion, nor based on the taboos of purity and pollution. The scene of spinning by young women of different castes and communities sitting together testifies to the absence of social barriers.[55] The scene represents a space for all women: women of well-off families (*mehretiana*), women of khatri caste (*khatranian*), women of Brahman caste (*bahmanetian*), women of carpenter caste (*tarkhania*), women of Jatts (*jattetiana*), women of blacksmith caste (*loharian*), women of tailor caste (*darzaniana*), whores, dancing girls (*malzadian*), wives of bards (*mirzadian*), female needle-vendors (*manharia*), wives of fishermen (*machhretian*), wives of minstrels (*bhatetian*), women haling from Sindh (*makretian*), those females who were engaged in the profession of twisting twine for stringing cots (*van vatetian*), wives of liquor vendors (*kalalnan*), females engaged in the profession of leeching (*gagrian*), temple dancers (*ramjtetian*), female drum-beaters (*bhrainan*), wives of watchmen (*barwalian*), females engaged in threshing reed fibres used for making ropes, strings or matting (*dhani kuttanan*), wives of boatmen (*metnan*), females who dwelt in huts (*pakhvarian*), wives of peddlers (*banjarian*), wives of the palmists, known in vernacular as *rawals* (*rawalanian*), female scent-vendors (*gandhilian*), female rope-walkers/acrobats (*natnian*), dancers (*bainan*), wives of those who performed the *ras*, i.e. the drama related to the life of Krishna (*vir-radhnan*), women of those who press oil-seeds (*telna*), women of cobblers (*chamariana*) and women of Khojas, Pathans, Banjaras, Rajputs, Bhatts, Sayyids, Shaikhs, Kalals, Jains, etc. Here we observe that women of about twenty different castes and professions sang together while spinning. The caste-collage sketched by Waris Shah on the canvas of *trinjan* underlines what Ibbetson said about conversion from Hinduism to Islam not having much effect on caste.'[56] For Ibbetson, 'the whole basis of diversity of caste is diversity of occupation'.[57] *Hir Waris* too displays caste in this light and the caste-collage of the *trinjan* substantiates it.

The caste-collage also needs to be studied from the viewpoint of the character of Islamic expansion, which had started from Arabia. It is premised by a sociologist that by the time this expansion began in India, its tribal character had undergone a significant transformation. Its contact with Persia fostered a hierarchal social structure in Islamic society; and the Islamic elite, as bearers of its Great Tradition, were now stratified into separate classes. The twelfth-century Muslim conquerors of India were 'distinctively divided into priests (including missionaries), nobility (ruling families and administrators), and all the others (including soldiers, merchants, artisans, etc.).'[58] Thus the early encounters with Islam reinforced the social structure of local society.

Waris Shah also apprises us that the mutual relationships were governed by the *jajmani* system. The *jajman* was a kind of 'patron', and hence the *jajmani* system was one of patronage. The *jajmani* system was marked by a village-wide exchange of services and goods between patron and client. There was a 'dominant caste' in almost all villages, whose members exercised influence, no matter what its position was in the region as a whole. In fact, it is generally a Rajput, Kshatriya, or peasant-proprietor caste.[59] References in *Hir Waris* speak of a cluster of twenty-one such caste groups (*patties*) or service-castes (*khidmatgars*): cobbler (*mochi*), oilman (*teli*), barber (*nai*), village watchman (*chowkidar*), village water carrier who carries water in cattle skin (*mashki*), waterman (*jhiaure*), bard singer (*marasi*), priests and saints (like *maulvi, faqir, brahman*), washerman (*dhobi*), blacksmith (*luhar*), carpenter (*tarkhan*), potter (*ghumiar*), minstrel (*bhat*), midwife (*dai*), fisherman (*machhi*), wrestler (*pahalwan*), etc. These *khidmatgars* were at the beck and call of the people of the dominant community.[60] In the qissa, Aulia barber, Alfu cobbler, Mojm herdsman, Dhidi fisherman, Changar *doom* and Billa sweeper all are the *khidmatgars* of Chuchak, the sardar. But they all lead their lives within the metaphors of kinship: *bhai* (brother) and *bacha* (son/daughter). A sense of shared honour (*izzat*) is strongly prevalent among them.[61] Marriage is arranged by collaterals or ritual intermediaries. The Kheras sought the services of a barber to convey to the Siyals the message about the former's intention of marrying their son with the latter's daughter.[62] A Brahman is consulted to fix the auspicious date for the wedding. Again, the house of a lower-caste bard (*doom*) is chosen to cure Hir of snake bite. Different from the feudal formation of Western Europe, Indian feudalism was community-oriented.[63]

Lived Islamic Life

The conversion of the fourteen clans of Rajputs, including the Siyals, Ranjhas, and Kheras, to Islam is said to have taken place during the time of Baba Farid in the thirteenth century,[64] but the qissa of *Hir* portrays a culture more Punjabi than 'Islamic'. Tribal names such as Mauju, Ajju, Dhido, Saida, Kaido, and Malki continued in use, which could not reveal religious identity. Conversion, thus, did not mean sudden and self-conscious rupture from the non-Islamic past. This was a period when neither British census officials nor zealous middle-class reformers, nor the print media, had intervened in public life. Punjabi folk visited the shrine of Shaikh Farid as his devotees, and probably did not perceive themselves as staunch adherents of their 'new' religion. They can be best described as enrooted Punjabi Muslims. There is obviously distinction between conversion that is fabricated as a 'rupture', and conversion that is an addition to existing social life. One needs to know that the dialectics of culture do not subscribe to the 'total' negation of the previous cultural phase.

Hir Waris illustrates the lived life of Punjabi Muslims. As mentioned above, a Brahman is consulted for the date of the marriage of Saida with Hir.[65] In Damodar's *Hir*, both a qazi and a Brahman perform the rituals of the Punjabi Muslim family.[66] The Islamic taboos regarding the use of alcohol and music do not intervene in the celebration of the marriage.[67] The five sufi pirs grant Ranjha the love of Hir only after hearing the music he plays on his flute.[68] Such transgressions were not only true at the folk level but also on that of the ruling class.[69] Drinking is said to be the etiquette of kingship.[70] Similarly, dance and music were also an integral element of enjoyment of elite gatherings.[71] Thus we discover in *Hir Waris* that the exuberance and vibrancy of folk or indigenous culture is retained in contrast to the puritanical concepts of Islam. The socio-cultural character of Punjabi Muslims, as revealed by Waris Shah, is indicative of the steady and sustained impact of tribal and sufi-cum-bhakti traditions. References to a large number of Hindu and Islamic legends and myths in *Hir Waris* further substantiate the existence of cultural fusion. While Sahiti, the sister-in-law of Hir, was involved in a scuffle with Ranjha who appeared in the disguise of a jogi, she said,

> We women have bridled Rajas like Bhoj,[72] / you cannot understand our ways. / Kings' jail their brothers for our sake, / and brothers-in-law to princedom raise. / You know how women can humble princes / like Rasalu[73] for all their pride. / Yusuf[74] suffered much harm because a woman / and Sassi's lover in the desert died burning. / Sohni lost her

Mahiwal and herself, / and Jalali Roda[75] was cut into pieces. / Ravana[76] got his Lanka reduced to ashes, / for Sita's[77] sake for all his learning. / The Pandavas[78] lost full eighteen hosts / in consequences of a woman's jibe.[79]

The absence of references in *Hir* to the basic Islamic practices, the profession of faith and the five obligatory prayers is significant. We do not find any reference to Muslim women veiling themselves. Hir wore a partial veil at the residence of her in-laws,[80] but that is condemned as an evil in the qissa. Ranjha, the jogi, exhorts Hir:

The veil deserves to be put in fire; /it is the cause of many ills. / It hides the splendour of a beautiful face, / and in the open ruin invites. / It drowns the lover's heart in sorrow, / or stifles it like a bird in a cage. / Come, see the world in all its glory, / let not the veil keep you in siege. / The veil binds even those who have eyes, / take off the evil, discover your lights. / Pearls ought not to be buried in earth, / nor flowers, Waris, scorched on coals.[81]

Punjabi Muslim women seem to have been ignorant about the prohibition regarding ornaments. It is stated that during the eighteenth century in northern India, Muslim women 'freely used the ornaments, some of which retained their original Hindu names, while others were given Persian names'. They also imitated many of the toilet custom used by the Hindu women.[82] In *Hir Waris* young unmarried women wear the *kurti* (a bodice reaching the waist) and *salwar*, whereas *choli* (a bodice covering only the breasts), *lungi*, and *ghaghara* were worn by married women. The *dupatta*, *chadder*, *phulkari*, and *chuni* served as headdresses. Hir is given a variety of ornaments on the occasion of her marriage.[83] Necklaces such as *har*, *chanan-hara*, *hemail-mala* and *jangerian* and nose ornaments were worn. One may find a good deal of references to *jangerian*, *machhlian* and *laung* nose ornaments in the folk songs. Among the varieties of the ear-rings worn by the women, Waris Shah mentions *bundey*, *pipal-pattian* (crescent-shaped), and *bir-balian* (a circlet with pearls worn in the ear). Arms, wrists, fingers and ankles were bedecked with different kinds of ornaments, such as *pochian* and *pazeb*. In addition to ornaments, women used perfumes and smeared their bodies with *vattna* (stuff made of maize flour, turmeric, and oil). They wore their hair in different styles.

Eyes were brightened with the use of *surma* (collyrium). *Surkhi* (lipstick) and *dandrasa* (peels of nut) were used to redden the lips.

An account of the Muslims of northern India during the eighteenth century, as presented by Muhammad Umar, testifies to the prevalence of cultural fusion. It describes the tradition of the groom's party being led with great pomp and show, accompanied by fire-works, light, music, and dancing parties; yellow and red garments of the bride and bridegroom, colouring of the palms of the bride and bridegroom, chanting of songs called *sithni*, etc., all originally Hindu practices.[84] On the marriage of Hir and Saida Khera, *naklias* (bufoons), *kanzreians* (professional women dancing parties) and *dooms* accompanied the groom's party. Various kinds of fireworks, stars, wheels, balloons, coloured rain-rockets, set pieces of elephants, stags, peacocks, coloured circles, moving thrones, and revolving moons (*atishbazi*, *phuljarian*, *charkhrian*) were lit as a mark of celebration of the marriage.[85] We also see women joining the barat. There was no burqa or purdah.

> Come beauties row on row such as / the houries of heaven would faint to see. / And peasant women, lotus-faced, / and fragrance-laden adorn the yard. / Of twelve creeds and seven traditions, / they are all of fair figure and face. / They sing and scoff and win applause / they chide, revile and even abuse. / With gossamer shawls they cover their heads, / and silken lungis skirt their waists. / They twist their necks to watch the show, / open their shawls to show their breasts. / With mirror-attested looks they come / into the arena of romance. / Wild peri-like village girls, they sing / in sweet, full-throated voices and dance. / Like peddlers they display their breasts / and musk-pod navels thinly veiled. / They clap their hands and sway and sing, / of high romance, knight-errantry. / They whirl about in ecstasy / and come and go in an endless line. / Till the koel-sweet turn raven-hoarse / and some indeed fall out of tune.[86]

The medieval rural society of Punjabi Muslims, it seems from *Hir Waris*, did not adhere to the Islamic rules of divorce. Hir, whose marriage with Saida Khera has been performed by a qazi according to the shariat, is given back to Ranjha in the end by the decree of Raja Adali. There is no mention of divorce in the concluding part of the legend. This peculiar characteristic of Punjabi Muslims makes them a community distinct from Muslims of other countries. In his works on ethics written in 1590–1 Abdul Qadir Badauni comments, 'what good customs have the people of India that they shun this practice and regard divorce as the worst word of abuse'.[87]

The indigenous life pattern narrated above seems to be incompatible with those norms that Shah Waliullah (AD 1703–62) was propagating for Muslims at the time. His text of Islamic life embedded in the grand Islamic *route* was in tension with that of Waris Shah's text of the legend of Hir that was grounded in the indigenous *roots*. Shah Waliullah's *Wasiyat Nama* and *Hujjatt-Allah-il Baligha* on the one hand, and Waris Shah's *Hir* on the other offer a contrast between a normative text for the Muslims in general and the particular conditions of life in Punjab. Shah Waliullah exhorted Muslims to part with un-Islamic lifestyles. He disapproved of luxurious dowries, playing the drum and other musical instruments, and wearing the bright and gaudy clothes at weddings.

But Punjabi Muslims seem to have been non-conformist and *quasi-Islamic* in view of the norms prescribed by the contemporary Islamic scholar, Shah Waliullah. He writes in his *Wasiyat Nama*: The Muslims in India were like a traveller because their ancestors came to this country as travellers. The Muslims should feel proud of both that they were Arabs by descent and their language was Arabic and these two served as a source of access to the last Prophet (Muhammad). They thank God first of all by not discarding the practices and rituals of the Arabs and by no means adopting the customs of the Iranians and the Hindus as desired by the Prophet. That is, when the Arabs went for *jihad* to Iran, Caliph Umar became worried lest they might adopt the customs of Iran and discard their own customs. Therefore, he wrote a letter telling them that they should tie *tahband* (a strip worn round the loins), and cover up their body with the sheet, and wear shoes, discard the use of stockings and should not wear trousers. They should adopt the dress of their ancestor Ismail and keep off from the pleasures and external appearance (of the Iranians) and sit in the light of the sun as it was the bathroom of the Arabs; adopt the practices of Ma'ad tribe to which belonged the ancestors of the Prophet. They were to wear the coarse garments and lead a hard life. Accustom yourselves to wear the old garments and eat the camels.[88]

An incompatibility between Islamic norms and indigenous or vernacular practices is illustrated by Ranjha. On his way to Jhang, he stays at a mosque. The mullah rebukes him for his improper physical appearance, not expected from a 'good' Muslim:

'Who are you to thus defy the law?' / at sight of Dhido the mullah cried. / 'For cads who do not cut their hair / to proper length we have no room. / A mosque is the house of God Himself, / and the lawless have in it no place. / Long locks like yours, long whiskers, too, / had best be singed, / And also a lungi that falls below / the ankle must be torn away. / A sinful friar, a prayerless man / and a fouling dog deserve no grace. / Hanged shall he be by the nearest tree / who breaks the law in Fikah laid, / And foes of God from a distance must / be shooed away like dogs indeed.'[89]

With reference to the mullah's objection to Ranjha's length of hair, it is interesting to note that the Mughals generally shaved their heads or kept their hair close-cropped, but the Rajputs and Pathans kept their hair long falling upon the back of the neck.[90]

Ranjha rejected Muslim priests who claimed to take a stand on the writ of *fiqh* and to shun and punish those who violated the Islamic law and skipped the daily prayer:[91]

The devil is hid behind the beard / of a Shaikh to ambush passers-by. / You mount the dais, Quran in hand, / and snares of spurious piety throw. / What can you teach of good and evil / to us who know already the law? / The foulness that you bring in here! / Thank God for His great charity. / A maid, a wife, a widow, a sheep, / a she-ass, none is safe from you.[92]

He chided the mullah:

O tell me what your prayer is like, / and where indeed was she born and bred. / Is she a woman with ears, nose, eyes, / sent down here to the bane of man? / Is she tall or short? / What would be her age? and what charms does she sport or own? / Or is she just a weaver's web / on half a dozen pegs spread?

In the house of God you let out farts, / and vaunt of it, devoid of shame; / And full of sloth, like lepers, / you throw the dice of life and death. / You smell of the pudding and taste of carrion, / and kill the living with pious breath. / You shelter under the mask of law / the wicked, steeped in sin and crime, / Then when in the small hours of the night, / hunger wakes you up, you crow for prayer. . . .[93]

The Muslims of rural Punjab, as revealed in *Hir Waris*, were nonchalant towards the rigidity prescribed by the ecclesiastical classes. When we study the expansion of Islam within the local ambience of the rural Punjab, we can dispel the cliché of the 'impact/influence' of Hindu society on the Muslims and vice versa. We can do away with the question of what part of the cultural life of the Muslims was 'borrowed' from the Hindus, as in the writings of Muhammad Umar, Aziz Ahmad, and many others.[94]

Let us appreciate that the discourse of 'impact', 'influence' and 'borrowing' does not stand for conflict-resolution: it underlines only an analytic compartmentalization; it refers to hegemony and domination; it subsumes the historic and creative cultural phenomenon of the meeting of numerous traditions, and of spontaneous cultural reciprocity. Such an approach devours that significant 'third space' which is neither Hindu nor Islamic but local and rooted; one that is syncretic, and hybrid, and 'offers important opportunities for understanding Muslim groups that appear to transcend normative expectations of behaviour, belief, and identity. . . .'[95]

Medicine, Magic and Religion

Descriptions of diseases and cures in *Hir Waris* reveal that in medieval Punjab there existed a combination of religion, magic, and medicine. People were not bound to follow the curative instructions of their particular religion or sect. References to Dhantar Vaid,[96] the founder of Ayurveda, Lukman Hakim,[97] and to Arabic and Persian books of medicine suggest that the system of healing cannot be categorized as Ayurvedic (Hindu) or Unani

(Islamic). Healing methods were typically indigenous and tribal, with an input of Ayurvedic and Unani systems. These systems had collaboration with each other. The efforts of Bahwa Khan, a minister of Sikandar Lodi, and Haqim Yusuf, a physician in the court of Babur and Humayun, to develop a composite and integrated medical system through a synthesis of Arabic, Persian, and Ayurvedic thought was an expression of this collaboration. A large number of medicinal plants of Indian origin were added by Unani physicians to their *materia medica*, just as Ayurveda incorporated in its pharmacopoeia several medicines from the Unani system.[98]

As *Hir Waris* suggests, the system had three salient features–herbal medicines, potions made of a variety of elements taken from the animal world, and cures effected by magical actions. The cure depended on how the cause of disease was identified. The causes may be grouped in three chief categories: (a) human agency in which it was believed that the disease was directly due to the action on the part of some human being, (b) the action of some spiritual or supernatural powers, and (c) natural causes. During his scuffle with Sahiti at Hir's in-laws, Ranjha (in the disguise of a jogi) makes a mention of folk medicines which must have been popular among the people.[99] Diseases like cough, pain in the stomach, headache, and cold were cured with *sharbat* and *kara* mixtures made of various roots, fruits, and leaves. Skin problems were cured with ointments. Sour curd was poured on head of a person suffering from the pain in his temple.[100] The magic mirror was shown to a paralysed person. The oil of *peen* was rubbed on emaciated arms and legs. *Dhania* (coriander seeds) was administrated as medicine to cool the excessive sensual passion of man or woman. Persons suffering from impotence were cured with the use of oil squeezed from *beerbotian* (a small scarlet insect which appears on sand in the rainy season).

Contemporary records of Europeans visiting Punjab during Maharaja Ranjit Singh's reign refer to various kinds of medicines prepared from herbs and plants that were available for sale in Amritsar. Medicinal plants and their indigenous names and effects were noted.[101] Steinbach, a Prussian adventurer who joined the military service of Maharaja Ranjit Singh in 1836, informs us, 'Certain old-wife remedies, such as decoction of the chicoree plant, are used with effect in combating jaundice, and it is not unusual to assail cholera with doses of the juice of onions, and dysentery with powdered charcoal or burnt cork.'[102] The later ethnographic survey of Punjab and North-West Frontier Province conducted by the state acquaints us with relationships between complex curative measures to combat disease on the one hand, and the animal world, religion, magic and herbs on the other.[103]

For treating many ailments, for the fulfilment of desires, and for psychic cures, jogis were greatly relied on. They claimed to have magical powers to cure impotence and frigidity. They resorted to magic for resolving conflict, curing the possessed, uniting lovers, removing all kinds of pain in the body, and exterminating evil spirits. Ranjha the jogi throws ample light on this kind of magic.

> Listen, O Sahiti, 'I am a cobra, / a student of the occult arts. / Ghost, jinn, pretence, we beat out all, / and exorcise the evil soul. / By blowing into a peasant's nose, / the shadow of evil we dispel. / Reciting texts divine and holy, / we root out evil from people's hearts. / From houses into which we cross, / we drive out distress, grief, and pain. / If we read a charm from the core of our hearts, / we can revive extinguished love. / And should we want to kill a man, / we nail him down in another's grave. / A charm on a clove will bring her round / should a wife rebel against her name. / We pass our hands over a woman's breasts, / the spell makes all her ailments go. / We break the teeth and cut the hair / of witches, however much their skill. / If a lover cannot get to his love, / we give him a magic flower to smell. / And should we bear a grudge against one, / we set a ghost to run him through. / A woman who rudely speaks to a yogi, / ought to be shaved, put on an ass. / We make our spirits and demons serve, / those whom we wish all well and good. / If nothing else avails, we spray / the herb of love on a person's head. / God willing, we shall pull out, Waris, / the fairest plant from the Khera's house.[104]

Ranjha the jogi, is a shaman, a medicine man. In him one may observe three traditional physicians of the Hindu Ayurveda, Siddha and Unani systems. He represents the special features of Siddha Order of Eighty-four Masters on this earth who observed no distinction of caste, creed, religion, race, or country. These Siddhas went about curing people with what is known as *siddha ausadhis* (medicines), teaching divine alchemy and employed miracles. They were poets, physicians, alchemists, musicians, and astronomers rolled into one. The following are the twelve particular perfections or attainment-marks which the historical Siddhas are said to have achieved: the power to fly in the air; to assume at will any shape, human, sub-human or super-human; to enter into and use another body, dead or alive; to transform anything into gold; to cure all diseases; to make any immoveable object move or any moving object stand still; to transfer power to the disciple by sight or by touch; to retain or regain youth and youth's charm; to see across time and space; to appear anywhere to anyone and to multiply oneself; to grant any boon; and to prepare the 'Elixir of Life'.[105]

Ranjha could cure disease with herbs and plants. He could also harness unseen spiritual powers to cure ailments. He foretold the future and intervened for good or evil in human affairs. Jogis were expert in 'healing and wizardry' and carried a variety of substances with them for the purpose: the roots of plants, herbal extracts, one-eyed coconut, the gallstone of a cow, and animal substances such as horns, hoofs, nails, hair, claws or excreta (for use as both charms and medicine).[106] In the thirteenth century, the popularity of Shaikh Farid, who distributed amulets to devotees for their welfare and that of their livestock, may also be seen in this context. Muslims, Hindus, and Sikhs did not draw distinctions between the sufi saint and the Hindu jogi. They followed every kind of prescription, whether their Great Religious Tradition permitted it or not.

In the *Umdat-ut-Tawarikh* (Daftar III, Parts i-v, 1831–9) Sohan Lal Suri acquaints us with the religious and medicinal curative methods prescribed to save the life of Maharaja Ranjit Singh, who had suffered a stroke which paralysed his face and right side. By June 1839 the Maharaja, had six European doctors—three sent by the Governor-General and three of his own—but preferred to rely on the indigenous medicines such as *esabaghol,* syrups, *kushta, tabashir, ilaichi,* pumpkin seeds, almond oil, *bezour*-stone, opium, or aromatics as prescribed by the *hakims* and *vaids* such as Faqir Azizuddin, Khalifa Nuruddin Mian of Noorpur. Astrologers, *sadhus,* and religious shrines of the Hindus, Sikhs and Muslims were in the background.

I have tried to highlight the significance of *Hir Waris* as a source of the history and culture of Punjabi Muslims. Unlike professional chroniclers, Waris Shah lets his people speak for themselves. He does not 'find' facts and then cook them to his taste in his own frying pan. Instead, he 'discovers' facts. As he weaves a complex plot, he introduces us to the multiple layers of Punjabi Muslim society.

NOTES

1. Rafiuddin Ahmed, 'The Emergence of the Bengal Muslims', in Rafiuddin Ahmed, ed., *Understanding the Bengal Muslims: Interpretative Essays*, New Delhi, 2001, p. 2.
2. S. Nurul Hasan, 'Medieval Punjab', in Harbans Singh and N. Gerald Barrier, eds., *Essays in Honour of Dr. Ganda Singh*, Patiala, 1976, p. 73.
3. *Hir Waris*, stanza no. 519.
4. Ibid., stanza nos. 102, 107 and 171.
5. Babur in his *Babur Nama* writes that 'if we go into Hindustan the Jats and Gujjars always pour down in countless hordes from hill and plain for loot in bullock and buffalo. These ill-omened peoples are just senseless oppressors! Formerly their doings did not concern us much because the country was enemy's, but they began the same senseless work after we had taken it. When we reached Sialkot, they fell in tumult on poor and needy folks who were coming out of the town to our camp, and stripped them bare. I had the silly thieves sought for, and ordered two or three of them cut to pieces.' Zahiruddin Babur, *Babur Nama*, tr. A.S. Beveridge, New Delhi, 1970, p. 454.
6. Andre Wink, *Al-Hind: The Making of the Indo-Islamic World*, vol. II, New Delhi, 1999, pp. 170–2. Also see Brajadulal Chattopadhyaya, *The Making of Early Medieval India*, New Delhi, 2006, pp. 55–88.
7. J.M. Wikeley, *Punjabi Muslims*, Lahore, n.d., pp. 140–3; Denzil Ibbetson, *Punjab Castes*, Delhi, 1993, pp. 147–8; S. Jabir Raza, 'The Jats of Panjab and Sind: Their Settlements and Migrations (*c.* 5th–12th Centuries AD)', in Vir Singh, ed., *The Jats: Their Role and Contribution to the Socio-Economic Life and Polity of North-West India*, vol. 1, Delhi, 2004, pp. 54–61.

8. Steedman, *The Jhang Settlement Report*, p. 244; Denzil Ibbetson, *Punjab Castes*, Delhi,1993, pp. 147–8; Lepel Griffin, *Panjab Chiefs*, p. 502 as quoted in Khaliq Ahmad Nizami, *The Life and Times of Shaikh Farid-ud-Din Ganj-i-Shakar*, Delhi, 1973, p. 108. Also see Gulshan Rai, 'The Mughal Province of Multan and its Subsequent History (1707–1849)', *Journal of the Panjab University Historical Society*, vol. II, pt. I, no. 3, 1933.
9. S. Nurul Hasan, 'Zamindars under the Mughals', in Muzaffar Alam and Sanjay Subrahmanyam, eds., *The Mughal State 1526–1750*, New Delhi, 2005, p. 295.
10. Wikeley, *Punjabi Muslims*, p. 143.
11. Veena Sachdeva, 'The Non-Sikh Chiefs of Punjab Plains and Maharaja Ranjit Singh', *Journal of Regional History*, vol. II, Amritsar 1981.
12. The river Chenab or Chanderbhaga (its ancient name) reverberates with the love-legends of Punjabis: Hir–Ranjha and Sohni–Mahiwal, and others. Here on its shores Hir and Ranjha fell in love, and Sohni, the beloved of Mahiwal, drowned one night deep in its bosom while crossing it to meet her lover on the other shore. The Chenab is a river with deep romantic associations for every Punjabi heart.
13. Ibbetson, *Panjab Castes*, p. 148.
14. Sohinder Singh Wanjara Bedi, *Panjabi Lokedhara Vishav Kosh*, Delhi, 1992, vol. 6, p. 1470.
15. *Hir Waris*, stanza nos. 8 and 9.
16. For these features of the *zamindar* class, see S. Nurul Hasan, 'Zamindars under the Mughals'.
17. *Hir Waris*, stanza no. 8.
18. Ibid., stanza no. 9.
19. Ibid., stanza no. 57.
20. Sant Singh Sekhon, *A History of Panjabi Literature*, vol. II, Patiala, 1996, p. 181.
21. Ibid., p. 176.
22. J.R. Puri and T.R. Shangari, *Bulleh Shah*, Beas, 1986, p. 323.
23. There are a large number of references to *mulak*, *vatan*, *pardes*, and *des* in *Hir Waris* which acquaint us with socio-cultural space-specific ideas of the country: the *root*.
24. Surjit Hans, 'The Idea of Country in *Hir* by Waris Shah', *Punjab Journal of Sikh Studies*, vol. XX, no. 2, 1996. Peter J. Bertocci, 'Islam and the Social Construction of the Bangladesh Countryside',

in Rafiuddin Ahmed, ed., *Understanding the Bengal Muslims: Interpretative Essays*, p. 82.

25. Irfan Habib, *The Agrarian System of Mughal India 1556–1707*, New Delhi, 2000, pp. 197–8.
26. *Hir Waris*, stanza no. 231.
27. *Hir Waris*, stanza no. 598. It would not be out of context to apprise the reader of Amir Khusrau's love for India, his *vatan*, in order to substantiate the argument about the significance of the *root* approach in the study of the Indian Muslims. In the third part of his famous historical masnavi, *Nuh Sipihr* (The Nine Skies), Khusrau takes pains to prove India's superiority to Khurasan, and is enthusiastic about the land of his birth: 'the love of one's native land (*vatan*) is a part of one's faith (*iman*)'. Mohammad Wahid Mirza, *The Life and Works of Amir Khusrau*, Delhi, rpt. 1974, pp. 181–9.
28. H.A. Rose, *A Glossary of the Tribes and Castes of Punjab and North-West Frontier Province*, vol. I, Patiala, 2nd rpt. 1990, pp. 49–55.
29. S. Nurul Hasan, 'Zamindars under the Mughals', p. 293.
30. The Arains are market-gardeners. They are in Jhang and Rawalpindi. They originally came from the lower Indus and spread up the five rivers. Denzil Ibbetson, *Punjab Castes*, pp. 189 and 194.
31. The Awans, or Qutubshahis as they claimed to be, are a tribe of the Salt Range, where they once held independent possessions of very considerable extent. They are said to be the descendants of Qutub Shah of Ghazni who himself was a descendant of Ali, the son-in-law of the Prophet Muhammad. But Qutub's mother was not the Prophet's daughter. She came from Herat, about AD 1035, and settled in the vicinity of Peshawar. Thence the Awans spread along the Salt Range, forming independent clans by whom the chief of Kalabagh was acknowledged as head of the tribe. The Awans employed Hindu Brahmans as family priests. Ibid., pp. 169–170.
32. The Syeds are descendants of Ali, the son-in-law of Prophet Muhammad, and the word properly applies to those who descended from Ali by Fatima, the Prophet's daughter. Ibid., p. 222.
33. Shaikh in Arabic means an elder or chief. Ibid., p. 206.
34. The Kambohs were one of the skilled cultivating castes in Punjab. They seldom engaged in market-gardening like the Arains, but they were equally industrious. Ibid., p. 201.
35. The Gakhars were the ancient rulers of the northern portion of the cis-Indus Salt Range. They confronted Mahmud of Ghazni in 1008

in the neighbourhood of Peshawar. They were mainly residents of Rawalpindi, Jhelum, and Hazara districts. Ibid., pp. 165–8.

36. The Jats, about whom no description is available before the seventh century, were agriculturalists. They made the transformation from pastoralism to agriculture between the eleventh and the sixteenth centuries. During these four centuries a great expansion of the Jats also took place. Irfan Habib, 'Jatts of Punjab and Sind', in Harbans Singh and N. Gerald Barrier, eds., *Essays in Honour of Dr. Ganda Singh*, pp. 92–103.
37. The Dogars were originally a shepherd rather than an agricultural tribe. They were practically all Muslims. Denzil Ibbetson, *Punjab Castes*, pp. 177–8.
38. The Pathans are apparently of Indian origin, although their language is Pashto. (It is this word of which Pathan is the Indian corruption.) They held in the early centuries the whole of the Safed Koh and northern Suleman hills from the Indus to the Helmand and from the sources of the Swat and Jalalabad to Peshin and Quetta. Ibid., p. 62.
39. Ibbetson is of the view that the distinction between Jat and Rajput is social rather than ethnic. He believes that 'those families of the common stock whom the tide of fortune has raised to political importance have become Rajputs almost by mere virtue of their rise; and their descendants have retained the title and its privileges on the condition, strictly enforced, of observing the rules by which the higher are distinguished from the lower castes in the Hindu scale of precedence; of preserving their purity of blood by refusing to marry with families of inferior social rank, of rigidly abstaining from widow marriage, and of refraining from degrading occupations. Those who transgressed these rules have fallen from their high positions and ceased to be Rajputs.' Ibid., p. 100.
40. The Mughal dynasty founded in India by Babur in 1526 ruled northern India up to 1857. It was a branch of the Timurid line. 'Mughal' derives from Mogul or Mogol, the Persian/Arabic term for Mongol. Timur, who invaded India in 1398, was a Mongol by origin. Zahiruddin Muhammad Babur was the fourteenth scion of Chengiz Khan in his mother's line, and the fifth scion of Timur in his father's line. Babur was born in 1483 in Farghana. Mughals are of Mongol descent, and their being described as Afghan or Turko-Afghan does not seem entirely correct. However, according to the French traveller Francois Bernier, by the late seventeenth century

the term 'Mughal' was applied by the Indians to any light-skinned Muslim of foreign descent, Persian, Turk, Arab, and even Uzbek. S. Devadas Pillai, *Indian Sociology through Ghurye: A Dictionary*, Mumbai, 1997, p. 165. Also see Richard C. Foltz, *Mughal India and Central Asia,* Karachi, 2001, pp. 12–17.

41. Mohan Singh, *An Introduction to Panjabi Literature*, Amritsar, n.d., pp. 21–2.
42. *Hir Waris*, stanza no. 519.
43. R.C. Temple, *The Legends of Punjab,* vol. II, 177.
44. P. Suri, 'Heer Waris Shah as a Document on the Social History of Punjab in the 18th Century', *Proceedings of Indian History Congress*, 1966.
45. Hamza A. Alavi, 'Kinship in West Punjab Villages', in T.N. Madan, ed., *Muslim Communities of South Asia: Culture and Society*, New Delhi, 1976, pp. 1–2.
46. *Hir Waris*, stanza nos. 169–70.
47. Hamza A. Alavi, 'Kinship in West Punjab Villages', p. 7.
48. Shafqat Tanveer Mirza, *Resistance Themes in Punjabi Literature*, Lahore, n.d., p. 11. Chuchak's inclination to marry his daughter Hir to his shepherd, and the rejection of this proposal, reflects differences in the norms of the Turkish ruling class and those of local society. Turks would promote a loyal slave to a position next to the master and the loyalty of a slave would even elevate him to the status of son-in-law. In the absence of a worthy male heir a slave was also destined to become a successor, as happened with Mahmud's father Subkatagin and grandfather Alptagin, and with Iltutmish and Balban, the most successful rulers of the slave dynasty of Delhi. In contrast, the marriage of Hir with Ranjha was not acceptable to the Siyal *biradari* because in local society Dhido Ranjha did not come up to the social status of the Siyals. Sant Singh Sekhon, *A History of Panjabi Literature*, Patiala, vol. II, pp. 63–4.
49. Ibbetson, *Punjab Castes*, 1993, p. 100.
50. H.A. Rose, *A Glossary of Tribes and Castes of Punjab and North-West Frontier Province*, vol. I, p. 57.
51. Ibbetson, *Punjab Castes*, p. 5.
52. *Hir Waris*, stanza no. 63.
53. Ibid., stanza no. 73.
54. Irfan Habib, *The Agrarian System of Mughal India 1556–1707*, p. 147.

55. *Hir Waris*, stanza no. 317.
56. Ibbetson, *Punjab Castes*, p. 2.
57. Ibid., p. 3.
58. Yogendra Singh, *Modernization of Indian Tradition: A System Study of Social Change*, Jaipur, 1988, pp. 67–8. Also see Khaliq Ahmad Nizami, *Religion and Politics in India during the Thirteenth Century*, New Delhi, 2002, pp. 95–186; Satish Chandra, *Medieval India: From Sultanate to the Mughals, Part One, Delhi Sultantate (1206–1526)*, New Delhi, 2000, pp. 158–74.
59. Richard Lannoy, *The Speaking Tree: A Study of Indian Culture and Society*, London, 1971, pp. 157–62.
60. Patron-client relationships prevailed in eighteenth-century Punjab. This is substantiated by recent studies on the artisan classes of the nineteenth century. For instance, Harish Chander Sharma informs us that, 'The *julahas* and *telis* were called upon to assist during the reaping season and were paid separately. The *chamaras, lohars, tarkhans, mochis* and *kumhars* were hired during both the sowing and reaping seasons to work as field labourers. On social ceremonies like marriages and births in their patron's house, the artisans were expected to perform certain specialized and ceremonial services for which they were entitled to a fee known as *lag*, and were thus called *lagis* on these occasions.' There was also *begar* or unpaid labour. 'The *begar* included white-washing the village guest-house, carry the luggage of the visiting officials from one place to another, and bringing fodder for the cattle of the agriculturalists from the fields.' Harish Chander Sharma, 'Artisans in Punjab under Maharaja Ranjit Singh', in J.S. Grewal and Indu Banga, eds., *Maharaja Ranjit Singh and His Times*, Amritsar, 1980.
61. *Hir Waris*, stanza nos. 123–4.
62. Ibid., stanza no. 171.
63. Irfan Habib in his 'Classifying Pre-Colonial India' states that Marx was 'right when he thought that Indian society merited analysis on the basis of its own specific features. He found, first, that here the village community rather than individual peasant represented the basic object of subjection by the exploiting class. He recognized that cultivation was undertaken by peasant households separately, but that community and caste ties bound the peasant and village-artisan into a single social and economic unit. As a result individual subjection, whether slavery or serfdom, could not become dominant.' Irfan Habib, 'Classifying Pre-Colonial India', *The Journal*

of Peasant Studies, vol. 12, nos. 2 and 3, 1985, p. 45; also see, D.N. Dhanagare, *Themes and Perspectives in Indian Sociology*, Jaipur, 1998, pp. 106–28.

64. Richard M. Eaton, *Essays on Islam and Indian History*, New Delhi, 2000, p. 215.
65. *Hir Waris*, stanza no. 183.
66. Jagtar Singh, ed., *Heer Damodar*, Patiala, 2000, stanza nos. 10, 126, 435, and 637.
67. *Hir Waris*, stanza no. 196.
68. Ibid., stanza nos. 116–18.
69. Despite 'some disapproval' from theologians and lawyers', P. Hardy is of the view that, 'music flourished early in the thirteenth century among Indian Muslims under the auspices of the Chishti mystic order. . . . Muslim singers at courts of such broad-minded Muslim rulers as Ibrahim Adil Shah of Bijapur (1535–57) would be expected to sing songs from Hindu mythology, while Hindu singers would be expected to sing Muslim songs. Probably it was in the sphere of music that Hindu and Muslim cultural traditions came nearest to a synthesis.' *The Muslims of British India*, New Delhi, 1998, p. 18.
70. K.M. Ashraf , 'Attributes of Medieval Muslim Social life', in *Indian Historiography and other Related Papers*, tr., Jaweed Ashraf, Foreword, Satish Chandra, New Delhi, 2006, p. 43.
71. Ibid., pp. 60–1.
72. Raja Bhoja (AD 1018–55) was a Paramara Rajput. Under him the Paramara dynasty flourished. He was an accomplished scholar and a great builder of dams and artificial lakes for irrigation. But he was also reputed to be an uxorious husband who on one occasion in his intimacies consented to become his wife's bridled horse. Sant Singh Sekhon, *The Love of Hir and Ranjha*, Ludhiana, 1978, p. 264.
73. Rasalu, a Rajput prince, was the son and successor of Raja Salvan of Sialkot. He is known in Punjabi literature as Raja Rasalu. His adventures are told and sung by Punjab people. His wife Rani Koklan gave her favour to a king named Hodi in his absence. See Charles Swynnereton, *The Adventures of the Punjab Hero Raja Rasalu*, Calcutta, 1884.
74. Yusuf was the twelfth and youngest son of his father, Yaqub. Ten of them were by one mother and Yusuf and Bin Yamin by the second. Yusuf was exceedingly handsome and clever. Yaqub loved him very much. The brothers became jealous. One day Yusuf saw a significant

dream in which the sun and the moon and eleven stars paid obeisance to him. The next morning he narrated it to his father who interpreted it to mean that Yusuf would become one day a king as well as a prophet, and his brothers would be his courtiers. The father told Yusuf not to tell this dream to his brothers lest they should feel jealous. But Yusuf's step sister had overheard, and she conveyed the news to her brothers. The brothers conspired to take Yusuf out on some pretext and make an end of him. One day they asked Yaqub's permission to go to the woods to hunt and take Yusuf along with them. While passing through a desert they threw Yusuf into a well. Taking away Yusuf's robe they smeared it with the blood of an animal they had hunted. Then they caught a wolf and put some blood on the wolf's jaw. They brought the wolf to Yaqub and told him that Yusuf had been eaten by a wolf. The next day, a caravan passed by that well. Noticing grass and water in the oasis, the travellers camped around the well. As they lowered a leather bucket into the well, an angel cleverly placed Yusuf in it. The caravaneers were astonished at Yusuf's good looks and decided to take him along to Misr (Egypt), where they would sell him as a slave. There, Zulaikha, wife of the king, was impressed with the good looks of Yusuf and she purchased him. In the palace Zulaikha made advances to him. Yusuf withstood the temptations and tried to escape. Failing in her designs, Zulaikha complained to the king that Yusuf had made advances to her. Yusuf was thus thrown in prison. But the then ruler saw a dream which could not be interpreted by his ministers. The king was told that his prisoner, Yusuf, alone could interpret it. Yusuf interpreted it as meaning that seven years of plenty would be followed by as many years of famine in the kingdom. The ruler of Misr was so pleased that he abdicated in Yusuf's favour and drove Zulaikha away from the palace. When the famine struck Canaan also, Yusuf's brothers came to Misr to buy grain. He recognized them and sent them back with camel-loads of grain and precious stones. But he detained Bin Yamin who was his real brother by the same mother. Yaqub came to Misr to ask for Bin Yamin and learnt the whole story from Yusuf. In the meantime Zulaikha had become an old hag and had taken her abode in a hut by the road. As Yusuf went in procession to receive his father, Zulaikha expressed her love and devotion to him. Yaqub heard the story and requested Yusuf to fulfil her wish as God had fulfilled the wishes of the family. Yaqub prayed for Zulaikha to become young again. Yusuf too was deeply affected by Zulaikha's consistency in love and gladly married her.

75. The legendary lovers of Punjab. She was the daughter of a blacksmith (*lohar*). She was seized upon by a local king, from whom Rode Shah or Roda spirited her away. Jalali's home is given variously as Patna, and somewhere in the Karnal or Multan districts. R.C. Temple states, 'About Rode Shah all I have been able to gather is that there is a tomb or shrine to him near Lahore on the Amritsar road, otherwise he is said to come from Multan, as a follower of Abdul Qadir Jilani, in which case we must place him about the 15th century at the earliest. . . .' Rode Shah is believed to have performed the miracle of 'making the invaluable *dub* grass of India green and sweet for ever'.
76. The king of Sri Lanka who had abducted Sita, and later was killed by Rama. The entire story is a part of the Indian epic, *Ramayana.*
77. Rama was the god-ruler of Ayodhya in the Gangetic valley. Sita was his wife.
78. These names remind one of the Indian epic the *Mahabharata.* The subject of the truly epic portion of the *Mahabharata* is the great war between the Kauravas, the hundred sons of Dhritarashtra, led by Duryodhana, and the Pandavas, the five sons of Pandu, brother of Dhritarashtra, led by Yudhishthira.
79. *Hir Waris,* stanza no. 351.
80. In the seventh century, Eaton informs us, when the Arabs had conquered Iraq and Syria, they absorbed many aspects of Greek and Iranian culture. 'This included what became known as the *purdah* system or seclusion of a woman from all men but her own—in private apartments at home, and behind a veil if she walked abroad—which had long been mark of privilege in upper-class Byzantine and Sasanian society.' Muslims of all social classes followed the court's example, with the result that by the fourteenth century, women had effectively disappeared from the public life throughout the Arab Muslim world. But this was not to be the case beyond the Arab world. 'Thus the great Arab traveller Ibn Battuta [d. 1377] expressed shock at seeing unveiled Muslim women in southern Anatolia, Central Asia, the Maldive Islands, and western Sudan.' Richard M. Eaton, *The Rise of Islam and the Bengal Frontier, 1204–1760,* Berkeley, 1993, p. 298.
81. *Hir Waris,* stanza no. 389.

82. Mohammad Umar, *Islam in Northern India during the Eighteenth Century*, Delhi, 1993, p. 432
83. *Hir Waris*, stanza nos. 183–93.
84. Muhammad Umar, *Islam in Northern India during the Eighteenth Century*, p. 430.
85. *Hir Waris*, stanza nos. 196–7.
86. Ibid., stanza no. 194.
87. See Athar Ali, *Mughal India: Studies in Polity, Ideas, Society, and Culture*, New Delhi, 2006, p. 111.
88. For details see Muhammad Umar, *Islam in Northern India during the Eighteenth Century*, p. 43n.
89. *Hir Waris*, stanza no. 35.
90. See J. Albert de Mandelslo, *The Voyage and Travels of the Ambassadors sent by Fredrick Duke of Hoslten to the Great Duke of Moscow, etc. (1639–69)*, tr. John Davies, London, 1869, p. 63; Edward Terry, *A Voyage to the East Indies*, London, 1655, pp. 125, 247, as quoted in Muhammad Umar, *Islam in Northern India during the Eighteenth Century*, p. 432.
91. Sant Singh Sekhon, *The Love of Hir and Ranjha*, Ludhiana, 1978, p. 23.
92. *Hir Waris*, stanza no. 36.
93. *Hir Waris*, stanza nos. 38–40.
94. Aziz Ahmad, *Studies in Islamic Culture in the Indian Environment*, New Delhi, 1999, pp. 164–5.
95. Peter Gottschalk, 'Mapping Muslims: Categories of Evolutionary Difference and Interaction in South Asia', in Imtiaz Ahmad and Helmut Reifeld, eds., *Lived Islam in South Asia: Adaptation, Accommodation and Conflict*, Delhi, 2004; also see Shail Mayaram, 'Beyond Ethnicity? Being Hindu and Muslim in South Asia', in the same volume.
96. *Hir Waris*, stanza no. 282.
97. Ibid., stanza no. 290.
98. K.N. Panikkar, *Culture, Ideology, Hegemony: Intellectuals and Social Consciousness in Colonial India*, New Delhi, 1998, p. 146.
99. *Hir Waris*, stanza no. 370.
100. The uses of numerous plants as medicine may also be read in the accounts of Jan Huyghen Van Linschoten. He was a Dutch traveller of the sixteenth century who sailed from Spain to Goa. *The Voyage of East Indies*, ed. A.C. Burnwell, New Delhi, 1988, vol. I.

101. For details see Baba Prem Singh Hoti, *Punjab Da Samajak Itihas (Khalsa Raj Vekhey)*, ed. Fauja Singh, Patiala, 1979.
102. Lieut-Colonel Steinbach, *Punjab*, Patiala, 1970, p. 45.
103. H.A. Rose, *A Glossary of the Tribes and Castes of Punjab and North-West Frontier Province*, vol. I, pp. 253–8.

'When a goat kills a snake it devours it and then ruminates, after which it spits out a bead (*manka*) which applied to a snake-bite absorbs the poison and swells. Dropped then into milk it is squeezed and the poison drips out. This cures the patient. If not put into milk, the *manka* will burst.'

'Piles can be cured by winding a thread of 5 colours, white, red, green, yellow and black, thrice around the thumb, and then putting it round the toe at night, for fortnight ending on a Tuesday, the day sacred to Hanuman.'

'Tiger's flesh has magical qualities. Khatris always keep a little by them dried and when a child is attacked by small-pox they burn a little near him to propitiate the goddess. Hence, when a disease is raging in a town the house of a Hindu who has a tiger's flesh is frequented by people begging for a small piece of it.'

'Hare's blood in a lump of cotton is used in many ailments, the cotton being soaked in water and the blood extracted given to the sick. It is said to be most efficacious in the fits of various sorts.'

'Owl's flesh, particularly the heart, is a potent love-philter, making the recipient fall violently in love with the giver.'

'Epilepsy is cured by administering a snuff made from dried worms snorted out by male camels during the rutting season, and which are believed to live on the animal's brain.'

'Blinders, provided it is not congenital, may be cured by antimony, applied for 8 days. Antimony is obtained at the Karangili hill near Pindi Dadan Khan.'

'Scorpion-sting may be cured in various ways by simple remedies, but charms are used. Draw a pentathlon in ink thrice over the wound at intervals of 5 minutes and the pain will disappear: or hang a scorpion's sting up in the house where children are playing and they will never be stung. Indra and Gaurja Devi are also invoked in a rhyme which will send the poison into the Kumbhi, the lowest hell.'

'To cure obstinate sores a little curdled milk is put over them and a dog allowed to lick them.'

'Remittent fever may be cured by taking a spinning-wheel and placing it on a cot in the sun.'

'A galled bullock may be cured by applying the ashes of a lizard killed on a Sunday and burnt.'

104. *Hir Waris*, stanza no. 367.
105. Mohan Singh, *Order of Siddha-Yogis*, Amritsar, n.d., pp. 14, 17.
106. Satish K. Kapoor, 'The Use of Drugs in Indian Tradition', *The Journal of Religious Studies*, vol. XXVII, Spring 1997, no. 1.

CHAPTER 7

Sufi, Shrine, and Sacred Space

> The arrival of the sufi saint
> Baba Farid Shakkar Ganj dispels the sorrows of Punjab
>
> WARIS SHAH

We have seen that *Hir Waris*, with its Punjabi Muslim protagonists, does not fall into a category of stereotyped text of Muslims in Punjab. The historians who rely on elite sources (as opposed to vernacular literature) are prone to such misconceptions. When the local literary sources are accorded a marginalized status in historiography, and Punjab historians dealing with Islam, Hinduism, and Sikhism make no mention of the works of jogis, sufis, bhaktas and qissa-kars, medieval Punjabi society is misrepresented as bifurcated on the basis of Islam and Hinduism. Instead of looking historically and anthropologically at how and through what medium the religious fusion took place among the common people of Punjab, historians habitually talk about the scriptural authority of the Vedas and the Quran, and of the classical languages like Sanskrit, Arabic, and Persian. They overlook the the people's/folk religion, liberated from the conventional religious boundaries, which was a significant catalyst for the maintenance of a social order and harmony. Whether the exclusion of this phenomenon from the colonial and post-colonial histories of medieval Punjab is deliberate or accidental is not my concern. But one thing is certain: since the colonial intervention, historians have been too absorbed in the Great Religious Traditions to concern themselves with the popular religious domain. Like the ecclesiastic classes, they too have looked down on folk religion as profane, savage, and often confusing and contradictory. Of the number of achievements of colonialism, one is that its Indian educated middle classes succeeded in, to great extent, smashing the holistic unity of folk religion under the programme of socio-religious reform movements—a success which medieval theologians like Shaikh Ahmad Sirhindi and Shah Waliullah could not achieve. However, if one is ready to accept folk religion as historically evolved, and the importance of the social function it performed, then religion is as essential to the working of society as are morality and law. Religon is part of a complex system by which people may live together in 'an orderly arrangement of social relations'.[1] Let us begin our discussion with the sufis.

SUFIS AND THE SPREAD OF ISLAM

Vernacular literature speaks of a variety of socio-cultural sensitivities and the specificities of Islam. It reverberates with the voices of sufis who may be said to have been the single most important catalyst in initiating and promoting socio-cultural reciprocity, and in the vernacularization of Islam. In other words, the sword and the theology of the priestly class were less effective in comparison to the multifarious activities of the sufis in spreading Islam among the masses. In *Hir Waris* the five sufis/pirs grant their blessings to Hir and Ranjha whom the orthodox priest and patriarchs considered to be 'outlaws'. It was the sufis who advocated the removal of mediation or intervention by the socio-religious patriarchs. If the Islamic theologians were concerned with framing the rules that God had commanded to govern everyday life, the mystics attempted to acquire an immediate and personal experience of God's reality'.[2]

In a little over three centuries (say, 1200–1530), sufism became immensely important in India, although Islam had previously enjoyed only a sequestered following.[3] How this happened may be understood with reference to Punjab. India is one of the five great centres of sufism, together with Iran (including Central Asia), Mesopotamia, Syria, and North Africa.[4] Sufism is intrinsically grounded in the Quran. The Prophet himself was the teacher of the external laws (*shariat*), the mystic path (*tariqat*) and gnosis (*haqiqat*). Also the vernacular character of Islam was more a cultural phenomenon than simply a religious/theological one, and needs to be understood from the viewpoint of its variegated vernacular shades. In medieval Punjab, Islam percolated to the grassroots through sufis, their monasteries (*khanqahs*), their mausoleums (*mazars*) and shrines (*dargahs*), their network of disciples (*murids*), their literature, their charitable activities, their love of music and their miraculous powers or charisma (*karamat*) and their use of the vernacular.

What I wish to suggest is that the phenomenon of vernacularity as expressed by sufis and their followers illustrates the nature of Islamic fusion in the socio-religious ambience of the 'others' and vice versa. The sufis carved out a space for Islam, the new religion, in the everyday life of villages and towns—a space which was historically and culturally more significant than were political domination and theological hegemony. In other words, the sufis made Islam a popular religion that could be understood by the masses at the level of their *commonsense.* The sufis assimilated and imbibed elements from *other* cultures and religions. They appealed to the socio-religious ethos of the masses and thus gained popularity. They understood the human predilection to a personal, direct, and intense experience of God or of the religious truth.[5] Thus the sufis and their mysticism stood in direct contrast to the ideology of the ecclesiastic class of Islam that monopolistically claimed to be a necessary and inevitable bridge between the Almighty and people. The sufis de-hegemonized the dominating mediation. They represented a reaction against 'over-intellectualism, formalism, and hair-splitting theology', as well as rebellion of conscience against social injustice.[6] Western Punjab, where sufism and sufi literature developed prominently, was more 'Islamicate' than 'Muslim'. The latter, like 'Hindu' (in contrast to 'Indic'), is a rigid category with communitarian overtones; 'Islamicate', for its part, refers to an area influenced by Muslim rulers[7] but not restricted to the practice of Islam as a religion.[8] Punjabis, who converted to Islam, adhered to their pre-Islamic socio-religious practices, beliefs, and customs. In this connection the Punjabi qissa, *Hir Waris* included, is an instance of Islamicate ambience.

One needs to remember here that strains of anti-intellectualism in the Indic bhakti movement coincided with those of sufi mysticism. Both were more popular than the formal disciplines of the elite religious classes. This is the reason that sufis, saints, and bhaktas mustered popular support and response. They joined in a common cause. It has been rightly observed that

> differences of Muslim and Hindu doctrines were so blurred in some cases as to result in the formation of sects and mendicant bands whose denominational identity had almost completely dissolved. Among the most notable examples of the new syncretists were the bhakti saint, Ramananda, and the Muslim weaver-poet, Kabir.[9]

'Muslim' sufis and the 'Hindu' saints alike appealed to the sentiment of inter-caste/community fraternization and focused less attention on particularistic community ethics than on the universal ideal of harmonious equilibrium. In Punjab, for example, Shaikh Farid, Guru Nanak, Shah Husain, Sultan Bahu, and Bulleh Shah, over a long span from the twelfth to the eighteenth centuries, were against religious intellectualism and formalism.

Legitimacy of Sufis

The sufis, both saints and the poets, who shaped and sharpened the cultural narrative of Punjab, were its natives. Their ancestors were either immigrants or converts to Islam. The area of their activity was that part of (west) Punjab where indigenous political power had been displaced by the military campaigns of Mahmud of Ghazni and Muizzuddin of Ghor. It was also that area where Brahmanical taboos regarding caste purity and pollution were almost absent. Another significant factor, which facilitated the legitimacy of the sufis, was the location of their khanqahs. Since these were situated on the principal land routes, they offered shelter and hospitality to merchants and travellers.[10] They served as focal points of Islam—centres of fervour, ascetic exercises, and sufi training. The khanqahs of Punjab grew up around a holy man and became associated with his order (silsila). The organic relationship between a sufi, his silsila and his khanqah created a specific territorial identity. The sufi monasteries (*jamat khanahs*) stood for collective and egalitarian life. Devotees converged on them without distinction or discrimination. The principles, practices and ambience of the khanqahs were different from those of the religious institutions which promoted segmentation and segregation. Thus the sufis, their silsilas and their khanqahs created what Annemarie Schimmel calls a 'mass movement'. She comments that ordinary people required outlets for their emotions towards holy men and had the opportunity to participate in festivities with music and often with whirling dance. 'The corporate pursuit of the Way was easier for most people than the lonely spiritual struggle of the mystical seeker; the common prayer meetings gave them strength and warmed their faith.'[11] The sufis preached the essentials of Islam without bothering much about its Turko–Persian or Arabic cultural trappings. Their khanqahs were the platforms for gaining 'emotional experience of religion'.[12] This is why the holistic vision of the sufis elicited a mass response of the people, whose friends, preachers, and protagonists they became.[13] The sufis were not just spiritual saviours. They protected the common people from the wrath of invaders. For instance, during the invasion of Timur the population of Ajodhan fled to Bhatner, while the few remaining people were spared by the invader out of respect for the shrine of Shaikh Farid.

Indian Islam is considered essentially a holy-man Islam.[14] It was the sufi, not sufism, who attracted the regional folk. Sufis recognized and respected popular beliefs and practices that appealed to the heart, not the mind. They created an aura of saintliness which inspired devotion among the rank and file. As formal Islam preached and propagated by the ulema had little to offer to the folk, the blend of sufi silsilas with the saint cult represented the popular religion. The sufis responded to the mundane and spiritual needs of the tribal and agrarian population, besides protecting them and their livestock, through their alleged miraculous powers, from the distress caused by nature and disease. Thus sufism became a cult of personality. The *Gulzar-i-Faridi*, *Baharia*, *Manaqab-i-Sultani* and *Bagh-i-Auliya-e-Hind* praise sufi poets of Punjab such as Shaikh Ibrahim Farid Sani, Shah Husain, Sultan Bahu, and Shah Inayat Qadiri (the preceptor of Bulleh Shah) for their ability to perform miracles (*karamat*).[15]

It is also significant that sufis of various silsilas did not set themselves up as rivals. They had a clear notion of the territorial boundaries of their spiritual jurisdiction.[16] They administered the spiritual world on behalf of God, as the governor (*subedar*) did the temporal world on behalf of the sultan.[17] It may be noted that during the time of the Prophet, and 'in the language of the Quran, the word *sultan* usually meant 'authority' in the spiritual rather than temporal sense of either power or argument'.[18] The sufis released the forces of socio-cultural fusion and removed social, ideological, and linguistic barricades between the numerous cultural groups. As a result, a common cultural outlook developed.[19] In fact, a sufi is

> one who seeks to transcend the world of forms, to journey from multiplicity to Unity, from the particular to the Universal. He leaves the many for the One and through this very process is granted the vision of the One in the many. For him all forms become transparent, including religious form, thus revealing to him their unique origin.[20]

With such a holistic vision, the sufis maintained amicable relations with non-Muslim religious men. *Amritkund*, a Sanskrit document of the thirteenth century, apprises us of the practices of Hindu jogis as an integral part of Indian sufism. The interaction of the Chishti saints with Hindu jogis acquainted the former with the latter's religious philosophy. The Chishtis evinced interest in the translation of Sanskrit treatises on spiritual exercises and philosophy.[21] Behind the powers, mystical and magical, of saints like Shaikh Farid lay 'deep cultural sympathies which made the person of the sufi and his teachings attractive to non-Muslims'. A sufi who renounced worldly gain, devoted himself to prayer, and expressed himself in poetry, corresponded in popular imagination to the bhakti preacher who had given up his past life and had access to higher wisdom.[22] The popularity and legitimacy of the sufis could also be discerned in their concern with the worship of local gods and in their adoption of Hindu devotional songs.[23]

Sufis were not sectarian, nor were their dwellings. The *jamat khanah* of Shaikh Farid would remain open till midnight not only for devotees but also for the Hindu jogis and *qalandars*.[24] Shaikh Nizamuddin Auliya is said to have met a jogi in the khanqah of his master Shaikh Farid.[25] The Shaikh is also said to have conversed with the jogi in the earliest form of Urdu, i.e. Hindawi and the khanqah of Shaikh Farid is thus one of 'the earliest cradles of the Urdu language'.[26] The deep sufic interest in Indian thought may be measured from sufi attempts to reconcile the Advaita, Vedanta, Yoga, Vaishnavism and other Indian religious strands with sufism. During the reign of Akbar, Jahangir, and Shahjahan, a close association developed between Hindu and sufi mystics. Both appreciated their inner fundamental similarities and discarded the external forms of religion.[27] The significant commonality among both the communities of mystics was a holistic vision that transcended barricades of caste, community, and creed. The Qadiri sufi, Mian Mir, had a close association with the fifth Sikh Guru, Arjan Dev. A sufi pir was identical with a non-Muslim guru. The devotion of *murid* to his *pir* thus is strikingly similar to the devotion of the *chela* to his *guru.*[28]

Another factor which helped the sufis to establish themselves in Punjab was their chain of successors who maintained the spiritual lineage of their respective khanqahs. In the tribal and agrarian milieu of Punjabi society, where lineage and genealogy in the context of close kinship ties had their own socio-cultural space, the sufis and their khanqahs created a distinct legitimacy. For instance, Shaikh Farid and his khanqah at Pakpattan associated the Chishti order with the region of Punjab. Shaikh Farid contributed much to the wider diffusion of the Chishti sufi lineage and genealogy. Apart from his descendants (five sons and three daughters),[29] he initiated many disciples and successors (*khalifas*)[30] who moved to different parts of India and established their hospices, where succession became hereditary. It was sufi shrines, not mosques, that became the symbol of Islam.[31] With regard to genealogy, Lawrence writes:

> There were two kinds of family tree: one pertained to the Shaykh's [Shaikh] biological heritage, and was particularly important to confirm him as related by blood to the earliest generations of Muslims, and perhaps even to the Prophet Muhammad himself, in which case the title *Sayyid* could be affixed before his name. Usually, however, biological ties were subordinate to a second kind of genealogy, a spiritual genealogy that linked the Shaykh to the other, already established, Sufis of earlier

generations. Many of these affiliations were traced back to the tenth century Baghdadi ascetic, Junayd.[32]

Sufi responses to vernacular literature were also a significant factor so far as legitimacy is concerned.[33] The sufis adopted popular Punjabi poetic genres, *dohira, kafi, baramaha, athvara, siharfi, qissa,* and *var*[34] to express and communicate Islamic mysticism, history and mythology. Most of these popular poetic genres were also used by the Sikh gurus who constructed their own discourse on devotion and social issues. Music too is said to have played a significant role in the spread of Islam at the popular level. For example, the distinctive feature of the Chishti silsila in Punjab 'was the use of music for devotional texts'. Muinuddin Chishti, the founder of the silsila, found that 'music was a significant component of worship, and the Brahmins sang *sloks, sabads,* and *bhajans* with percussion and wind instruments'. The sufi followed the same practice and subsequently wooed many Hindus. It is also said that the same sufi integrated the Iranian practices of *qawwali* or *sama* into Indian devotional rituals.[35]

Thus the sufis, who began to appear in Punjab in the beginning of the eleventh century, had moored themselves in the local space after a generation or two. It was the pattern of daily life in which the mystic experience was articulated and expressed. The entire expression became such as was native to Punjab, 'except that the content was Islamic and Sufic—with certain key-terms taken from Persian and Arabic; but constant use rendered them familiar'.[36] Two points need to be observed here. First, sufis in the Punjab used a number of common vernacular words as metaphors and motifs: *musafar* (traveller), *saran* (tavern), *pani bhardian kurian* (girls drawing water from a well), *suhra* (in-laws), *peka* (paternal house of a married girl), *suhagan* (married woman), *vesva* (whore), *vanjara* (mobile vendor), *gahk* (customer), *sui* (needle), *dhaga* (thread), and so on. In Shah Husain's poetry one finds a large number of words associated with the popular non-Islamic religious and devotional expression: *satgur, thakur,* and *har* (Almighty), *japna, simran,* and *Ram bhajan* (remembrance of God), *jamn* (satan), *dhian* and *tari* (meditation), *bibhut* (smearing of ash), *darshan,* and so on.[37] Second, it is equally important to observe that the sufis, sufi poets and the qissa-kars of Punjab acquainted the people with Islam through their discourse on *ibadat* (prayer to God), *ishq* (love of God), *tarq* (renunciation of all worldly desires), *marfat* (knowledge of God), *wajd* (ecstasy of contemplation), *wasl* (union with God), and *finah fillah* (absorption into the eternal being)—the seven stages of spiritual experience. The use of Arabic and Persian words for Islamic concepts such as *malik* (master), *parvardigar* (cherisher), *reza* (divine will), *mehar, karam, bakhshish, nazar, nadar* (divine grace), *dargah* (portal), *fakir* and *darvesh* (saint/holy man), and *dar* (door) is also remarkable in Punjabi society. Gradually these ideas and terms became an integral part of the people's language.

Certain words enriched the religious discourse of the Sikh faith too:

> *fateh* (victory) which coming from the Arabic is an inalienable part of the Sikh situation. *Deg* (Persian: cooking cauldron—figurative meaning: charity or the shared blessings of life), and *teg* (the sword) are a part of the esoteric Sikh formula whereby the two-fold ideal of the Sikh faith—service to mankind and crusading for faith and righteousness—is expressed. *Dastar* (a Persian word for turban) is a part of the Sikh sacred canon, as this article of dress is indispensable for a Sikh, and none of the synonyms for it from the native sources has the ceremonial sanctity of this word. *Sidq* (truth, sincerity—Arabic) defines Sikh orthodoxy more intimately and comprehensively than any other equivalent term.[38]

In fact, this was a vernacularization of Islam. During the eighteenth century when the Mughal empire was in decline, the sufi poets in Punjab had developed a clear vernacular character, as exemplified by Waris Shah, Bulleh Shah, and Ali Haider. During this period, they expressed their sense of identification and association with local space—a phenomenon which may be characterized as commitment to the *vatan* or homeland.

The practices described above, operating through the vernacular, played a significant role in diluting the character of 'Muslim' sufis as *alien* and *other*,[39] because from the eighth to the fourteenth centuries the 'natives', Rajput, Brahman, and others, identified people from the Iranian Plateau 'not by their religion, but by their linguistic identity—most typically, as Turks (Turuska)'.[40] It is rightly observed that an indigenous model of Islam that evolved in the subcontinent through sufism contains in itself the beliefs of a myriad local cultures and populations.[41]

Posthumous Significance of Sufis

The shrines, mazars, and dargahs of the sufis facilitated the spread of Islam among the people of Punjab. A shrine was a sacred space encapsulating the presence of a particular sufi saint. It signified a continuous relationship between a living devotee and a saint who had *departed* to the other world but was not dead.[42] People visited shrines in order to seek favours from the saints buried there.[43] This kind of worship and devotion was similar to the ancient *guru-chela* practice prevalent among Hindus. Such forms of worship were the heritage of the Muslims of India through their Hindu origin and it became easy for saint-worship to become an integral part of Muslim religious life.[44] The rationale of this perpetual relationship (between shrine and a devotee) was the unflinching faith and devotion which a devotee reposed in the saint, through his *baraka* or charismatic self. The devotee discerned the presence of a saint in his tomb. He perceived that his patron (*murshid*) listened to his petitions and would plead with God to sanction his requests. This intimate relationship which the devotee constructed and his belief that the departed saint reciprocated, formed the basis of shrine worship.

Ali bin Usman Hujweri, popularly known as Data Ganj Bakhsh, migrated from Ghazni during the mid-eleventh century and settled permanently in Lahore, where he wrote the first ever treatise on Islamic mysticism, *Kashf-ul-Mahjub* (The Opening of the Veil). His opinion on the insignificance of pilgrimage in the Great Tradition appealed to the religious ethos of the Muslim folk. 'Anyone who is absent from God at Mecca is in the same position as if he were absent from God in his own house, and anyone who is present with God in his own house is in the same position as if he were present with God at Mecca', he writes. The 'true object of pilgrimage is not to visit Kaba, but to obtain contemplation of God'.[45]

Sufism hence tended to devalue the *hajj* in favour of pilgrimage to local tombs and shrines.[46] Belief in the particular sanctity of saints' graves is connected with a number of concepts about consecrated graves. In Muslim belief, God forbade the soil to consume the bodies of prophets, martyrs, theologians and *muezzins* lying buried in it. Disturbance of a saint's grave is, therefore, considered desecration, to be avenged by divine wrath.[47] A local pilgrimage and its merit or *ziyarat* attained the status of *hajj*.[48] Within the framework of institutional sufism, the quasi-divine status of a pir or sufi saint has significant ramifications. Though he experienced death of the body, the spirit of the saint was considered to live on eternally in the presence of God. The pir pierced the 'curtain of death through the tomb' that enclosed his physical remains. His presence was stronger in the tomb than elsewhere. Also, here in the tomb, the pir was 'more receptive to the intercessory pleas' of his followers.[49]

The mazar and dargah[50] played a significant role in the cultural integration of different religious communities.[51] It is stated that after AD 1000 the tombs of sufi saints began to take on public importance when rulers started to see the political advantages of associating with them. 'Thus the Seljuk Turks constructed a tomb for the Persian master Abu Said ibn Abi al-Khayr (d. 1049), and the Mongols erected one for Bayazid Bastami. Paying reverence to saints' tombs also constituted an important ritual practice for the sufi orders, which began to emerge about the same time.'[52]

As regards shrines in Punjab, Oberoi points out that their popularity in the countryside was also part of 'standard curative practices'.[53]

After Shaikh Farid died (in 1265) his shrine continued to inspire devotees and others. His austere lifestyle, his charismatic or spiritual power, and the exceptional qualities of his immediate successors were among the important factors which made his shrine popular.[54] It is stated that it was 'really his popularity that led his sons to bury him in his khanqah against his will, votaries being anticipated from Ajodhan (modern Pak-Pattan) to offer prayers, invoke his blessings for the fulfilment of their desires and thereby to financially help his survivors. Since Ajodhan was situated on the merchant caravan route linking Multan . . . with Delhi . . . merchants, nobles, and soldiers . . . paid visits to the dargah and invoked the saint's help and blessings.'[55] After the demise of Shaikh Farid, the construction of the vast shrine above the tomb began.[56] It had a mosque, a welfare kitchen (*langar*), and a number of related buildings that were raised during different times. Various places in the dargah complex became specific spots blessed with spiritual powers. For instance, the door of paradise (*bahishti darwaza*), which leads to the grave of Shaikh Farid, is believed to save visiting devotees who pass through it from the fires of hell. C.M. Wades writes:

> [This] doorway is about two feet wide and cannot be entered without stooping, and the apartment itself is not capable of containing thirty people crowded together. Yet such is the care which the saint takes of his votaries on the occasions, that no accident or loss of life has ever been known to occur. A superlative heaven is open to those who are first to enter the tomb on the day mentioned. The rush for precedence may, therefore, be better imagined than described. The crowd of pilgrims is said to be immense, and as they egress from the sacred doorway, after having rubbed their foreheads on the foot of the saint's grave, the air resounds with the shouts of Farid! Farid ![57]

For Eaton, the shrine of Shaikh or Baba Farid (not the saint himself) was a catalyst in the conversion of the agrarian and pastoral population of Punjab to Islam.[58] By the thirteenth century, the descendants of Baba Farid and his burial place became organically linked with his spiritual power (*baraka*). Eaton identifies the institutionalization of the shrine with, first, the patronage of the Delhi court, and second, the extension of mass devotionalism into the countryside. During late Khalji times, the governor of Dipalpur, Ghiasuddin Tughluq (who later on became Sultan), was one of the local notables attracted to the spiritual power and piety of Diwan Alauddin Mauj Darya, the grandson of Baba Farid. Ghiasuddin would frequently visit the Diwan at Ajodhan. On one such occasion, the latter prophesied that Ghiasuddin Tughluq, his son Muhammad bin Tughluq, and his nephew Firoz Shah Tughluq were destined to be the rulers of Hindustan, and the prophecy proved to be true. Later Sultan Muhammad bin Tughluq conferred the city of Ajodhan on the shrine, allocating local revenues for the shrine's support. Firoz Shah Tughluq (1351–88) had the tomb of Baba Farid repaired and granted 'robes of honour to his descendants and confirmed allocated villages and lands.[59] Much later, the entire Mughal dynasty, believing that the blessings of Chishti shaikhs underpinned their worldly success, vigorously patronized the order.[60]

On entering India in 1526, Babur prayed at the shrine of the Chishti sufi, Qutbuddin Bakhtiyar Kaki. In 1571 Akbar built a tomb for his father Humayun near Shaikh Nizamuddin Auliya's shrine.[61] In the same year, he began building his new capital of Fatehpur Sikri at the hospice site of Shaikh Salim Chishti. Jahangir built gates and other buildings at or near the Chishti shrine at Ajmer. That the spiritual power of the shrine had spread far and wide is evident from the fact that in the early fourteenth century small memorial shrines to Baba Farid, built by the common people, appeared across the countryside and that the '*baraka* and authority of Baba Farid became physically established over the land in much the same way that political/administrative authority was'.[62] H.A. Rose provides us the list of known Chishtis and their shrines at towns such as Delhi, Karnal, Panipat, Ambala, Thanesar, Pak-Pattan, Lahore, Jullundar, and other places.[63]

The shrine of Sakhi Sarwar at Nigah, 22 miles west of Dera Ghazi Khan, is of great interest.[64] By race, the saint, whose parents had migrated to Multan some time in the twelfth or thirteenth century, was a Syed of Baghdad. The cult of his presence illustrates a process of socio-cultural fusion. The influence of the cult on the Hindus and Sikhs was extensive, and the followers of Sakhi Sarwar were found both in Cis-Sutlej and Trans-Sutlej right up to Saharanpur. His shrines throughout Punjab were under the control of Muslim attendants (*mujawirs*) and priests (*pujaris*) of Khatri, Brahmin and jogi communities. One may also mention Pir Hassu Taili, said to have been born some time in the sixteenth century at Makhiwal on the bank of the Chenab, and died in Lahore in 1603. M. Athar Ali highlights the social diversity of the disciples of this saint. Muslims and Hindus had accepted his bondage and recited his name day and night. Landed aristocrats and *zamindars* owed allegiance to him. He was believed to belong to the line of the *naths* of Gorakh Nath. While he appears to have remained formally a Muslim, he did not follow the five basic observances of Islam.[65]

A reading of Schimmel's *Islam in the Indian Subcontinent* obliges us to further illustrate the form and nature of the relationship between people and their saints:

(1) Typical is the story of Diwan Gidumal, the Hindu minister of the Kalhora, who offered the invading Ahmad Shah Abdali (1749) a little bag which, as he said, 'contains the most precious thing Sind has to offer: dust from the tomb of Sayyids and saints.

(2) Quite a few places in the subcontinent can boast of relics, such as a hair from the Prophet's beard; one such hair is in Delhi next to the Great Mosque, one in Bijapur, and again another one (acquired in 1545) in Rohri (Sind) where it is exposed in a beautiful gold case set with rubies and emeralds, in the month of March.

(3) Even more important is the *qadam-i-rasul*, the Prophet's footprint in stone, examples of which pious pilgrims brought from Mecca or Medina and around which remarkable architectural structures were built; the *qadam rasul* mosques in Bengal bear witness of this veneration. One may see here a typical Indian relic, for to touch the foot is an act of humility, and long before Islam India had known the Buddha's footprint and 'feet of Vishnu'.

(4) The Qadiri *dargah* in Uch preserves a hair of the Prophet along with Abdul Qadir's turban and other relics.

(5) In Lucknow the horseshoe of Husain's horse, which was lost in the battle of Karbala, is preserved.

(6) The tombs of saints, even more than the mosques, reflect the character of both the builder and the saint: the small tomb of Salim Chishti in Fatehpur Sikri resembles a beautiful white pearl in the vast landscape of red stone buildings; and the windows of Muhammad Ghauth Gwaliori's grey marble tomb seem to translate into visible forms the constellations of the stars which he knew so well. Ruknuddin's tomb in Multan belongs to the most impressive constructions of Indian architects, its colossal body being here and there adorned with blue and white tiles.[66]

Lack of literary evidences is considered as the most formidable obstacle to the historical identification of a village khanqah, the tomb of a local pir, and the grave of a local martyr.[67] However, one may read in H.A. Rose's *Glossary*, a detailed account of the important shrines, the Muslim saints and of their miracles meant for alleviating the sufferings of the people. His account covers the Kurram valley,

Hazara, Kohat, Dera Ghazi Khan, Muzaffargarh, Shahpur, Multan, Bahawalpur, Ferozpur, Ambala and Lahore.[68]

Let me sum up what I have intended to convey in the preceding pages. The sufi saints survived in shrines, tombs, and dargahs as well as in the space of folk magic and religion. Dietrich Reetz remarks, though in a different context, that 'the sufi-inspired and pir-based network of devotional Islam represented majority of real existing Islamic practices in sub-continent'.[69] In Punjabi folk literature, we find references to charms and amulets read and written in the name of Baba Farid to cure a person who was afflicted with tooth-ache or snake-bite or scorpion-sting.[70] To protect a milch animal under an evil eye, a written charm with reference to Khawaja Hodi and Zahir, placed in kneaded flour, was given to the animal.[71] The influence of sufi mystic love was predominant on Punjabi folk literature, as is evident from the songs about Hir–Ranjha, Sassi–Punnun, Sohni–Mahiwal and Laila–Majnu. A large number of catch-songs (*bolian*) about these lovers constituted a significant segment of Punjabi folklore.[72] Many verses of Baba Farid and Bulleh Shah are used as proverbs and sayings in Punjabi.[73] In the atmosphere of communal harmony created by the sufis, Rattan Nath who was by birth a Kshatriya and a disciple of Machhander Nath became 'Baba' Rattan Nath (Baba is a Persian word which means patriarch). After Rattan Nath, Shaikh Farid was popularly called 'Baba' Farid. Later, Gorakh also became 'Baba' Gorakh instead of Guru Gorakh Nath. Later still, Guru Nanak was addressed with the same title.[74] This signifies that non-conformist jogis, sufis, and bhaktas came together in the domain of the folk practices of popular religion that transcend time and space. Thus was constructed the cultural narrative (and also the cultural genealogy) of Punjabi society.

Sufism in Punjab was a protest against denominationalism, priestly ritualism, and dogmatism.[75] As a tradition of people's poetry in people's idiom, it (Punjabi sufi poetry) stood parallel to the classical Sanskrit and Persian elite literature.[76] While the orthodox protagonists of Islam influenced Punjabis with their political and economic clout, the sufis wooed the commoners by adapting to the people's culture. Thus to a large extent the sufi presence 'mitigated the harshness of the Muslim military conquest'.[77] The sufis obliterated the difference between *momin* and *kafir*. They identified themselves not with the Muslim ruling class but with the subalterns. Shah Husain (1538–1601)[78] was proud of being of the weaving profession and expressed his mystic love through it. Similarly Bulleh Shah[79] was proud of being the pupil of a gardener (*arain*), named Shah Inayat Qadiri. When his sisters and sisters-in-law came to argue with him that they were the descendants of the Prophet (*nabi*) and he was dishonouring them, Bulleh replied:

He who calls me a Sayyid will be punished in hell. / He who calls me Arain, /will ride swings in heaven. / If you want to get comfort and pleasure, become a client of the Arain.[80]

I have attempted to show that the spread of Islamic culture and the creation of its aura were not the byproduct of political and military campaigns or of Muslim immigration or fear and force, nor of the role of the qazis and mullas; it was more the result of a process which was gradual, zigzag, non-antagonistic, and spontaneous. Punjabi people responded more enthusiastically to the process of cultural fusion initiated by the sufis than to the orthodox process of Islamization. However, it must not be construed that the sufis were not inextricably connected with Islam. They indeed were, but they were different in their orientation from the ecclesiastical class of ulema. In contrast to the latter, they preached Islam in an emancipatory discourse. They refrained from the politicization of religion or from advocating the cause of a theocratic polity. They were more aware than their orthodox counterparts of social realities and considered themselves to be the part and parcel of the local societies they lived in. They preached Islam not as technicians and politicians, but as mystics committed to devotion. Their Allah was omnipresent rather than omnipotent as the *ulema* saw Him. For the sufis, the essential relationship of man with Allah consisted in their relationship of love, whereas the ulema propagated that relationship in the master–slave context. Bulleh Shah in one of his *kafis* pronounced:

I have learnt now, what relation is there between shariat and love, / When one quaffs the cup of love, one forgets everything. / The Lord is

Lord of every home, recognizable in every shape. / The Preceptor lives within me, through love I have learnt it. / Logic semantics, symbols, rhetoric, all that was learnt is wasted. / Prayer and fasting do not avail when one is intoxicated with wine. / Bulleh has turned deaf and dumb by coming / into the company of the Master.[81]

Thus the sufis, in contrast to the ulema, aimed at achieving union with Allah, not Paradise. The sufis made their five daily prayers (*namaz*), but insisted on the constant remembrance of God. Instead of fasting only during Ramzan, they advocated austerity for the whole of one's life. Instead of advocating only *zakat*, they offered the ideal of renunciation of all possessions. It was preferable to visit the pir's khanqah than to go on a pilgrimage to Mecca.[82] In his verses, Bulleh Shah elevates the status of Takht Hazara, the village of Ranjha, to the level of Islamic pilgrimage.[83] The renunciation of rituals and pilgrimage and, at the same time, the advocacy of love are boldly reflected in the verses of Bulleh Shah:

God is neither in the shrines nor at the Mecca. / Whosoever sees him brightens up in the face. / Burn the prayer mat / Don't carry rosary, cup or stick, / Lovers are shouting all along, / Discard religiously purified meat, eat the carcass, / A lifetime is wasted in a mosque. / Filled inside with impurities, / you never prayed or worshipped. / Why raise now a hue and cry? / Love has made me forget paying obeisance to you.[84]

Punjabi sufis (for instance, Mian Mir who laid the foundation of Harmandir Sahib, the supreme religious shrine of the 'other' non-Muslim community) tried to impart a holistic vision to the Mughal state and its religious allies. They never allowed their concern for Punjab to be nourished on sectarian and discriminatory lines: their concern was rooted in the cultural soil of Punjab, not in theology. They facilitated the creation of a Punjabi ethos among the people. Their poetry and their living styles had deep effects on the history and culture of the region and saved the three major communities from perceiving and conceiving each other as aliens. It was the sufis who kept Punjabi people away from fanaticism, and created an aura of communal harmony. This was the reason that Ghani Khan and Nabi Khan, the Pathan horse dealers, saved the life of Guru Gobind Singh by presenting him as *Uch Ka Pir* when the Mughal imperial army was in hot pursuit. A large number of Punjabi Muslims joined the Khalsa struggle against the Mughals and the Afghan invaders. The century-long Khalsa struggle against the oppression and plunder of the state could not prevent Ranjit Singh from paying homage at the royal mosque constructed by Aurangzeb, with whom the Sikhs had been in deadly confrontation.

If the sufism of Punjab is to be understood as the expressive manifestation of a basic drive towards meaningful life, a longing for social and communal harmony, for justice and creative expectations, then the sufis of Punjab may be characterized as critical of an unequal society and institutionalized religion which tended to hegemonize an individual and constrain his/her freedom. Their aim was to create and construct self-determining and concrete historical being, as Hir and Ranjha endeavoured to be, while fighting the mullah and qazi and taking on the feudal patriarchy. The non-sufic Islamic message of liberation lost its appeal when it allowed itself to be put to fanatical use, as is evident from the cold response of the Muslims of Punjab to the orthodox ideology of Shah Waliullah or to the call for *jihad* raised by the Wahhabi Syed Ahmed Barelvi against the 'Sikh' Maharaja Ranjit Singh. The sufis of Punjab became popular because they rejected theocracy and autocracy alike.

One is now able to draw a distinction between religion as source of social creativity and a sacred foundation on the one hand, and religion as a reason for social conflict and power politics, on the other. In the latter case, the Islamic orthodox or fundamentalist movement was by no means immune to trivialization. Friendly meetings between sufis and the yogis/jogis were frowned on.[85] The popular religious movement that began to emerge in the sixteenth century in the form of the sufi poetry of Shah Husain, the *sulh-i-kul* of Akbar, and the compilation of the *Adi Granth* by Guru Arjan Dev had far-reaching consequences. It facilitated the spread of an ideology of conflict-resolution inspired by the sufis and the Sikh gurus, and which countered the Islamic and Brahmanical orthodoxies.

The Cult of Pirs

Had Punjabi Muslims been thinking in terms of a narrowly-defined religious identity with their invaders or priests, no community based on a historically-evolved cultural fusion would have evolved in the land of Punjab. The historical, cultural, and literary cohesion of the region negates the existence of a medieval Muslim population as a monolithic community of a diasporic character. Such views tend to overlook the significance of the cultural boundary of a community that 'cannot be appropriately articulated without reference to a socio-territorial identity, i.e. a linguistic and cultural heritage shared by its members who have collectively inhabited a common territory'.[86]

Waris Shah offers to his readers a kaleidoscopic canvas of the religious life of Punjabi folk who worshipped a number of gods and pirs/sufis. Each god or pir was a patron of a certain situation and a certain group of people. Guru Nanak, Shah Madar, Kabir, Tehra, Shams, Nam Dev, Lukman, Khawaja Khizar, Raja Nal, Satan, Suleman Paras, and others were patrons of ascetics (*udasis*), jugglers (*madaris*), weavers (*julasis*), cobblers (*mochi*), goldsmiths (*suniars*), tailors (*chhimbas*), carpenters and blacksmiths (*tarkhasis* and *lohar*), folk buffoons (*marasis*), barbers (*nais*), oilmen (*telis*), sailors, and gamblers.[87] Different from the 'living' class of mullas and pandits who maintained a social distance from the masses, these pirs and gurus, signified five important socio-cultural and religious dimensions.

First, the said cluster underscores the fact that the bulk of the Indian Muslims retained the culture of their castes or professions.[88] Thus local converts, with their vernacular heritage, were distinct from the descendants of the immigrants who began to be classified as Sayyid, Shaikh, Mughal, or Pathan. Second, ethnic, linguistic, regional, and class differences played a significant part in Muslim lives, and prevented the emergence of a unified Muslim *umma*.[89] Third, the cluster reflects a pluralism that was quite different from sectarianism. The former is defined as spontaneous and based on a positive attitude towards religion and the lived social reality, while the latter is said to be ideological and in that sense self-conscious, constructed, and sceptical.[90] Fourth, the cluster signifies that the agricultural and rural communities (like that of Jhang, Rangpur Khera, and Takht Hazara) could not conceive the idea of bhakti in the *nirguna* tradition, beyond attributes.[91] Inherently grounded in the cosmology of kinship relationship, the rural folk, unlike the urban populations, had their own pirs/gurus/gods. The peasantry believed in the concretization of relationships, be it a living or non-living thing or be it a god. It is said that bhakti, literally 'participation' (of the soul in the divine), is emotional worship, the intimate adoration of a personal deity/pir/guru in a spirit of love and deep affection and self-surrender. A life of bhakti is not necessarily a life of inaction or passivity. It involved listening to the accounts of deity/pir/guru, his praises, singing his songs and eulogies, meditation on his name and deeds, worshipping his image, prostration, subservience, friendship and surrendering one's life to him.[92] The rural folk's relationship with the mazars of sufis illustrates this well. The patron saints whom we meet in *Hir Waris* have a close relationship with certain classes of work and particular classes of individuals. The saints have their own significance and spheres of influence, which may be the immediate vicinity or village, or a quarter of a city, or else a universal space. In the domain of folk religion, one may come across a number of saints—historical, legendary or imagined, universal or local. Ranjha frequently seeks the intercession of gods and pirs to counter the social and religious injunctions of the patriarchs and priests. On a number of occasions he remembers Khawaja Khizar,[93] Farid Shakarganj (Baba Farid), Lal Shahbaz,[94] Bahauddin Zakariya[95] and Syed Jalal Bukhari.[96] They bless, support, and encourage him.

'Mother, father, and qazi all went for me, / but I have failed not in my part.' / Says Hir, and Ranjha invokes the saints / as he hears from her to this effect. / He prays to them with folded hands / and the flow of tears is not checked. / 'My Hir is brought to bay, the qazi / and all her people threatening worse. / 'Help me for the sake of God, O saints, / my love will go to ruin else.' / 'What trouble besets you, child,' they ask, / 'that puts such tremors in your heart?'

The saints bid him be of good cheer, / and put the lover quite at ease. / 'To help your Hir is now the charge / of the most revered Jahania, / Who as you know is one of us. / And let us have some music now.' /

And the peasant [Ranjha] plays the flute so well / that the saints are moved to lend him grace.

Well pleased, the saints say, 'You shall have / whatever be your heart's desire. / To you we give this day this girl [Hir], / so steeped in love's celestial hue. / But we will not give you the beggar's sack, / nor make her a beggar to tramp with you. / Not a beggar-maid at her father's house, / elopement is not best for her. / Nevertheless we are pleased with you / and grant your prayer. / Hir shall be yours, / And you shall have whatever you wish, / for we will be your providence. / Go, play your flute to your herds and make / the wood resound with music, and dance,' / Ah, Waris, in this way the saints / bestow on man unlimited favours.[97]

The motif of pir as a counter-hegemonic, charismatic, force is prevalent in the legend of Hir–Ranjha whether versified by Damodar, or Muqbil or by other qissa-kars. Even the love in Hir and Ranjha is sparked off by the pirs in Damodar's *Hir*. They meet Ranjha, who is about to leave for Jhang, on the shores of the Chenab and bless him with the love of Hir, and then appear in the dream of Hir and suggest she accept Ranjha as her lover.[98] Last, the cluster of pirs and gods underlines the synthesis of bhakti and sufi traditions.

Hir Waris falsifies the idea of monolithic religious communities of Hindus and Muslims, imagined by some scholars. In a number of Punjabi folk songs exists a space where 'Hindu' gods and goddesses (Devi, Hanuman, Krishna, Indra) and pirs or faqirs (Haider Shaikh and Baba Farid) plus jogis (Gorakh Nath and Bal Nath) and gurus (Nanak) meet on a common ground.[99] Generally speaking, the people of medieval Punjab, in view of their hybrid religious space, were neither restricted to a particular religious space, nor the domain of the five pirs was fixed in the broad cosmology of the religion, either of the Muslims or of the Hindus. The denominational status of the five pirs varied. Sometimes they stand for five Pandavas; sometimes they appear as the Prophet Muhammad, Fatima, Ali, Hasan and Husain. In the Gujranwala district, Shaikh Samail, Shah Daulat, Shaikh Fateh Ali, Pir Fateh Khan, and Shah Murad are the five patron-pirs of the Bhattis. In the centre and west of Punjab a queer mixture of five figures (Sultan, Devi, the

Guru, Khawaja and Gugga Pir) can be observed. In Ludhiana, Khawaja Khizar, Durga Devi, Vishnu, Sakhi Sarwar, and Guru Gobind Singh constitute the five, whereas in Shimla, Gugga Pir, Balaknath, Thakur, Sakhi Sarwar and Shiv enjoy the same status.[100] The 'confluence' of Muslim and Hindu thought, according to Schimmel, 'becomes clear from new combinations of spiritual "helpers" such as the *Panj Piriya*, a group of five saints whose cult is quite common in the fluvial plains of Indo-Pakistan'.[101]

The Chenab valley was 'famous for its saints'.[102] Conceived and considered generally as a political and religious space of the Muslims, the Jhang district deserves special mention because of its Hindu saints, namely Ram Piara, Mula Sant, Baba Shahana, Jinda and Kaliana. Ram Piara was a bhakta who generally resided in Jhang and Dera Ismail Khan and professed Vaishnava tenets. Mula Sant was a famous Gaur Brahman of Wazirabad who lived in the beginning of the sixteenth century and migrated to a place called Suliman in the Chiniot tahsil of Jhang. The tenets of Mula Sant were also Vaishnava. Similarly, Baba Shahana was not originally a native of the Jhang district. He was Gauri Khatri of Satghara who lived in the sixteenth century. His original name was Mihra and his original occupation was boiling gram or chickpeas. One of his customers was a Muslim faqir who made him his disciple and conferred on him the name of Mihr Shah. The followers of Jinda and Kaliana, two saints said to have lived in the early part of the sixteenth century,[103] constituted another sect of the locality. These pirs and saints stood as alternatives to, what Gellener calls the 'legalistic, restrained and arid Islam of the *ulama*'.[104] Many stories are told in Pakistan 'about the necessity of having at least one saint's tomb in a village so that life can properly continue with his blessing'.[105]

The Cult of Jogis

Ranjha the 'Muslim' did not hesitate to visit the hillock (*tilla*)[106] of Bal Nath, a Hindu jogi. The syncretic Punjabi character of the 'Rajput/Jatt' Ranjha and the 'Muslim' Ranjha emerges prominently in this incident.

'Prize of my life I have lost,' says Ranjha / 'and to recover it now must I / Renounce all caste and creed, assume / a beggar's robe of ochre hue. / Yes, there the grace of God [*rab*] is served / in platters, as it were, and now / For me remains only to turn / a mendicant and I must try.'

Thus fanned, the smouldering fire of love / leaps into flame, and taking the oath / of turning into an ear-cleft *yogi* [*jogi*], / Ranjha makes his way to the hermit's cave. / His hair long nourished on butter and cream, / is timed now for a close, clean shave. / Driving out all thought of birth and creed, / he goes to sell himself to the Nath, / To serve a master who should teach / the art of tripping a woman on the sly. / Ah, Waris, these lovers are not afraid / to lose their lives for love, and why?

At the hermitage with folded hands / begs Ranjha to be initiated. / 'I come across wild wood and marsh, / for a glimpse of your divinity. / Inspired by faith and truth I come, / admit me to your order, pray. / God is the king of all the worlds, / faqirs His ministers of state. / Without you we cannot find the path, without milk no pudding can be made. / You meditate on God alone, / and from the world aloof you rest. / And yet you are its true support / more than the prince or even the priest. / No father or mother or brother have I, / no kinsman, and no friend or mate. / I am lost in the mazes of this world, / pray cut the shackles off my feet. / Where else to go when you seem to me / so patently a man of God?'[107]

Punjab Rajputs had a long association with the cult of nath-yogis or jogis. It was the Rajput prince, Puran, son of Raja Salvan of Sialkot, who was rescued by Gorakh Nath when the former with his mutilated limbs was thrown into the well by his father (on the charge of molesting Luna, his step-mother). If in the *Qissa Puran Bhagat* life is bestowed on Puran by Gorakh Nath, in *Hir Waris* Ranjha is blessed with the love of Hir by Bal Nath. Interestingly, the blessings of the five 'Muslim' pirs and that of the Hindu jogi combine when Ranjha is blessed with the love of Hir by Bal Nath. Bal Nath's prayer to God for the fulfilment of Ranjha's wish is of interest:

His eyes shut fast, now Bal Nath prays / to God, and supplicates His aid. / Unstinting is Thy court, O Lord, / where man is not ashamed to beg. / The sky Thy limitless expanse, / Thou art the Lord of heaven and earth. / This roguish Jatt has turned to Thee / giving up all pride of name and birth. / He seeks not aid of kith and kin, / with faith in Thee he craves for *yoga.* / The shafts of the eyes of a woman have pierced / his heart, and drained it of its blood. / Having shaved his head and beard and bored / his ears, the cup of hemp he has drained. / Out of the nest of a home he comes / to far-off lands, flying like the crane. / Thou art Lord-guardian of the poor, / grant prayer, too, of this mendicant. / 'Say, Lord, what is thy will, this Ranjha, / the new-shorn *jogi* begs Hir of Thee./ Recommending him for a tiger-skin, / the five *pirs* too join his prayer. / The word of heaven descended then: We grant him Hir, he may not despair.' / The Nath [Bal Nath] then opened his eyes and said. / 'Go now, the Lord has granted your prayer. / Hir shall be yours without doubt, / the ruby is now strung with the pearl.[108]

Like the sufi pirs, the jogis were non-conformist. As the sufis were critical of the priestly class of mullah and qazis, so were the jogis critical of Brahmans and pandits. They may be said to be first non-conformist trend setters in the evolution of the Punjabi cultural fusion. They expressed their receptiveness to vernacular discourse as against the domination of Sanskrit. They developed a rapport with the masses in the popular tongue. The existence of a pretty long pre-Nanak era of Punjabi literature is warranted by 'the actual presence of works attributed to writers like Pushya, Chand, Gorakh Nath, Charpat Nath, Gopi Chand, Khusro, Farid, etc.'[109] Disregarding the Brahmanical ritualistic formalism, the nath-yogis inveighed against the vanity and hegemony of the priestly class. The canons of the caste-system were defied; and the principle of purity and pollution was countered. The naths may be said to be the harbingers of the movement of dissent expressed by the bhakti and sufi saints in medieval Punjab.

Commonly known as jogis, siddhas and rawals, the naths were born either Hindu or Muslim. Their cult had non-Brahmanical elements. The costume of the jogis, their everyday things, and their life pattern signified a revolt against Brahmanism, and simultaneously underlined the tribal and agrarian overtones of Punjabi society. This is evident from the following characterization of a nath by Wilson and Briggs. To the sacred thread around their neck was attached a ring called *pavitri* made up of deer's or rhinoceros' horn. It could also be that of a bone or be made of brass. To a ring were attached a whistle (*singnad*) and single *rudraksa* berry. The *singnad* was blown before meals and for the evening and morning prayers. Its use was ordered by Shiva (the Destroyer, third in the Hindu triad, the first being Brahma, the Creator, and the second being Vishnu, the Sustainer). One may read a phallic significance in the association of ring (*pavitri*) and *singnad*, a symbol of creation and fertility. Some jogis wore around the loins a special rope of black sheep's wool, to which they fastened their loin cloth, the *langoti*. A rosary of *rudraksa* berries was also worn. It was hung around their neck. *Rudraksa* signified the eye of Rudra (Shiva). Like Shiva, all yogis smeared their bodies with ashes, indicating mortality, renunciation, and rebellion against the hegemony of the Brahmans and their patrons.[110] Gorakh Nath spoke in his verses against formalism of every shade and variety.[111] To shift the emphasis from idol worship and Vaishnavistic devotion to the Unseen and Infinite, Gorakh Nath deconstructed the appellation *Bhagwan*, and replaced it with the discourse of *Alakhkh* (Unseeable), *Agama* (Unknowable), *Para* (Transcendant), *Amurata* (Formless), and *Nirakara* (Unformed).[112] The nath sect was a 'peculiar manifestation of social protest',[113] but, its stress upon the physical and spiritual perfection of an individual (by means of ascetic feats and resignation from worldly pleasures) did not let it spread on the social scale. The sect could not survive as a social mass movement like the one launched by the Sikh gurus.

Let me add here that the medieval Punjabi cultural matrix, the one which we also discover in *Hir Waris*, resonates with the religious non-conformists like jogis, sufis, saints and the Sikh gurus. From their sacred spaces like tillas, khanqhas, dharamshalas or gurdwaras, they constructed and communicated a vernacular discourse against the priestly classes who held a monopoly over language, education, religion, morality, and justice, and were organically bound to a patriarchal structure. It is, therefore, necessary and important to study 'in-depth' which religious element of the society of Punjab assumed the role of vanguard. Medieval socio-religious movements succeeded in introducing certain liberalizing tendencies, apart from enriching the regional literatures 'by providing new ideas and visions, new mores and modes, new moods and emotions as well as new contents, which in turn opened up new release-windows for the mind and imagination of perceptive individuals and groups'.[114]

Non-Scriptural Devotion and Pragmatic Concerns

Hir Waris reveals that the religious life pattern of rural Punjabi Muslims was not a scriptural and codified religion. It was locally confined. The pirs, sants and gurus of different communities of a village had intimate relationships with their clients. No priestly ritual was required to invoke them, a remembrance or meditating on the divine name (*yaad* or *dhian* or *zikr*) being sufficient to seek their help and blessings. The relationship to God was more a matter of faith and love than of doubt, fear, or reason. The universe was limited and simple to understand. Confronted with the dangers to life and property from nature, and living in constant fear of destruction, the peasant-tribal societies had developed the idea of God which happened to be close to the sufi and bhakti traditions, advocating a direct association between devotee and God. As human action emanated from divine will, the theologian's distinction between right and wrong did not prevail at the popular level. For instance, some of the deeds in the love affair of Hir and Ranjha are not socially permissible, but God's will and grace is mentioned time and again in the text. Hir says, 'Along with all my friends, / your bond-slave ever I shall stay, / For now that God [*rab*] has brought you [Ranjha] to me / all youthful friendships back I fling.'[115]

Later she tells her mother that the herdsman Ranjha was a gift of God bestowed on them.

> 'This herdsman is a gift of God [*rab*], / O mother you are so fortunate, / That a man like him should come to hand, / the whole world would bend low in prayer. / As God has willed, so has it happened.'[116]

Thus instead of looking at the institutional function of religion, the people of the medieval Punjab looked on religion as something that helped them in their day-to-day life. Their existence and identity were organically linked with the way they conceived and practised religion. Pirs and jogis exerted their influence by virtue of their charisma, made manifest by miracles and revelations. But the conflict of Hir and Ranjha with the maulvi and qazi signifies that the Punjabi Muslim folk had not yet given recognition to what Max Weber calls, the 'professional equipment of special knowledge, fixed doctrine and vocational qualifications' of the priestly class.[117] This signifies a tension between scriptural religion and paganism.

Waris Shah throws light on the identity of Punjabi Muslims within their indigenous religious milieu. Their cultural specificity and sensitivity, as revealed in *Hir Waris*, is in tension with the standardized social and religious parameters. Their 'vernacular' self-emerged boldly and they became increasingly aware of their identity when they were confronted with the oppression of the ecclesiastical class. This phenomenon can be visualized when the characters in *Hir Waris* refer to their mythological heritage. In these legends and myths the protagonists do not belong exclusively to one or other religious faith.[118] If people preferred to many Muslim customs, they also consulted a Brahman for the fixation of the auspicious date for the wedding. Their belief in one God did not make them actually perceive any contradiction with their belief in many gods and pirs. The hybrid character of the legend of Hir and Punjabi Muslims may also be discerned in Ranjha's reply to Hir when she asks him, 'Tell me truly: what is the relationship between us?' Ranjha's reply alludes to a Hindu (or pre-Islamic) and Islamic synthesis in the self of a Punjabi Muslim:

> When I, Ranjha, was in the house of Indar, you were a maiden there. / When I, Ranjha, was Namanand [the medieval Hindu reformer], you were my wife Gorkhan. / When I, Ranjha, was Radha Kishn [Krishan], you were Brikhban's daughter. And then when I, Ranjha, was born in Takhat Hazara, you were born to Mihar Chuchak.[119]

Thus in order to understand the socio-cultural character of Punjabi Muslims, one needs to traverse the Punjabi literary and cultural space. One of the fundamental contradictions in the text of *Hir Waris* is that between the sectarian orthodoxy and the syncretic religious ethos of the people. When the jogi Bal Nath persuaded Ranjha to follow the orthodox injunctions of his cult with regard to celibacy, the young peasant revolted. He confronted Bal Nath in anger:

Bal Nath: 'A woman is like the sugar-cane / exposed alike to pest and thief. / We must not foul ourselves with sin / feed properly this body's beast. / Be humble, celibate and austere, / and both in mind and body chaste. / Chop off this troublesome lump of flesh, / O Waris, with a keen-edged knife.'

Ranjha: 'Had I been pure and chaste, O Nath, / should I have brought this on my head? / Could I refrain from love, need I / have left my home and brothers and peers. / If I could truly subdue the self, / need I have ventured on this course? / 'Should I have grazed the herds of the Siyals / if I could live as a hermit in the wood? / I would not let you shave my head / and pierce my ears, had I abstained. / And had I known of your imposts, / I would not take your rings to burn. / I would not come to foul this mount / had I known from women you would warn.'[120]

It may be argued that the medieval agrarian society like that of Punjab, facing a variety of natural and social confrontations and hardships on a geographic and political frontier, may have developed a pragmatic approach to religion to meet the demands of everyday life. Such an approach would have cut across any imaginary boundary we now construct between Hindus and Muslims, and even the syncretic ethos obliges us to give credence to the needs of pragmatism. Hir suggested that Ranjha become a jogi and 'manage' to meet her at her in-laws' house. Ranjha invoked the five pirs with the aid of his flute and visited the tilla of Bal Nath jogi, because he desired to be blessed with love of Hir, otherwise denied to him by the die-hard norms of the patriarchs. What was religiously and culturally important about the pirs and Bal Nath was that they dealt with 'the pragmatic concerns of survival'.[121] People (like Ranjha) adopted a *hybrid* life pattern in their devotion to the pirs, gods, saints—a devotion which otherwise was not permitted by the injunctions of the Great Traditions—because they knew that these divine figures wielded the charisma to make their lives better or fulfil their desires. Harjot Oberoi's explanation of the Sikh participation in popular devotion at the shrine of Sakhi Sarwar, Gugga Pir, goddess Devi (worshipped under numerous names like Sitla Devi, Mansa Devi and Naina Devi) may further enrich our understanding of the syncretic culture and religious boundaries. Oberoi offers us the following four arguments to explain the enchanted universe of the Sikh (and for our purpose it may be a universe of the Muslim medieval rural society where Hir and Ranjha lived):

> Formulating this popular religion in the nineteenth-century Punjab, which was predominantly an agrarian society rooted in peasant household production, might begin by delineating the four features. . . . First, everyday life within it was marked by an absence of scriptures and other such religious codes, be they in Gurmukhi, Sanskrit or any other language. Second, participation in this religion was restricted to common people who lived in the rural tracts: in this sense one could call it a village religion. Third, the focus of religiosity was not on analysis but on pragmatic results. Whereas scriptural religion is concerned with explaining reality, popular religion seeks to manipulate reality to the advantage of its constituents, be it through the intercession of spirits, magic or other rituals. . . . Finally, popular religion had its own cultural agents.[122]

The god of the people of medieval Punjab was not one who dispassionately or ruthlessly dispensed justice, but an anthropomorphic god who protected his people. Having no philosophical view on the subject, peasants had a romantic (or common sense) view of the intimate relationship between life, matter, and mind. In popular religious culture, then, the boundaries between Islam and Hinduism were more flexible than in formal doctrine. As Lapidus has put it, 'Islam entered into the Indian environment sometimes by assimilating converts into a new communal identity and religious beliefs and sometimes by being assimilated into the indigenous culture.'[123] If the participation of the 'Muslim' folk of medieval Punjab in the enchanted universe was a matter of existential concern, the same concern can be discerned among the ruling class and its patronage of sufis and their shrines, patronage which was otherwise not recommended by the theologians. True, there was a difference between the pragmatic concerns of the general masses and those of the ruling elite. Richard Eaton's narration of the Delhi sultans' patronage of a sufi order may be cited here to illustrate the point:

Among all South Asian Sufi orders, the Chishtis were the most closely identified with political fortunes of Indo-Muslim states, and especially with the planting of such states in parts of South Asia never previously touched by Islamic rule. The pattern began in the first several decades of the fourteenth century, when the order's rise to prominence among Delhi's urban populace coincided with that of the imperial Tughluqs. The two principal poets in India of that time, Amir Hasan and Amir Khusrau, and the leading historian, Zia al-Din Barani, were all disciples of Nizam al-Din Auliya. As writers whose works were widely read, these men were in effect publicists for Nizam al-Din and his order. And since the three were also patronized by the Tughluq court, the public and ruling classes alike gradually came to associate dynastic fortune with that of the Chishti order. Moreover, as the spiritual power of a charismatic Sufi was believed to adhere to his tomb, shrines at such tombs were patronized by Indo-Muslim rulers just as they were frequented by Muslim devotees. And since the tomb-shrines of the greatest shaikhs of this order were located within South Asia, and not in distant Central Asia or the Middle East as was the case with those of other orders, a ruling dynasty's patronage of Chishti shrines could bolster its claim to being both legitimately Islamic and authentically Indian. . . . On entering Delhi in 1526, Babur prayed at the shrines of India's second great Chishti Shaikh, Bakhtiyar Kaki (d. 1235), and the new emperor's brother-in-law rebuilt the tomb of Nizam al-Din Auliya.[124]

An interesting point concerning the pragmatic concerns of survival occurs in Gurbaksh Singh *Preet Lari*. Before I explain the point, I wish to give a brief account of this writer.

Gurbakhsh Singh (b. 1895) was a prolific prose writer. He turned to literature first of all as a means of transforming society. He graduated from an engineering college at Roorkee. Apart from being determined by a variety of influences like Sikh traditions, Christianity, the ideas of Thoreau and Emerson, the philosophy of Mahatma Gandhi, as well as the ideological climate of the national liberation movement of his epoch, Gurbakhsh Singh's ideas and concepts bore the strong imprint of Marxism. To propagate his views, he started a Punjabi journal, *Preet Lari.*[125] In his narration of the love legend of Hir–Ranjha, pirs are conspicuous by their absence. There is a reference to the jogi in the narration, but he does not bestow his blessings on Ranjha. He does not grant Hir to Ranjha with his charisma. Thus the charismatic elements which we find in *Hir Waris* are absent and, hence, obviously do not serve as pragmatic concerns for the survival and success of Hir and Ranjha in Gurbakhsh Singh's version. As a modern, progressive, and Marxist writer, Gurbakhsh Singh aims to render the story in a purely social (and patriarchal) idiom. There is no place for the supernatural element. The struggle of Hir and Ranjha is not disturbed by the intervention of the charisma of pirs and jogis. Pragmatic concerns for survival and success are dictated by enlightenment and reason, not faith and belief. Gurbakhsh Singh brings the folk legend of Punjab out from the sufic or devotional ambience and plants it in a subaltern-oriented struggle of lovers who do not seek the blessings and benedictions of mystical forces.

Sufism and Bhakti: A Fusion

From the beginning to the end of the *Hir Waris,* Ranjha exemplifies a synthesis of sufi and bhakti traditions. Both traditions cultivated the pleasure of personal absorption in God, while negating the mediation of the priestly classes. They had existed as a more popular vehicle for religious feeling than the colder and formal discipline of the priestly classes. Ranjha obliterates the difference between a Muslim and a non-Muslim Punjabi. The *raga* and *ragnis* that he sings[126] to appease the five pirs allude to the devotional songs of bhaktas and sufis. An explanation of some of *ragas* and *ragnis* sung by Ranjha speaks of the fusion of Shaivite, bhakti and sufi traditions of devotion. Of the many *ragas* and *ragnis* sung by him, mention may be made of Lalit, Bhairon, Deepak, Malhar, Basant, Handol, and Ramkali.

Lalit, the name of a *ragni,* is performed in the evening. Pictorially it is described as a pretty young girl, with a radiant complexion. She holds a *vina* and a cuckoo perches on her lotus-like hand. She is seated under the *kalpa-taru* (a tree which fulfils all wishes) with her breasts highly adorned. She is exceedingly amorous.[127] Bhairon, a *raga*, invokes fear. Bhairon is the name of a deity developed from Bhairava; and Bhairava means 'Terrible', 'Frightful', a terrifying form of Shiva.[128] The pictorial aspect of the *raga* Bhairon is described variously (i) as the sea of notes and micro-notes, with nectar of all varieties of rhythms and time measures, the fulfilment of the desire of the worship of Shiva, with body always besmeared with ashes, decked with matted locks, with the shine of the young moon on the head, with skulls as decoration; (ii) as white in complexion, clad in white, carrying crescent, the horn, Shiva's trident, the skull and the lotus and wearing garland, jewelled pendant on his two ears and matted locks; and (iii) as Ganges sparkling and playing on his locks, his large forehead is clasped by snakes; his three eyes offer emancipation from all woes.[129] This *raga* is performed in the early morning before the sun rise. Deepak *raga* causes fire when it is sung (Fire Melody). The magical feature of the *raga* is evident from a legend. The famous singer, Naik Gopal was ordered by the Mughal Emperor Akbar to sing the *raga* Deepak. The singer started singing. As he was singing while standing in the river Jamuna, the water became increasingly hot, and then suddenly flames burst from the artist's head and he perished. Malhar *raga* is performed during the rainy season or monsoon which lasts from the middle of June to the end of September. The *raga* is said to have a complexion of a blue lotus flower, and his face is beautiful like the moon. Dressed in yellow, he resides in the clouds. Sweetly smiling, it is the bravest of the brave.[130] Basant *raga* is performed in the month of spring (Basant Melody). Basant is described as surrounded by cuckoo and parrots and as dancing in the garden of love in the company of several lovely women.[131] Handol *raga* is performed in the morning during the spring season (March–April). The word *hindola* means 'swing'. In pictorial representations of this *raga*, Krishna is shown seated on a swing that is suspended from the sky.[132] Ramkali *ragni* is performed in the morning after sunrise. Holding a *vina* in her hand, she is seated on a mountain.[133]

Ranjha's total devotional absorption reminds us of synaesthesia. This is a personal experience of sensation emanating from the synthetic effect of music, dance, poetry, ritual and emotional religiosity. The devotional songs, music and dance that have a universal appeal, would have aided inter-community fraternization. Ranjha sings the Vaishnavite songs, called *bishanpatey* in Punjabi vernacular, and performs a sufic dance (*Jalai*) for the pirs. Despite opposition from the ulama, tradition of *sama* [audition] had come to stay and prosper in the Muslim world.[134] Ranjha substantiates the belief of Al-Ghazali (1058–1111), a theologian and philosopher of sufism, that only the foolish, the frozen, and the hard of heart were shut off from the pleasure of music and poetry.[135] Sufis were of the view that with their charisma, and their convivial ceremonies they would gain more adherents than would the educated but aloof ulama.[136] Among the Chishtis, the *hajj* was never given much importance and *sama* was never discarded in spite of opposition from the ulama. Isa Jund Allah, a saint who lived in Thatta during the seventeenth century, was bold enough to equate sama with ritual prayer.[137] Similarly, the singing of devotional songs (*kirtanas*) and dance being salient features of the bhakti cult, sama, bhajan, dance, *zikr*, *simran*, and *sarban* constituted a popular Punjab mode of religious expression different from the chanting and recitation of scriptures by the priests. Mira Bai, Baba Ramdas, Surdas, and Swami Haridas had made wide use of music for the propagation of their ideas, and Ranjha made use of the various *ragas* to persuade the pirs to bestow the love of Hir on him.

Waris Shah is the first folklorist of the region to document the culture of Punjabi Muslims. He is the founding father of the study of Punjabi folklore. He records not only its cultural, religious, and social ethos, but also offers us valuable empirical evidence about castes, saints, pirs, jogis, incarnations, and matters such as religious books, ornaments, dress, varieties of food and sweets, utensils, diseases and methods of treatment, and animal life. He makes us familiar with a variety of mythological figures, and with a number of *ragas* and musical instruments. In presenting the vast canvas of Punjab social and cultural life in a single text, Waris Shah remains unsurpassed to this day.[138]

NOTES

1. A.R. Radcliffe-Brown, *Structure and Function in Primitive Society*, London, 1979, p. 154.
2. Ira M. Lapidus, *A History of Islamic Societies*, Cambridge, 1989, p. 109.
3. Bruce B. Lawrence, *Notes from a Distant Flute*, Tehran, 1978, p. 88.
4. A.M. Shushtery, *Outlines of Islamic Culture: Historical and Cultural Aspects*, Bangalore, 1954, p. 413.
5. Khaliq Ahmad Nizami, *Religion and Politics in India during the Thirteenth Century*, New Delhi, 2002, p. 53.
6. Ibid., p. 54.
7. The western provinces of India became part of the Muslim empire in 711, when an Arab conquered Sind and adjacent provinces, north to Multan.
8. It is Marshall G.S. Hodgson who coined the term Islamicate. *The Venture of Islam: Conscience and History in a World Civilization*, Chicago, 1974, pp. 57–60.
9. Richard Lannoy, *The Speaking Tree: A Study of Indian Culture and Society*, London, 1971, p. 230.
10. Nizami, *Religion and Politics in India during the Thirteenth Century*, pp. 220–30.
11. Annemarie Schimmel, *Mystical Dimensions of Islam*, Lahore, rpt. 2003, p. 239.
12. Gurbachan Singh Talib, 'Brief Life Sketch of Baba Farid', in Gurbachan Singh Talib, ed., *Baba Sheikh Farid: Life and Teachings*, Patiala, 1973, p. 9.
13. Gulwant Singh, *Islam Ate Sufiwad* (in Punjabi), Patiala, 1994, p. 75.
14. J. Spencer Trimingham, *The Sufi Orders in Islam*, London, 1971, p. 22.
15. Lajwanti Rama Krishna, *Panjabi Sufi Poets AD 1460–1900*, New Delhi, 1973, pp. 24, 34, 47–8 and 62. Riazul Islam lists the following kinds of miracles, wonderworks and thaumaturgies that are mentioned in the sufi literature: 'raising the dead; curing the sick with immediate effect; killing (sometimes by a movement of hand or staff, and sometimes by a mere angry glance, etc.); telepathy; clairvoyance (seeing the out of sight); clairaudience (hearing the inaudible); divination (knowledge of the unseen or of the future by

supernatural means); telekinesis (moving objects without touching); bilocation (presence at different places at the same time); teleportation; levitation (moving in the air or on water without support); miracles wrought on inanimate objects; miracles wrought on animals (one rather rare variety being turning a dog or a cat into a saint); controlling nature, such as starting or stopping rain, or stopping the movement of the sun; and passing through physical objects such as a wall; etc.' Riazul Islam, *Sufism in South Asia: Impact on Fourteenth Century Muslim Society*, Karachi, 2003, p. 411.

16. This is evident from the following instance. Shaikh Bahauddin Zakariya's relationship with Baba Farid was cordial. Once a musician, named Abdullah, had to leave for Multan from Ajodhan. He asked Baba Farid to pray for his safe journey. The Baba replied that the limit of his spiritual domain extended to a certain water tank and that beyond it lay the territory of Shaikh Bahauddin whose prayers he should seek. The musician acted on the counsel of Baba Farid and reached his destination safely. S.A.A. Rizvi, *A History of Sufism in India*, Delhi, 1986, vol. I, p. 193.
17. M. Waseem, 'Introduction', in M. Waseem (ed. and tr.), *On Becoming an Indian Muslim: French Essays on Aspects of Syncretism*, New Delhi, 2003, p. 7.
18. J.P.S. Uberoi, *Religion, Civil Society and the State: A Study of Sikhism*, Delhi, 1999, pp. 37–8.
19. K.A. Nizami, *The Life and Times of Shaikh Farid-ud-din Ganj-i-Shakar*, Delhi, 1973, p. 105.
20. Seyyed Hossein Nasr, *Sufi Essays*, London, 1972, p. 146.
21. In the thirteenth century, a Sanskrit classic on yoga philosophy, *Amritkund* was rendered in Persian, and entitled *Hauz-ul-Hayat.* The introduction to this work tells us that a Brahmin in Bengal had become curious to acquire knowledge of the religion of his conquerors. He acquired knowledge of Islam and subsequently converted to it. Asked by sufis about Hinduism and the spiritual exercises prevalent among its ascetics, he began to help in a translation of the *Amritkund* into Arabic and Persian. Neither the original Sanskrit manuscript nor the Arabic translation (*Hauz-ul-Hayat*) are extent, but the Persian version, also entitled *Hauz-ul-Hayat*, exists. Iqtidar Husain Siddiqui, 'Sufi Cults and the Making of a Pluralistic Society', in Anup Taneja, ed., *Sufi Cults and the Evolution of Medieval Indian Culture*, Delhi, 2003, p. 37. Also see S.A.A. Rizvi, *A History of Sufism in India*, vol. I, p. 335; Muzaffar

Alam, *The Languages of Political Islam in India, c. 1200–1800*, Delhi, 2004, p. 83.

22. Lapidus, *A History of Islamic Societies*, pp. 445–6.
23. Ibid., pp. 446, 449.
24. Nizami, *The Life and Times of Shaikh Farid-ud-Din Ganj-i-Shakar*, p. 50.
25. Ibid. Also see Khwaja Hasan Sani Nizami, 'Sufi Tradition and its Impact on Religious Thought', in Asghar Ali Engineer, ed., *Islam in India: The Impact of Civilization*, Delhi, 2002, pp. 66–74.
26. Nizami, *The Life and Times of Shaikh Farid-ud-Din Ganj-i-Shakar*, p. 106.
27. See Malik Mohammed, 'Indian Sufism as Harbinger of Inter-Religious Harmony', in Gurbachan Singh Talib, ed., *The Sikh-Sufi Quest for Harmony*, Patiala, 1980, pp. 55–73.
28. John A. Subhan, *Sufism, Its Saints and Shrines: An Introduction to the Study of Sufism with Special Reference to India and Pakistan*, New Delhi, 2002, p. 141.
29. Khwaja Nasiruddin, Khwaja Shihabuddin, Shaikh Badruddin Sulaiman, Shaikh Nizamuddin, Shaikh Yaqub, Bibi Masturah, Bibi Sharifah and Bibi Fatimah. Nizami, *The Life and Times of Shaikh Farid-ud-Din Ganj-i-Shakar*, pp. 59–78.
30. Among them were Shaikh Najibuddin Mutawakkil, Maulana Badruddin Ishaq, Shaikh Jamal-ud-din Hanswi, Shaikh Nizam-ud-din Auliya, Shaikh Arif, Shaikh Ali Sabir and Maulana Fakhr-ud-din Safahani.
31. Trimingham, *The Sufi Orders in Islam*, p. 67.
32. Bruce B. Lawrence, 'Islam in India: The Functions of Institutional Sufism in the Islamization of Rajasthan, Gujrat and Kashmir', in Richard C. Martin, ed., *Contribution to Asian Studies: Islam in Local Context*, Leiden, vol. 17, 1982, p. 31.
33. Carl W. Ernst observes that generally scholars of Islamic sufi poetry have adopted the cultural hierarchy, regarding 'Arabic as the central language for Islam, with Persian as a close second, barely conceding some importance to Turkish for literature and history. For the most part, other languages used by Muslims outside the "heartlands" of Islamic civilization have been often dismissed as local and presumably deviant in some way.' This gives short shrift to the cultural riches of a great number of non-Arab Muslims. *The Shambhala Guide to Sufism*, New Delhi, 2000, p. 175.
34. See Mian Mohammad Bakhsh Jehlmi, *Qissa Saif-ul-Maluk*, Patiala, 1971, pp. 655–6.

35. Shemeem Burney Abbas, *The Female Voice in Sufi Ritual: Devotional Practices of Pakistan and India,* Karachi, 2003, p. 14 (henceforth *The Female Voice*). Carl W. Ernst, *The Shambhala Guide to Sufism,* pp. 179–98.
36. Gurbachan Singh Talib, 'Guru Nanak's Teaching in Relation to Sufism', *The Journal of Religious Studies,* vol. III, 1971, pp. 41–2.
37. Mohan Singh 'Diwana', *Shah Husain,* Amritsar, 1952, pp. 70–4.
38. Gurbachan Singh Talib, 'The Surviving Muslim Influences in the Speech of Punjab', in Attar Singh, ed., *Socio-Cultural Impact of Islam on India,* Chandigarh, 1976, pp. 27–41.
39. To quote Alam Khundmiri, 'The universal character of the Sufi movement does not lie in its supposedly uniform teachings, but in the manner in which these universal teachings were presented to the different peoples through different languages and cultures, and the manner in which these principles were practiced so as to draw different peoples towards them.' M.T. Ansari, *Secularism, Islam and Modernity: Selected Essays of Alam Khundmiri,* New Delhi, 2001, p. 237.
40. Richard M. Eaton, 'Introduction', in Richard M. Eaton, ed., *India's Islamic Traditions, 711–1750,* New Delhi, 2003, p. 10. To support his statement Eaton cites Brajadulal Chattopadhaya, *Representing the Other? Sanskrit Sources and the Muslims,* New Delhi, 1998, pp. 28–43, 92–7.
41. Abbas, *The Female Voice in Sufi Ritual,* p. 19.
42. Belief in the worship of shrines and tombs of the sufis was not a peculiar religious sensitivity of Indian Islam. It came with those who brought the religious orders to India from Afghanistan, Persia, and Iraq', Murray T. Titus, *Indian Islam: A Religious History of Islam in India,* New Delhi, 1979, p. 131. In Syria and Iraq the graves of known Muslims, spiritual mentors, scholars, and pious people had turned into places of pilgrimage. Mausoleums were constructed over these graves and fairs were held.
43. M. Waseem, 'Introduction', in M. Waseem (ed. and tr.) *On Becoming an Indian Muslim,* p. 6.
44. Murray T. Titus, *Indian Islam: A Religious History of Islam in India,* New Delhi, 1979, p. 131.
45. Al bin Usman al-Hujwiri, *Kashf ul-Mahjub,* tr. Reynold A. Nicholson, Delhi, 1982, p. 329.
46. Imtiaz Ahmad, 'Introduction', in Imtiaz Ahmad, ed., *Ritual and Religion Among Muslims in India,* New Delhi, 1981, pp. 17–18.

47. Ignaz Goldziher, *Muslim Studies*, tr. C.R. Barber and S.M. Stern, London, 1971, p. 286.
48. Ibid. 287.
49. Bruce B. Lawrence, 'Islam in India: The Function of Institutional Sufism in the Islamization of Rajasthan, Gujrat and Kashmir', p. 30.
50. Marc Gaborieau draws a distinction between mazar, dargah and khanqah. The first is a notch above the common *qabr* or simple grave. This is transformed into a mazar once a dead person begins to be venerated as a saint. Dargah, on the other hand, applies to more complex types of shrines, with courtyards, pool, and *naubat khana* (music house). The khanqah is a hospice and comes into existence if the saint was also a member of a sufi order. Marc Gaborieau quoted in A.R. Saiyed, 'Saints and Dargahs in the Indian Subcontinent: A Review', in Christian W. Troll, ed., *Muslims Shrines in India: Their Character, History and Significance*, New Delhi, 1992, p. 242.
51. Iqtidar Husain Siddiqui, 'The Early Chishti Dargahs', in Christian W. Troll, *Muslims Shrines in India*, pp. 1–3.
52. Ernst, *The Shambhala Guide to Sufism*, p. 71.
53. Cures were administrated at these shrines for any number of afflictions: 'intestinal disorders, eye diseases (including blindness), tetanus, leprosy, localized paralysis and psychosomatic disorders. In a peasant society, crippling, permanently disabling arthritis and chronic rheumatism of the joints are highly prevalent.' However, 'not all diseases were treated at the same shrine: there was a kind of medical specialization among different pirs and shrines'. Harjot Oberoi, *The Construction of Religious Boundaries: Culture, Identity and Diversity in the Sikh Tradition*, Delhi, 1997, p. 156.
54. Iqtidar Husain Siddiqui, 'The Early Chishti Darghas', p. 14.
55. Ibid.
56. Baba Farid died as he had lived, without worldly means. The door of his house was pulled down to provide unbaked bricks for his grave. 'The man whose offer of constructing a *pucca* house for the Shaikh was refused by Baba Farid, built a dome over his grave. This tomb was later repaired by Firuz Shah Tughluq.' K.A. Nizami, *The Life and Times of Shaikh Farid-ud-Din Ganj-i-Shakar*, p. 58.
57. *Journal of the Asiatic Society of Bengal*, 1837, p. 192 as quoted in Iqtidar Husain Siddiqui, 'The Early Chishti Dargahs', p. 16.
58. Sources like *Jawahir-i Faridi*, H.A. Rose's *Glossary*, and the oral

tradition speak of the fourteen clans (Bhan, Chhina, Dhudhi, Dogar, Gondal, Gondaal, Hans, Joiya, Khokhar, Siyal, Tiwana, Wattu, Kharral, and Arain) converted to Islam by Baba Farid. However, some believe that the conversion of non-Muslims to Islam was not a function of early sufis of the Chishti order (Mohammad Habib, 'Shaikh Nasirudin Mahmud Chiragh-i Delhi as a Great Historical Personality', *Islamic Culture*, 1946). Eaton attempts to reslove the problem: 'If one were to hypothesize that the agent of the clans' conversion, instead of Baba Farid himself, was the shrine of Baba Farid as a highly complex religious and social institution, a number of problems fade away. Baba Farid resided in Ajodhan only sixteen or twenty-four years, which is a very short time span for many eponymous clan founders or *maliks* who are claimed to have met him actually to have been there. The shrine, on the other hand, has been there all along, sustaining the powerful *baraka* of the saint through its line of *diwans*. The identification of the shrine with the spirit of Baba Farid has been so thorough, in fact, that by the sixteenth century the very name of the city containing the shrine, Ajodhan, became known as Pakpattan ('the holy ferry'), in honour of Baba Farid's memory. Under these circumstances it would hardly be surprising that the clans, in reconstructing the story of their own conversion to Islam, should recall the name of the saint himself and not that of any particular diwan.' Richard M. Eaton, *Essays on Islam and Indian History*, New Delhi, 2000, p. 216.

59. Ibid., pp. 207–9. Also see Ahmad Nabi Khan, 'The Tomb of Baba Farid Ganj-i-Shakar at Pakpattan', *Journal of the Pakistan Historical Society*, vol. XXVII, pt. II, 1979.
60. For the political implications of the support and devotion given to sufism see Carl W. Ernst, *The Shambhala Guide to Sufism*, pp. 125–6.
61. Richard M. Eaton, *Essays on Islam and Indian History*, pp. 101–3.
62. Ibid., p. 210.
63. H.A. Rose, *A Glossary of the Tribes and Castes of Punjab and North-West Frontier Province*, vol. I, Patiala, 2nd rpt. 1990, pp. 580–1.
64. Ram Chand Manchanda 'A Panjabi Saint', *Journal of the Panjab University Historical Society*, vol. III, pt. I, 1934.
65. M. Athar Ali, 'Sidelights into Ideological and Religious Attitudes in Punjab during the 17th Century', in K.A. Nizami, ed., *Medieval India: A Miscellany*, vol. II, Bombay, 1972.

66. Annemarie Schimmel, *Islam in the Indian Subcontinent*, Lahore, 2003, pp. 126–7.
67. S.A.A Rizvi, *A History of Sufism in India*, vol. II, New Delhi, p. 458.
68. H.A. Rose, *A Glossary of the Tribes and Castes of Punjab and North-West Frontier Province*, vol. 1, pp. 574–617.
69. Dietrich Reetz, *Islam in the Public Sphere: Religious Groups in India, 1900–47*, New Delhi, 2006, pp. 124.
70. For the Punjabi text see Karnail Singh Thind, *Punjab Da Lok Virsa*, Patiala, 1996, p. 135.
71. Ibid.
72. Ibid.
73. Ibid., p. 116.
74. Mohan Singh, *An Introduction to Panjabi Literature*, Amritsar, 1956, p. 41.
75. Attar Singh, *Secularization of Modern Punjabi Poetry*, Chandigarh, 1988, p. 44.
76. Ibid.
77. Eaton, *Essays on Islam and Indian History*, p. 188.
78. Shah Husain was a popular Punjabi sufi. He was a vociferous critic of religious orthodoxy and formalism. He belonged to that period of history when Emperor Akbar had been spreading the message of communal harmony, and Guru Arjan Dev was about to compile in the *Adi Granth* the compositions of sants and sufis who would later be categorized as 'Muslim', 'Hindu', 'Sikh', and 'dalit'. Shah Husain made sufi poetry a prominent genre in the history of Punjabi literature. He made love the basis of his mysticism and expressed himself in the genre of *kafi*. Born in Lahore, he was the first sufi to belong to a family of converted Muslims. His great grandfather, Kalas (or Kuljas) Rai, a Dhada Rajput, embraced Islam in the reign of Feroz Shah Tughluq. His father, Usman, was a weaver by profession.
79. After Shah Husain, Bulleh Shah was the most prominent and popular sufi poet of Punjab. He was born in a Saiyyid family of village Pandoki of Kasur in the Lahore district. Bulleh Shah was, as per the information contained in *Khazinat-ul-Asfiya*, 'a disciple of Hazrat Shah Inayat Qadiri of Lahore. 'He lived in the town of Kasur. The common people recite by heart his verses of divine knowledge and unity. The Qawwals sing his *kafis* in sufi gatherings and augment the passion of the listeners. People narrate many miracles of Mir

Sahib.' Like Shah Husain, he expressed his mysticism in *kafis*. These are regarded as 'the pinnacle of Sufi literature'.

80. For the Gurmukhi text see G.L. Sharma, *Bulleh Shah: Vivechan Te* Rachna, Amritsar, n.d., p. 39.
81. Sant Singh Sekhon, *A History of Panjabi Literature*, vol. II, Patiala, 1996, pp. 218–19.
82. J.S. Grewal, 'The Sufi Beliefs and Attitudes in India', in Asghar Ali Engineer, ed., *Sufism and Communal Harmony*, Jaipur, 1991, pp. 27–8.
83. For the Gurmukhi text see Sutinder Singh Noor, ed., *Punjabi Sufi Kav*, New Delhi, 1997, p. 228.
84. Sant Singh Sekhon, *A History of Panjabi Literature*, vol. II, pp. 221–2.
85. The sufis conducted their dialogue with *kanphata* (split-eared) yogis or the Nath followers of Gorakhnath. From them they learnt about medicines for long hair, yogic postures, and breath control. The *Hatha* yogic treatise *Amritakunda,* translated into Arabic and Persian in the thirteenth century, had a lasting effect on sufism. The topics discussed at *jamat khana* gatherings of Baba Farid were of great interest to visiting Sidhhas, whose beliefs were founded on Hatha Yoga. See S.A.A. Rizvi, *The Wonder That Was India*, vol. II, Calcutta, 1993, p. 256; S.A.A. Rizvi, *A History of Sufism in India*, vol. I, p. 323.
86. Rafiuddin Ahmed, 'The Emergence of the Bengal Muslims', in Rafiuddin Ahmed, ed., *Understanding the Bengal Muslims: Interpretative Essays*, Delhi, 2001, p. 2.
87. *Hir Waris*, stanza no. 342
88. S. Nurul Hasan, *Religion, State and Society: Collected Works of S. Nurul Hasan*, ed., Satish Chandra, New Delhi, 2005, p. 71.
89. Ibid.
90. T.N. Madan, 'Religions of India: Plurality and Pluralism', in Jamal Malik and Helmut Reifeld, eds., *Religious Pluralism in South Asia and Europe*, New Delhi, 2005, p. 72.
91. Satish Chandra is of the view that although '*nirguna* and *saguna* forms have been included in popular *bhakti*, the popular base of the two was different—one was more artisanal and urban, and the other more agricultural and rural'. *Essays on Medieval Indian History*, New Delhi, 2005, p. 13.
92. Jan Gonda, *Medieval Religious Literature in Sanskrit*, Wiesbaden, 1977, pp. 12–13.

93. He is intimately associated with water, and so naturally becomes the patron saint of sailors, and also of washermen and water-carriers (*dhobis* and *bihishtis*).
94. He was a thirteenth-century ascetic who came from Seistan and settled in Sehvan, in the lower valley of the Indus.
95. He was a thirteenth-century saint of Suhrawardi *silsila.*
96. He was a disciple of Bahauddin Zakariya's grandson.
97. *Hir Waris,* stanza nos. 115–18.
98. Jagtar Singh, ed., *Heer Damodar,* Patiala, 2000, stanza nos. 182–7.
99. See M.S. Randhawa and Devendra Satyarthi, eds., *Punjabi Lok Geet* (An Anthology of Punjabi Folk Songs), New Delhi, 2002, pp. 160–5.
100. Rose, *A Glossary of the Tribes and Castes of Punjab and North-West Frontier Province,* vol. I, p. 572.
101. Annemarie Schimmel, *Islam in the Indian Subcontinent,* Lahore, 2003, p. 137.
102. Rose, *A Glossary of the Tribes and Castes of Punjab and North-West Frontier Province,* vol. I p, 389.
103. Ibid., pp. 390–1.
104. E. Gellner, 'Doctor and Saint', in Nikki R. Keddie, ed., *Scholars, Saints and Sufis: Muslim Religious Institutions Since 1500,* Berkeley, 1972, p. 309.
105. Schimmel, *Mystical Dimensions of Islam,* p. 239.
106. Cunningham described this *tilla* thus: *Tila* means simply a "peak or hill", and the full name is *Gorakhnath-ka-Tila.* The more ancient name was *Balnath-ka-Tila.* Both of these are derived from the temple on the summit, which was formerly dedicated to the Sun, as *Balnath,* but is now devoted to the worship of *Gorakhnath,* a form of Siva. The latter name, however, is very recent, as Mogal Beg, who surveyed the country between AD 1784 and 1794, calls the hill '*Jogion-di-Tibi,* or tower of the Jogis, whose chief is called *Balnat.* Abul Fazl also mentions the "cell of Balnat", and the attendant Jogis, or devotees, from whom the hill is still sometimes called *Jogi-tilla.* Alexander Cunningham, *The Ancient Geography of India,* Varanasi, 1963, pp. 138–40; also see Irfan Habib, *An Atlas of the Mughal Empire,* Delhi, 1982, 4A and sheet 4B.
107. *Hir Waris,* stanza nos. 244–8.
108. Ibid., stanza nos. 277 and 278.
109. Mohan Singh, *A History of Panjabi Literature,* Amritsar, 1956, p. 12.

110. H.H. Wilson, *The Sketch of Religious Sects of the Hindus,* Delhi, Cosmos Publications, rpt. 1977, pp. 205–19. George Weston Briggs, *Gorakhnath and Kanphata Yogis,* Delhi, 1982.

111. (a) 'Wander not to sacred places, O siddha, / The truth in thee abides in thy own form. / He who is enmeshed in this passing show / A slave is he to objects and objectivity, / And miserable, helpless, despairful, / while the renouncer abides joyous / Within the Fort of the Unknowable. / Hear, O dissatisfied one, / These few words of Gorakh : Center thy awareness in the Formless One alone', Mohan Singh, *Introduction to Panjabi Literature,* p. 33.

(b) 'Not everyone who leaves his home and hearth is an ascetic, / Not everyone who runs a home is an enjoyer. / Not everyone who studies sacred books knoweth Jnana, / Who merely indulges in philosophical hair-splitting, / Blind is he.' Ibid., pp. 34–5.

(c) In a similar tone, Charpat Nath (890–990), the disciple of Gorakh Nath, spoke against the priesthood, formalism, and the forces of vested interest : 'You may put on white dress / or change it for blue; whatever faith you assume, / you pray only your own stomach.' I Serebryakov, *Punjabi Literature: A Brief Outline,* Chandigarh, 2000, p. 20.

112. Mohan Singh, *Introduction to Panjabi Literature,* p. 30.

113. Serebryakov, *Punjabi Literature: A Brief Outline,* p. 19.

114. Niharranjan Ray, 'Socio-Religious Movements of Protest in Medieval India', *Proceedings of Indian History Congress,* 1975.

115. *Hir Waris,* stanza no. 65.

116. Ibid., stanza no. 93.

117. Max Weber, *The Sociology of Religion,* tr. Ephraim Fischoff, London, 1965, p. 29.

118. *Hir Waris,* stanza no. 351.

119. Based on R.C. Temple, *The Legends of the Panjab,* vol. II, Patiala, 1963, p. 523.

120. *Hir Waris,* stanza no. 272.

121. I have barrowed this phrase from Tony K. Stewart, 'Alternate Structures of Authority: Satya Pir on the Frontiers of Bengal', in David Gilmartin and Bruce B. Lawrence, eds., *Beyond Turk and Hindu: Rethinking Religious Identities in Islamicate South Asia,* New Delhi, 2002, p. 23.

122. Harjot Oberoi, *The Construction of Religious Boundaries: Culture,*

Identity and Diversity in the Sikh Tradition, New Delhi, 1997, p. 142.
123. Ira M. Lapidus, *A History of Islamic Societies*, p. 446.
124. Richard M. Eaton, 'Temple Desecration and Indo-Muslim States', in David Gilmartin and Bruce B. Lawrence, eds., *Beyond Turk and Hindu: Rethinking Religious Identities in Islamicate South Asia*, pp. 252–3.
125. I. Serebryakov, *Punjabi Literature: A Brief Outline*, pp. 96–7.
126. *Hir Waris*, stanza no. 116.
127. Walter Kaufmann, *The Ragas of North India*, Calcutta, 1968, p. 323.
128. Narendra Kumar, *An Encyclopaedic Dictionary of Indian Culture*, p. 61.
129. Kaufmann, *The Ragas of North India*, pp. 234–5.
130. Ibid., pp. 394–435.
131. Ibid., p. 285.
132. Ibid., pp. 114–16.
133. Ibid., p. 243.
134. J.S. Grewal, *Guru Nanak in History*, Chandigarh, 1979, pp. 97–8.
135. Ibid., p. 98.
136. Bruce B. Lawrence, 'Islam in India: The Function of Institutional Sufism in the Islamization of Rajasthan, Gujrat and Kashmir', p. 33.
137. Annemarie Schimmel, *Mystical Dimension of Islam*, p. 185.
138. Sant Singh Sekhon states: He 'gives an ample proof of his learning in Islamic lore, through Persian and Arabic, and shows himself well-versed in Hindu folklore also. The extent of his knowledge is wide, indeed, so that whenever he chooses, he gives detail upon detail, for instance, about astronomy, Islamic mythology and history, Hindu mythology, the Greek system of medicine, the social rites of Hindus and Muslims, the various items of clothing and jewellery, sweets and delicacies served in marriage feasts, kinds of buffaloes and horses in context of dowry given to daughters, and so on, which he interprets in the course of narration just to show off his wide knowledge.' *A History of Panjabi Literature*, vol. II, p. 92.

CHAPTER 8

Challenge to Patriarchy

> What is a rebel? A man who says no: but whose refusal does not imply a renunciation.
>
> ALBERT CAMUS

> I got my Ranjha from the court of heaven.
>
> HIR in *Hir Waris*

It is necessary to recall that Waris Shah versified Hir's rebellion at a time when a desperate war was being fought by the people of Punjab under the leadership of the Khalsa against the internal and external oppression. In an atmosphere charged with martial values and masculinity, the revival of the story of Hir's rebellion indicates that Waris Shah was a progressive literary artist who enriched the political uprising by adding to it a social dimension. This qissa-kar lived in an age when, on the one hand, Shah Waliullah showed deep concern for the protection and propagation of Islam (both at the level of the state as well as the church), and, on the other hand, sufi poets like Bulleh Shah critiqued the religious formalism of Islam and Hinduism. The text of *Hir Waris*, with its overtones of a sufi-oriented concept of love, not only reveals the tension between Islamic theologians and the sufis, but also a tension in the social domain between the social patriarchs and theologians and priests on the one hand, and those who did not seek the mediation of priests on the other.

Waris Shah enables us to discern that patriarchy, which was ingrained in the character of the medieval state, filtered down to the lower social orders through the rural aristocracy as represented by Chuchak Siyal, the father of Hir, and the local state functionaries like the panch and qazi. Waris Shah predisposes us in this direction from the very beginning of his narrative, when we are told that after the death of Mauju Chaudhari (the father of Ranjha), the corrupt qazi and the panchs demarcated the ancestral land for his sons in a dishonest and discriminatory manner:

In the qazi's presence, with the elders attending, / paternal acres were surveyed. / By graft the brothers acquired the best, / to Dhido's share fell bog and marsh. / The sisters-in-law poked fun at him, / their jesting was unkind and harsh. / The villagers talked and laughed and grieved / how Dhido had been fleeced and flayed.[1]

Waris Shah is specially skilled at constructing an alluring and charming picture of the patriarchal and religious institutions, and then dismantling the rosy picture. Waris Shah reveals to his reader the retrogressive character of patriarchy, something not evident in the literature or records of the elite. His vision of the world comprises 'an ironical dualism'. He 'centres his text around the most significant moment in the legend, omitting all that is not relevant to his design and by violently accentuating contrasts', says Matringe.[2]

Note that Hir does not fight partriarchy for her 'empowerment'. The story of the daughter of a rural aristocrat is not a story of feudal ambition and power. A queen of the Mughal empire like Nur Jahan came to power with the aid of a man 'who recognized in her great personal strength and skills necessary for a sovereign',[3] but Hir suffered because the patriarchs discerned in her character a strong streak of non-conformism and rebellion. In choosing Dhido Ranjha the herdsman as her life partner, Hir initiated a personal struggle against the feudal patriarchal class to which she herself belonged. She de-classed herself in the first instance. Thus her struggle is not only unique for medieval times, it is also unique for colonial Punjab, when the educated middle classes of the Hindus, Sikhs, and Muslims controlled women under the pretence of social reform of their respective communities. It is observed that 'the tasks of redefining and reformulating separate identities and boundaries focused on the role of women while retaining the existing family-structure, gender-roles and property-relations grounded in the patriarchal ideology'.[4] Like the reformers of the middle classes in the colonial Punjab, Hir did not fight the forms and instruments of patriarchy such as *purdah*, child marriage, or female infanticide. She understood the social laws behind the subservient position and status of women. Her fight was ideologically revolutionary in character, so far as the patriarchal hegemony was concerned.

Hir confronts those who oppose the social liberation or autonomy of a woman. She appreciates the logic concealed in the social discourse that revolves round parenthood, parentage, and parenting. She fights against the historically evolved united front of the social patriarchs and ecclesiasts who have a domineering sway over the society, not as individuals but as instituted realities. She rebelled on this issue many decades before Guru Nanak revealed, in his verses, the social significance of women in the community. Hir's revolt went so deep in the heart and mind of the people of Punjab that she is frequently remembered in the sufi and Sikh poetry of Punjab.[5] Hir's struggle for social autonomy is no less important than that of the Khokhars in the fifteenth century, and of the Khalsa in the eighteenth century. The latter two fought state hegemony, while Hir rose against social and ecclesiastical hegemony. Hers was, of course, an individual's defiance and rebellion, not a movement.

During the entire history of social struggle waged by the marginalized of medieval Punjab, Hir's is the voice of the women. She constructs the social discourse of non-conformism. A study of the political and social struggles launched by the Khokhars, the Khalsa, and Hir may enable us to appreciate the nature and character of Punjabi society which is otherwise presented as torn by communal conflict.

Hir's rebellion against her own father, her community of the Siyals and her priest, may be compared with other love-legends of the Punjab such as Mirza–Sahiban and Sohni–Mahiwal. We see that Hir is conscious, not blind, in conducting her love affair, and she is bold enough to deal with those in authority. She is tactful and astute. She has the knack of humouring the patriarch of her family, Chuchak. To perpetuate her love of Ranjha, she plans to employ him as a herdsman in her own house. Before introducing him to her father, she wins the latter over with her oratory:

Ah, father, I would give/ my life in ransom for your sake. / For in the sunshine of your day / in Sandal Bar[6] here I have played. / On swings of silk among its trees / with friends of my heart I have swayed. / You are my prop, as the Ox of the earth, / and here is the herdsman you will like.[7]

After having pleased her father, Hir switches to the qualities of Ranjha: 'Smart and clever, and wise, / he can be put at the head of our guards. / He will prod the cattle soft and kind, / and will not hit them churlishly', she says.[8]

After having been married to Saida Khera, it is 'careful' Hir who suggest that Ranjha come to her in-laws in the guise of a jogi. Her wisdom and bravery in dealing with the patriarchs and the qazi surface gradually as the story of her struggle unfolds.

In the beginning of the qissa Waris Shah presents Chuchak, the sardar of Jhang, and father of the rebel daughter, Hir. Economically and socially dominant, Chuchak does not let his beautiful daughter encroach on his exclusive patriarchal space. The inherent tension is between 'to domesticate' and not 'to be domesticated'. The patriarchal image of Chuchak is introduced to the reader through the first appearance of his daughter, Hir:

Followed by her sixty maids, she comes, / full of youth's pride and beauty's charm. / Bunches of pearls hanging from her ears, / she looks a hourie of heavenly birth. / The bright red bodice over her breasts, / makes one forget both heaven and earth. / Her nose-ring like the pole-star dares / the fury of the summer's storm. / O reckless one, relent, for here / so many have pitched their tents and gone! / The squire's daughter sweeps all before,/ so arrogant she, so proud and vain.[9]

Hir herself is aware and proud of her patrilineal heritage and status. Seeing a stranger (Ranjha) resting in her boat on the shores of the river Chenab, she flies into a fury:

Proud of her youth and her father's power, / what does she care for man or God? / 'I'll pull him down my couch, / is he a royal prince or what? / Let him a hundred thousand times, / crawl at my feet, I care not a jot.'[10]

The daughter of the sardar is provoked to punish the boatmen there and then:

The boatmen are all bound and whipped, / on orders from the virago. / She rebukes them: / 'You let a lout lie on my couch, / you dare commit such sacrilege!'

The poor men beg pardon:

Dear maid, but we are innocent. / Why do you fly into such a rage? / We never invited this strange guest, / have a fear of God, O, arrogant one! / Great has been our reward indeed, / for being at your services day and night![11]

Waris Shah, however, makes sure her pride is shattered. Throughout the narrative she fights for her choice of a husband, and comes to realize what it means to be a helpless person fighting a powerful rival. She seems to expresses her own helplessness *vis-à-vis* the mighty patriarchy through the metaphor of 'orphans'. Administering a rebuke to Sahti, her sister-in-law, who engages in a physical and verbal fight with Ranjha (disguised as a jogi), Hir tells her: 'Fight, if you must, your equals, girl, / do not flourish your stick at a shiftless beggar.' Hir's concern may have been grounded in the ethos of the Punjab where many invaders and plunderers had appeared in the past. The same concern is crystallized in the verses of the sufis and Sikh gurus who defied social and religious authorities, caste boundaries, and gender inequalities.

Watching the general massacre of the innocent inhabitants of the town of Sayyidpur by Babur during his third invasion on Punjab in 1520–1, Guru Nanak declared:

Thou art part and parcel of all things equally, O Creator; / If a strong man attacketh another who is equally strong, / Where is the grief in this, or whose is the grievance? / But when a fierce tiger preys on the helpless cattle, / The Herdsman must answer.

Profile of a Rebel Daughter

The description of the glamour and beauty of Hir and of her body-image by Waris Shah, with the aid of a variety of metaphors and similes, may look to some readers as a sensual exposure of the female soma. However, his intention was to convey a deeper meaning to his readers. His Hir confronts the community elders who are physically, socially and theologically strong. Waris Shah portrays the female rebellion:

In Hir's brows which are like arches of Lahore a full moon shines. Her cheeks pulsate like petals of rose and they are red like the colour of wine. Her lips red like rubies are brilliant. Her chin resembles with the pear-fruit of Iran. Her teeth form a chord of lilies and look like the seeds of a pomegranate. She is tall like a cypress brought from the paradise. Her neck is like that of a swan. Her arms are rolls of kneaded butter; and thighs round and slender and camphor-white. On her bosom, which heaves like a wave, two silken spheroids rise and fall and her navel like a musk-pod floats on the crystal of a heavenly pool. Her loins are velvet-soft, and her white shins are slim like the shafts of a minaret.

The winsome make-up of Hir's face reminds Waris Shah of the beautiful calligraphy of a book, most probably of the Quran, because he says that to behold Hir is like a pilgrimage to the Prophet's cenotaph. Hir outshines the beauty of the loveliest queens. Waris also alludes to her determination: 'Hir shines like a sword that is just unsheathed to fall upon the fatal block, she sways in the air, and she marches like a victor as hosts have marched ever from Punjab to Hindustan on conquering raids.'[12]

Such a female image is strong enough to confront the reason, ego, and physical power of the older men. Hir's external and internal strength is illustrated by her scuffle with Kaido and by her debate with the qazi of Jhang, and Chuchak, Malki and Sultan, the last three being her father, mother, and brother. She does not succumb to their pressures. She does not let Saida Khera come near her as he was imposed on her by others.

The Subalterns

The politics of the Siyals is determined and defined by their own class interests. Hir suffers as a woman with no voice and also because she is not allowed to marry Ranjha. The Ranjhas of Takht Hazara were poorer than the Siyals of Jhang. The latter are extremely conscious of their clout, particularly when they form their matrimonial relations. Moreover, Ranjha was only the herdsman of the family of Chuchak. The Siyals converse among themselves:

We never allied ourselves with the Ranjhas, / their sons could never marry our girls. / To add to it, he is a servant, / and she the daughter of the best of us. / Let us give her to a youth of the Kheras, / with whom our clan has age-old ties.[13]

The qazi of Jhang reminds Hir of the social position and class status of Chuchak Siyal. He prescribes the code of 'good' conduct expected from Hir, daughter of the sardar of five villages. Also, the council of elders assembles in the house of Chuchak, where Hir is instructed.

As Hir comes home back from the wood, / she finds the qazi waiting for her. / Her father and mother around him, he / asks her to come and listen to them. / And in words all sift and honey sweet, / he tenders advice that is ever the same. / 'It will not do to be free with servants [Dhido Ranjha]; / what do we know where they belong? / At home among friends of the spinning wheel, / good girls beguile themselves with song. / In a spinning match on a brand new wheel, / how sweet the songs of the Chenab are! / You know, O, Hir, your father, Chuchak, / is head and chief of village and tribe. / Give due regard to their honour, your people / bear among the Jats a name. / It's not for maidens to roam about; / one of these days messengers may come. / Move modestly, with downcast looks, / for that is what the wise prescribe. / We are making arrangements for your troth / and elsewhere there is equal stir.' / Ah, Waris, in few days now / the Kheras will come with fan and flare.[14]

The Spinning Wheel

This code of feminine conduct was a notion of the patriarchy that controls women as she is an 'object/instrument' of utility in the feudal socio-economic dispensation. A patriarch (in his/her position as husband or father or mother) is the direct oppressor and beneficiary of the subordination of women.[15] The qazi, Shamsuddin of Jhang, was spokesman of 'private patriarchy' and its code of conduct. His advice to Hir to stay at the spinning wheel in her house is, in fact, a longstanding preference against female freedom. Here mention may be made of the two poets of the sultanate period, Amir Khusrau (d. 1325) and Isami (b. 1311).

Amir Khusrau, in the first *maqala* of his *Matla-ul-Anwar*, marks the superiority of man over all other creations. His view about male ability to rise to immeasurable heights through discipline and training further accentuates his masculine prejudices.[16] He speaks skeptically of the loyalty of women, and advises them to observe *purdah*, tells them the way to domestic peace and amity, and winds up with a tirade against women of loose character.[17] He suggests that a woman should stay with the spinning wheel and needle. To save her from all calamities, he advises her to remain indoors, between the wall in front of her and the door behind her. The poet further writes,

> The secluded ones [women] are applauded and those who wander about in the streets are disgraced. The woman who runs in the street is not a woman but a bitch. The swing and tambourine which the women play upon are no better than pillories and rope for them. Songs and melodies appear at first to be simple affairs, but when carried to extremes they serve as virtual invitation to drunkenness. Wash your face of the false cosmetics, and try to be honourable without the red colour on the face. The real meeting of the bride and bridegroom is not that to look like a bedecked idol or fairy before the husband, but to be bashful, modest and fearful and to be known and seen from behind the curtain mounted with the fringe of the veil.[18]

Similarly, Isami characterized Sultan Raziya (1236–40) through his male prism. Raziya succeeded her father Sultan Iltutmish. Her intimate relations with her *Amir-i-akhur*, Yaqut, a slave of the Negro race, led Isami to comment, 'All women are in the snare of the devil, in privacy, all of them do Satan's work.' 'When the passions of a pious woman are inflamed, she concedes to an intimacy even with a dog', he wrote. Hence Isami is of the view that a woman cannot be a ruler, 'for she is essentially deficient in intellect'. The poet suggests, therefore, that 'it is better for a woman to occupy herself with spinning wheel' as any high position would make her intoxicated.[19]

Such prejudices persisted into the Mughal and post-Mughal

period. For Shah Waliullah, the eighteenth-century theologian, and Maulana Thanawi (d. 1943), a graduate of the theological academy of Deoband, for instance, women were not only unequal but also dispensable. In his *Hujjat Allah al-Baligha*, Shah Waliullah, apart from many other things, 'discovers' the male ability to think rationally.[20] Similarly, in Maulana Thanawi's *Bihishti Zewar* written during the last decade of the nineteenth century, a girl is imparted a lesson in her proper relationship to her husband, who is superior, the major crime she can commit against him is ingratitude, just as it is toward God. A woman is expected to follow her husband's aspirations, will, and eccentricities in all matters. She must seek his permission on all issues. The emphasis on *aql* (wisdom) in *Bihishti Zewar* is significant because women are often thought deficient in that quality. This book found its influence largely among the *ashraf* or elite.[21] In another nineteenth-century patriarchal discourse, a male is presented as active, progressive, defensive: creator, discoverer, and defender. His intellect is for speculation and invention; his energy for adventure, for war, and for conquest. Conversely a female's intellect is not for invention or creation.[22]

The medieval patriarchal discourse of the spinning wheel, as opposed to that of the sufi poets like Shah Husain and Bulleh Shah, tended to create passivity in woman and promoted her confinement and exploitation in the domestic economy. In the customary gender-division of labour, much hard work, for instance spinning, was done exclusively by women. Before the spinning-wheel came into use, rotating the hand-spindle was extremely stressful for women's fingers. Above all their work remained practically unpaid at home, or heavily underpaid when it was done outside the home.[23] Anthropologists in general believe that women were the key innovators in basketry, weaving, pottery, in domesticating grain and improving its seed-bearing ability.[24] The time and labour of women involved in spinning can be gauged from collective spinning (*trinjan*) in the rural Punjab. Waris Shah draws a picture of the *trinjan*, where women of various castes and sub-castes came together. A *trinjan* would run in two shifts: the first, called *raat katni*, lasted all night. The second shift, called *chri-chirunga*, extended from dawn to dusk. Collective spinning contributed tremendously to the medieval village economy. It was also a private female landscape, echoing with the lyrical voices of sorrow and the dreams of the marginalized.[25] Poets like Shah Husain and Bulleh Shah recognized the significance of woman's spinning. Bulleh Shah says,

Do your spinning, O girl, roam not aimlessly. / Take off the hank of yarn, put it in the basket. / Your parents have fixed your wedding day, / And you are still unmindful of it. / The days are few, you waste your time. / You will not come again to your parents' house. / Do your spinning, O girl, roam not aimlessly. / If you go to your in-laws without dowry, / you will not be liked by anyone there. / How will you ever please your Spouse? / Take counsel from the fakirs, O girl. / Do your spinning, O girl, roam not aimlessly. / Your companions have got their garments dyed for dowry. / They have bright red clothes on their persons. / Why have you set your feet in the wrong direction? / When you reach there, you will discover the truth. / Do your spinning, O girl, roam not aimlessly.[26]

In another song Bulleh Shah says:

Light the lamp lying near you; / Spin the cotton, put in your basket; / keep awake throughout the night, / And work tirelessly on your wheel! O, girl / Put your mind in spinning, O, girl.[27]

Thus the *trinjan*, amongst other things, was an important testing ground of a young woman's ability to work hard and of her skill. Hir is a rebel. She is not ready to conform to the image of an ideal woman at the spinning wheel. She is not ready to use the wheel as her catharsis, nor does she want to be used. She defies the advice to remain confined to spinning and to the domesticated space associated with it. What is ideal for the patriarchs is idle and slavish for Hir. She does not wish to share her aspirations with the mute wheel. She is determined to spin her own destiny. Hir sees herself as a tiger (the symbol of male bravery and agility) who by nature is liberated and assertive. She is a love-addict. She says:

O, mother, never can, / an addict give up opium. / I cannot live without Ranjha, / inveterate habits know no care. / The tiger cannot live without flesh, / with a tearing blow he earns his fare. / Like taint of mango-juice or steel, / the taint of love for ever remains. / Heads may be felled, the love-disease / does not admit of remedy. / I will respect your every wish, / but one wish I cannot obey. / So is it willed by fate, indeed, / none can undo what fate ordains. / For I got my Ranjha from the court of heaven, / God himself made me a gift of him.[28]

Spinning and the space of *trinjan* are social structures that embody patriarchal domination and a certain mode of domestic production; other forms of patriarchal hegemony are in the state, in sexuality, and in education. In different times and places some of these structures assume more significance and domination than others. The elimination of any one does not lead to the collapse of patriarchy as a system of social control.[29]

Peripheral Space and Patriarchal Space

So long as the love affair of Hir–Ranjha was confined to the woods and pastures there was no crisis. In the woods Hir brought him (Ranjha) things like *churi* to eat. But once the news of the love affair spread, the tragedy began.

While Kaido, the lame, is after her [Hir], / a dog pursuing a sumptuous scent. / Ah, Waris, the limping fellow will raise / mischief worthy of devil, indeed.[30]

Kaido deceptively procured some *churi* from Ranjha and produced it before Chuchak as evidence of Hir's clandestine meetings. In the culture of the time, *churi*, a symbol of a close kinship relationship, was not supposed to be given to a herdsman.[31] Hir is alarmed when she comes to know how Kaido managed to procure *churi* from the innocent Ranjha:

O dear, you have made a blunder. / This limping fakir is such a cad. / Given day and night to evil, he / will go and tell against us both. / He sows disunion everywhere, / works for breach of all pledged faith. / Now will he traduce me in the village, / and carry report to mum and dad.[32]

Kaido is a cad. He typifies a social parameter of patriarchy which restricts freedom in both love and marriage. Waris Shah draws a difference between the space of pasture and the social space under the domination of the Siyal fraternity. Ranjha takes his cattle to the pasture and Hir visits it with her friends. Waris Shah narrates the pleasures of the riverside and pasturage:

> If one [Hir's maids] would wring her braids in his [Ranjha] face, / another would leap right on his head. / And yet another of fragrant limbs / cling to his waist, rub cheek on cheek. / And still another would throw a challenge, / and run and, as he chased her, dive. / Another would shout, 'Herdsman, beware, / beware, your cow is going to calve'./ While Hir herself cuts a circle round Ranjha / or swims like a rainbow-coloured fish.[33]

In the qissa, the water game signifies the liberating quality of the riverside and woods in contrast to the prohibitions prevalent in the social space. It also stands for the mystical eroticism and aroma of the bhakti and sufic traditions that pervade most of the Punjab love legends told in the genre of qissa. The water game in Hir–Ranjha resuscitates the love game of cowherd Krishna with his *gopis*. Krishna courts the both (cows and *gopis*) with the sweet melodies of his flute. Like Krishna, Ranjha too plays a flute and Hir's girls sing in chorus or parts. The aim of the mystical eroticism is to create unity from the man–woman duality prevalent in 'rational' discourse. Waris Shah presents to us the social and mystical implications of riverside pleasures. It has been observed that Krishna is 'a god of transgression'.

> Though religion has become associated with law, reason, and so-called moral propriety, this was not always so, nor is it always the case in modern Hinduism, especially of the villages. In ancient times, worshippers were encouraged to commit excesses during festivals as the surest way to achieve *catharsis*, ecstasy, the purging climax of the orgiastic feast, the surmounting of duality.[34]

There is a tendency to associate the water game of Hir–Ranjha with the 'cult of the cowherd god of the pastoral semi-nomadic castes of north-west India' more than the myth of Krishna. Matringe states that even now 'this cult is alive in Punjab villages through the Dhadhi, a wandering caste of Muslim bards, who are identified in the popular imagination with Dum and Mirasi, who have descended from the great pastoral tribe of the Yadavas, among whom Krishna was born.'[35]

One also comes across the non-patriarchal space of *trinjan* at the home of the in-laws of Hir, in Rangpur Khera. When Ranjha enters the village as a jogi, the village girls take him to the trinjan. Trinjan is not only non-patriarchal, it is also imbued with the ambience of sufic and bhakti tradition of eroticism. Like Krishna, Ranjha is surrounded by spinning girls. And here the love-game begins:

> 'Come, yogi, let us show you where / young women sing to the spinning wheels'. / They took him to a house in the village / where women had come to spin together / He saw them dance in reckless frenzy / or play the sweeper-maid with a grin, / Or other parts in which they seemed / to emulate professionals. / Some look into Ranjha's eyes from near, and much admire his handsome face, / Bewitched by his looks they seem to fall / into his snare like forest-deer. / 'Perhaps he has loved one in his teens / whose fickleness he could not bear'. / One wipes his face with her shawl / with all her youthful tenderness. / Another approaches cheek to jowl, / and asks what is his heart desire. / One cuddles to him and teases him much, / stripping him of his stole and staff.[36]

The implicit presence of the cult of Krishna in the qissa may also be noticed in the beginning of Waris Shah's narrative. After Ranjha leaves his village Takht Hazara, he reaches a mosque as beautiful as holy Mecca or the great mosque at Jerusalem. When hunger, cold, and weariness fall upon him at midnight, he plays his flute and fills the air with melody. On hearing it, some become senseless and other hearts yearn.[37] For M. Mujeeb it is 'curious that of the two embodiments of the divine in the Hindu pantheon, Rama does not seem to have appealed to the imagination or the religious sentiment of the Muslims, but Krishna, the naughty boy of Gokul, whose spirituality evolved out of fun and frolic, who was god, lover, and beloved all in one, caught their fancy'.[38] It may be suggested that Krishna's pastoral, non-caste, and erotic image was close to the Muslim masses and the sufi concept of *ishq* and devotion.

Elders and the Daugher

The politics of manoeuvre in past patriarchal advice is followed by a threat of physical violence in case Hir does not adhere to the terms set by the 'elders'. The rebel is apprised of a myriad of atrocities. Before being done to death, she could face the 'pulling out of her hair', 'wringing her neck', 'battering of her skull with a churn', and so on.[39] The first threat comes from Malki, Hir's mother. She warns her daughter of the degree of the wrath of Chuchak, the sardar. The horrible consequences of the anger of the patriarch in case he is not obeyed are explained by the mother:

> She (Hir) will get her head chopped off her trunk, / should a daughter arouse her father's wrath. / And the severed head is thrown in a stream, / and the trunk is left to dogs and crows, / Indeed with injured pride, a father / may cast his daughter in a burning pit.[40]

The defiant Hir replies:

> O, mother, he who kills his daughter / shall be charged with cardinal sin. / He shall have to eat what he had killed, / to make a meal of the daughter's flesh.[41]

Hir is aware of the moral degradation and fall of her father.

A second threat comes from Hir's brother:

> Not a moment will I let her be, / if I see her ever again in the wood. / Henceforth, she must seclude herself, / otherwise she shall not keep her head.[42]

This threat too is rendered futile by Hir:

> I'll give my life for you, dear brother, / but there is a point of no return. / For no amount of effort can / divert a river from its bed. / When it is given a dagger thrust, / the heart, poor thing, cannot but bleed. / The fruit of love will ripen on / a severed head.[43]

In her struggle against patriarchy, Hir is ready to sacrifice her life. Let me add that the motif of 'lover' and 'martyr' (*ashiq* and *shaheed*) or love and martyrdom is prominently present in early Punjabi literature and culture. Guru Nanak pronounces it categorically:

> *jau tau prem khelan ka chau / siru dhari tali gali meri au / itu maragi pair dharijai / siru dijai kani na kijai*

> If you want to play the game of love, approach me with your head on the palm of your hand. Place your feet on this path and give your head without regard to the opinion of others.

In Islam sacrifice 'is the nourishment without which the tiny seeds of *iman* will not grow into mighty leafy trees, providing shade and fruit to the countless caravans of mankind'.[44]

The third threat comes from the qazi, Shamsuddin, as a last resort. With his legal authority to punish, he threatens Hir:

> O Hir, why are you courting death? / Fear God's own wrath. / Your tongue needs pulling out from your throat, / I am afraid of your blood being shed. / The moment I pronounce the law, / off from your shoulders flies your head.[45]

Hir's retorts help us understand her character as counter-patriarchal; they enrich the dramatic attributes of the text; and third, they help us understand Waris Shah.[46] The passivity/privacy/imprisonment/confinement involved in the counsel of the elders may be condensed to the term 'silence' expected by any patriarchy. Qazi, parents, and brother are annoyed with Hir because she is a vocal young woman. The 'silence' desired by them is connected with 'the patriarchal definition of ideal femininity' because it gives the proper grace to woman.[47]

The rebellious character of Hir emerges boldly when at her wedding she assumes the role of adversary of the qazi. In Mughal India the qazi used to control villages and towns within his jurisdiction.[48] He was one of the significant local components of the imperial power who would pronounce decrees in lawsuits, record all cases of adjudication, and put penal law into execution. He also determined the distribution of inheritance, and looked after unclaimed property, and the property of orphans. He used to supervise religious congregations in general and the Friday prayer in particular. He also performed all marriages and religious ceremonies.[49] Apart from this, the qazi was a model religious figure before the 'semi-Muslim folk of the countryside'.[50] Above all, he was corrupt, flourishing on heavy bribes.[51]

Hir decisively defeats the qazi of Jhang in a debate on the shariat. She holds the shariat supreme, but her shariat is in conflict with that of the qazi. She illustrates what is called the dynamic and revolutionary principle of *ijtihad* (creative interpretation). If she boldly faces the assembly of the patriarchs at her own house, she equally confronts the qazi on the occasion of her nikah with a man not of her own choice. During her argument with her family and qazi, Hir expresses herself in the rhetoric of a rebel. She refuses to be treated as an object, and on every point, she argues with the qazi to prove and debunk his narrow-mindedness and duplicity.

I have pledged my troth to Ranjha, O qazi. / why does my mother indulge in lies? / My faith I have bestowed on Ranjha, / she may give the Kheras all else there is. / She is churning only butter-milk, / to Ranjha I have given the cream. Like the devil she pours poison in my throat / while my poor life spills over the brim. / She looks for fish in a puddle of urine, / like a fisherman bereft of sight.[52]

Hir pleads her case in language understood by the qazi. Belittling the authority of the elders, she argues that 'she has received Ranjha from the court of heaven'. In other words, she tells the qazi that she is not ready to honour anyone else as her life partner. She also accuses her mother of breaking a pledge.

When did I ask you for a groom? / You have acted as from an ancient grudge. / Unwise are they, O mother, who lay / bricks meant for a tower in a drain of sewage. / Why do you now distort facts? / Like thieves you have carried out this deal. / You have joined the swan to an owl, indeed, / to a satyr given a fairy maid. / You are eager to stuck a cane of sugar / all at once, not node by node.[53]

To live is good, Sir qazi, / All things are mortal, only God / is deathless, is the holy word. / My mother has broken the pledge she gave, / I will complain in the court of the Lord. / 'All things I have created in pairs,' does He say not in the holy Quran?[54]

The qazi is not moved, even though he knows the theological semantic of terms like *kufr* (blasphemy) and *dargah* (God's Court) used by Hir. Hir and the qazi argue from different perspectives about loyalty and fidelity. If for Hir fidelity to her lover Ranjha is above everything, for the others, the case is the reverse. The qazi asks Hir to obey the *shariat* (obviously personified by him), if she wants to live. Besides, he says,

If you care to live, submit to the law, / the qazi pronounces, sharp and grim. / Keep true to the faith that after death / you may be admitted to paradise. / Then you will quaff in the garden of Eden / the sherbet of love of the sweetest relish. / Put on the veil of modesty, / why should you wear the sack of shame?[55]

However, what is truth for the qazi is not the truth for Hir. She knows that the qazi is too corrupt to listen to her. His vision of love and beauty is not as deep as is expected from the clergy. It is confined by his alliance with the self-centred patriarchs. He tells Hir:

Stray not from the path marked by Islam, / and from your heart root evil out. / Lay no store by this beauty and youth, / like spicy wine they go to the head. / The Lord's command, O peasant girl, / to man and woman is to wed. / So take the Khera as your spouse / by law, do not be obstinate.[56]

Hir for her part constructs a new discourse on God. She equates love with God, lover with believer, and the love-laden heart with the seat of God. She holds the qazi as a sinner when he persuades her to marry Saida Khera.

'The believer's heart is the seat of God, / O qazi!' She says. 'Do not demolish His throne. / Where the love of Ranjha has lodged itself, / the Khera cannot hold his sway. / A ball in the catapult of love, / I will not fall, swing hard as you may. / Why I should sell my faith indeed / for life that must fall a prey to death? / Where does, O Sir, the book allow, / that one may break one's promised word? / I have given up all other support / and rest my hope in the Merciful Lord.'[57]

Convinced that his religious authority is threatened, the qazi is inflamed. The rebel girl is warned.

I'll have you flayed by the Shara's command, / as Umar Khitab's own son was flayed. / Or get you thrown on the blazing pyre / for the world to see and learn / If you value your life, accept the Khera / and never breathe of Ranjha again. / Shut fast your eyes to the word's temptations, / no more than the shadow of a cloud.[58]

Hir recognizes a violent patriarch in the qazi. She has already experienced his threats in her own house, but remains silent. Now on the occasion of her nikah, when a decisive battle is being fought between her and the patriarchs, Hir unmasks the qazi, as corrupt and degenerate. Hir calls him wicked:

The wicked must ever be planning to put / asunder hearts made one in love. / That they should be bribed to sell their faith, / even qazis like you, learned and wise! / God wants them, may be, to feed the fires / of Hell, so sinners even have a use. / I find myself caught in a trap / and hardly know what to believe.[59]

Hir nullifies the threat of divine punishment after her death, as she says: 'For those who are steadfast in faith / find favour with the Lord above. / They shall attain both honour and rank / who chant the magic word of love.'[60]

In the debate over patriarchal reason versus a the rebel's faith, Hir wins. Yet she fails in the patriarchal court. The qazi has to conclude: 'Hard nut to crack. / She will not yield to law or reason. / Before she causes more ado, / let us gag her and perform the rites.'[61]

The conflict between the two poles, patriarch and female rebel, is the crux of the qissa. Hir, does not make petitions and prayers to the patriarchs. Flogging or threat of flogging is a typical aspect of the Islamic penal code; and it is remarked that Hir is perhaps the only female in Punjab history who has to face a shariat court. Nevertheless, she refuses to succumb.[62] In her revolt Hir seeks the principle of female existence. She is determined to lead her revolt to the logical end, achieve either death (in Punjabi sufi poetry she is a martyr) or social approval of her love with Ranjha. In both cases she seeks emancipation. She prefers to die on her feet than to live on her knees.

Hir places her love and self-respect above everything else and proclaims that they are preferable to life. She rebels; therefore, she exists gracefully in history, literature and memory of the people of Punjab. From beginning to end, she sticks to the sufi ideology of *ishq* of the five pirs (*panj pirs*) who address her and her lover:

Pray to the Lord, O children, you, / let not your love suffer ever a blot. / To keep our good will, you should know, / you must not waver in deed or thought.[63]

The rebel daughter apprises the oppressing patriarchs of the sacred status of woman and of her commitment to the path of love:

Enough, O mother, stop this swearing, / to swear, you know, is the devil's wont. / You slay a daughter to invite a curse, / for woman is the source divine. / O may some plague descend from heaven / and carry me from this place of sin! /But Ranjha I will never forsake, / though father, grandfather, great-grandfather rant.[64]

Packed off to the house of the Kheras, Hir, cries: 'The qazi and my parents have acted as tyrants.' The patriarchal medieval world of Hir–Ranjha is a world where only material considerations count.[65]

Social Relations

One may read in *Hir Waris* the practical aspect of the social relations which assume different forms and practices within the framework of patriarchy, joint family, individual *v/s* family, family *v/s* fraternity (*biradari*), and so on. A peculiar feature of the social cosmos is the man–woman relationship. Any individual, who attempts to transgress established norms and subsequently invents his/her own, is bound to provoke patriarchal reaction.

Hir and Ranjha are aware of this. Though they try to elope, social disapproval haunts them. Ranjha is against elopement. He tells Hir: 'There is no honour in love, O, Hir / if but elopement is the end.'[66] Similarly, when Hir is given back to Ranjha by the orders of the Raja Adli, he asks Hir to repair to Takht Hazara. But Hir rejects his proposal. She too desires their love to be socially accepted. We find that the existing value system obliges the lovers to seek social approval.

Now Ranjha proposes to take her home, / 'God has, my dear, given you to me. / He has delivered you from the Kheras, / and led you this way all along. / The saints too, have been kind to us, / and pearl with ruby is now strung. / You will be the lady of Takht Hazara, / so let us now make it our home. / You will be received there as my bride, /and I return as a happy groom.

However, Hir knows that the approval and blessings of God and the saints are not sufficient. What is necessary is the approval of the Ranjhas and Siyals. She tells Ranjha:

But going there like this, / I shall be said to have eloped, / Aunts senior and junior both will taunt, / decry me as a runaway.[67]

But in the patriarchal world the rebels are not destined to succeed. The Siyals enact a drama to give an impression to the lovers that their love is going to be approved and legitimized. Waris Shah debunks the humbug: 'A new fraud, Waris, is being played—inscrutable are the ways of God!' Hir and Ranjha are received warmly by the members of the family of Chuchak Siyal. Ranjha's earrings are removed and the bores in his ears are neatly sewn up. He is given a turban to wear and is fed milk and sugared rice. A couch is spread for him to rest on. Ranjha 'jogi' is initiated into the social space of the patriarchs. He is then told to go back to his village and come back with a marriage party (*barat*) of friends and relatives to wed Hir with grace and honour.[68] But before he reaches Jhang with a marriage party, Hir is poisoned to death.

The Siyals took counsel and resolved, / 'We'll guard our honour at any cost. / This girl is a blot on our good name, and / the tale has travelled far and wide. / We lose our honour to send our daughter /with our own cowherd as his bride. / These people repay kindness with ill, / and, winning our confidence, betray. / Infamy of daughters destroys households / as vices of sons and foul tongues may. / The law allows the killing of such, / and men of honour will not desist.' / Look at the Siyals by whose false wisdom / innocent lovers will be destroyed. / They poison Hir to death – such was / the will and glory of the Lord![69]

A messenger delivers the news to Ranjha at Takht Hazara. Waris Shah laments:

Like Farhad Ranjha uttered a moan, / his soul joined Hir's in the upper air. / Both passed to the House of Life Eternal, / whole and true from this House of Death. / Firm in this earthly shape of love, / they lived it out with utmost truth. / Waris in this place of dreams have many / blown trumpets and left for nowhere.[70]

Hir struggles and suffers simply because she aspires for autonomy and marriage with a man of her choice. The patriarchs do not allow it, and it is they who prevail. The patriarchal parameters regarding the freedom of a woman do not even care for Raja Adli who had ordered the Kheras to return Hir to Ranjha.

Gender equality is not just women's concern. It also deeply concerns men.[71] Second, the character of the medieval patriarchy is complex. These propositions can be understood with reference to the legend of Puran Bhagat as narrated by Qadiryar during the Khalsa Raj of Maharaja Ranjit Singh (1799–1839).

In *Hir Waris*, Hir is not allowed to marry a lowly shepherd. But this patriarchal justification loses its legitimacy in case of Luna in the qissa of *Puran Bhagat.* In this legend, the aged king, Salwan, a Hindu Rajput, transcends social barricades of caste and class. He marries Luna, the daughter of a tanner. Also, the qissa throws ample light on the psychological and sexual violence committed by patriarchs like Salwan on women like Luna, young enough to be his daughter. When Luna meets the handsome prince, Puran, she is captivated. She longs for love from a man of her age. But her longing is suppressed by the feudal lord Salwan. Qadiryar, who seems to be under the influence of feudal patriarchal morality, sees her longing as infidelity to the aged king. 'In her heart the son becomes the lover; the rope of her constancy snaps in the middle.' The sudden snapping of rope used for drawing water from a well, symbolizes Luna's transgression of the social bounds of a feudal code and a plunge into the well of immorality and disorder.[72] According to Qadiryar, Luna's attempt to fill her inner vacuum with love for Puran is like an attempt to divert the flow of a river in the opposite direction. Qadiryar seems to accuse her of defying all 'sacred' laws of marriage. The tide of her passion for love of Puran mounts and she objects to Puran addressing her as mother. 'When did she feed him with her breast?' But Puran is steadfast in his role as 'son', and does not discern the intensity of her craving. He is conditioned by the established morality.[73] He tells Luna, 'If such things begin to happen / the sky will be rent, stars fall, / and chaos reign.' When Luna's longing is not reciprocated, she turns against Puran in reprisal. She fabricates a story of Puran's advances towards her. Salwan orders the mutilation of the limbs of Puran and subsequently that he be thrown into a well.

The accounts of Luna and Puran, and that of Hir and Ranjha reveal the prevalence of domestication within the social institution of patriarchy. Hir and Ranjha suffer at the hands of patriarchs because the lovers refuse to be domesticated within the parameters of the Siyals and their qazi. Saida Khera, with whom Hir is forcibly married, also suffers because the 'undomesticated' Hir refuses to accept him as her husband. As long as she lives in Saida's house she does not have any physical relations with him. She has already told Ranjha, 'I will never accept the Khera, / disharmony shall ever prevail'.[74] Similarly, Luna and Puran too suffer because they are domesticated entities. Luna, the daughter of a tanner, is domesticated by the aged king. Living in the feudal space, she craves the love of a youth. Puran suffers at the hands of Luna because as a 'domesticated' prince he is burdened with patriarchal morality. He cannot respond to her and endures the mutilation of his limbs.

Lovers and Their Sacred Status

A number of love legends of medieval Punjab speak of lovers who rebelled against patriarchal domestication. They never deviate from their objectives despite all the counsels and warnings of the 'social elders'. A few instances may be cited here. The Baloch fraternity failed to stop Punnun from meeting his beloved Sassi. She too was determined to search for Punnun in the burning sand dunes, despite all the efforts of her mother. Sohni, knowing that the unbaked pitcher would dissolve into water and she would drown, plunged into the Chenab on the pitcher in order to swim across to her lover Mahiwal. Shirin, on hearing the news of the death of her lover Farhad, jumped from the walls of her palace and died. Ranjha in one of his replies to his sisters-in-laws defines the determination of those who are in love.

> Mauju Chaudhri's son is a grazer now; / is not indeed a miracle? / But the brave have always fought for love, / and hosts have thus gone under the earth, / Only he will run away from love / who is an imbecile from birth. / The likes of me, by harsh words stung / will go back at no summons or call.[75]

These are 'archetypal patterns of Punjabi behaviour' with the ideals of 'honour, loyalty, steadfastness, courage and fortitude'.[76] They are given spiritual status in the verses of sufis and Sikh gurus.

The sufi-poets speak of them in the female voice.[77] Shah Husain states:

(i) Without the Beloved, the nights are long. / Ranjha is the yogi, I am his spouse, / Maddened and deserted, / I am addressed as mad.

(ii) It would be excellent if I get together with the Beloved, / Friend Ranjha stands on the farther bank, / let us all swim across the stream.

Similarly, Bulleh Shah states:

What should Bullah know? What is the caste of love? / He is fair to look at, difficult to please, / I can neither sleep nor wake. / Ranjha and I are one and the same, / we are just testing the people. / I take on myself all the woes, / of the wood in which my love lives. / Bullah, I will not go to the wood, leaving my love who is so close to me.

In 'Sikh' religious verses, the rebellious lovers are 'canonized as saints'.[78] For instance, Bhai Gurdas (1559–1639) holds out their example:

The lovers Laila and Majnu are well known in all the quarters of the world. The excellent song of Sorath and Bija is sung in every direction. The love of Sassi and Punnun, though of different castes, is everywhere spoken of. The fame of Sohni who used to swim the Chenab river in the night to meet Mahiwal is well known. Ranjha and Hir are renowned for the love they bore each other. But superior to all is the love the disciples bear for their Guru. They sing it at the ambrosial hour of morning.[79]

Guru Gobind Singh approves of such expression of love when through a 'transference of imagery' he alludes to the romance of Hir–Ranjha:

Go and tell the Beloved / The state of His devotees: / Without Him, the material comforts are an agony to us, / And to live in the comforts of our households / Is like living with Snakes! Our water pots / Have become like pikes on which men are impaled. / The cup we drink from has an edge like a dagger! / Beloved, thy turning away from us, / Is like what a beast endures from the slaughterer! / With the Beloved, a mattress of strew would please us; / Without Him in rich houses of Kheras (the in-laws of Hir), / We are burnt alive![80]

The relentless struggle of Hir and Ranjha against patriarchs and priests places them in the sacred category of *mai* and *miyan*—a status accorded to the saints as a sign of devotion and respect. The lovers and rebels have entered the deep recesses of the Punjabi folk mind. In the qissa of Hir–Ranjha recorded by Temple in 1885, Ranjha is remembered as the sixth pir.[81] Waris at the end of his qissa conceives Hir as the soul and Ranjha as the body. This kind of love and rebellious spirituality in *Hir Waris*, originally the legacy of the sufis, the saints and the Sikh gurus, might have led to the construction of the tomb of Hir at Jhang as a posthumous tribute to the Punjabi girl.[82] This is the reason, it seems, that the Punjabis throughout the world irrespective of their religious affiliations and political boundaries have been responding to *Hir Waris* for centuries. Hir represents the Punjabi ethos of non-conformism and dissent.[83]

Ishq Mijazi and Qissa

The rebellious lovers who fought the patriarchy also need to be assessed from the viewpoint of their social praxis, if these narratives in the qissas are to be used as a source for writing the socio-cultural history of Punjab. These lovers and their struggles reflect social history. In other words, though the Punjabi romances are not chronicles of the exploits of particular men and women who appeared in time and space,[84] they need to be framed or contextualized in historical perspective. The injustice done to the lovers is often repeated in contemporary historical and literary approaches when we confine their love affairs to the dominant sufic theme of *ishq haqiqi* and try to justify this within the framework of sufism. The reconstruction of social history from devotional and mystical literature needs to be viewed analytically. Attar Singh states, 'Even independently of conceiving of heroism in love in a religious framework, love as a human emotion and experience is also of paramount importance within Sikh devotionalism and Sufi mysticism.'[85] When we assume *ishq mijazi* (the earthly romance with all its patriarchal implications) as a step towards *ishq haqiqi* (to be one with God), the peculiar characteristic of Punjabi qissa as a narrative of social struggle sinks into oblivion. Viewing qissa from the single prism of *ishq haqiqi* renders this poetic genre devoid of scope, devoid of its multiple contexts. The use of a literary folk text as a source of history, depends on the agenda of the researcher and on which element he gives priority. It depends upon his flare for making a text multi-contextual or else reductionist. With regard to qissa as source, the analyses that attempt to delink the qissa from its social base and, in the process, search for the metaphysical concerns, do injustice to the entire genre. Intrinsically, qissa is rooted in the soil. The life force of its survival lies in its concern with social praxis.[86] One of the reasons, indeed a significant one, for not adequately using the sufic literature like qissa as a source for the gender question is that both sufism and the gender issue have not yet grown into a social movement.

NOTES

1. *Hir Waris*, stanza no. 12.
2. Denis Matringe, 'Hir Waris Shah' in M. Waseem, ed., *On Becoming an Indian Muslim*, New Delhi, 2003, pp. 217, 219.
3. Ellison Banks Findly, *Nur Jahan: Empress of Mughal India*, New Delhi, 1993, p. 3.
4. Kamlesh Mohan, 'Clamping Shutters and Valorizing Women: Tensions in Sculpting Gender-Identities in the Colonial Punjab', in Pritam Singh and Shinder Singh Thandi, eds., *Punjabi Identity in a Global Context*, New Delhi, 1999, p. 178.
5. Shemeem Burney Abbas writes about the popularity of Hir: '. . . there is now substantial recorded material of Waris Shah's *Hir* available [in Pakistan], both on audio cassettes and videos sung in the folk traditions. Many renowned folk artists in the Punjab, such as Reshma, Zahida Parvin, Nazir Begum, Sabiha Khanum, Tufail Niazi, and Iqbal Banu, have sung it.' Shemeem Burney Abbas, *The Female Voice in Sufi Ritual: Devotional Practices of Pakistan and India*, Karachi, 2003, p. 92.
6. The land between the Chenab and the Ravi.
7. *Hir Waris*, stanza no. 70.
8. Ibid., stanza no. 71.
9. Ibid., stanza no. 53.

10. *Hir Waris*, stanza no. 57.
11. Ibid., stanza no. 56
12. Ibid., stanza nos. 53–5
13. Ibid., stanza no. 170
14. Ibid., stanza no. 107.
15. Sylvia Walby, *Theorizing Patriarchy*, Cambridge, 1994, p. 178.
16. Mohammad Wahid Mirza, *The Life and Works of Amir Khusrau*, Delhi, 1974, p. 193.
17. Ibid., p. 195.
18. S.H. Aksari, *Khusrau's Works as Sources of Social History*, New Delhi, 1975, pp. 160–1.
19. For details I.H. Siddiqui, 'Socio-Political Role of Women in the Sultanate of Delhi', in Kiran Pawar, ed., *Women in Indian History*, Patiala, 1996, pp. 87–101.
20. Gulfishan Khan, 'Shah Waliullah Dihlawi: A Traditional Perspective of Feminism', paper presented at a seminar on 'Sufi and Bhakti Movement in Medieval India', Department of History, Aligarh Muslim University, January 2004.
21. Barbara D. Metcalf, 'The Making of a Muslim Lady: Maulana Thanawi's Bihishti Zewar', in Milton Israel and N.K. Wagle, eds., *Islamic Society and Culture*, New Delhi, 1983.
22. John Ruskin, *Sesame and Lilies*, London, 1879, pp. 110–80.
23. Irfan Habib, 'Exploring Medieval Gender History', *Proceedings of the Indian History Congress*, Diamond Jubilee Session, Calcutta, 2000.
24. Vern L. Bullough, *The Subordinate Sex: A History of Attitudes Toward Women*, Urbana, 1973, p. 5.
25. For the songs see M.S. Randhawa, ed., *Punjab* (in Punjabi), Patiala, 1960, pp. 220–1. For further details about *trinjan* see Sohinder Singh Wanjara Bedi, *Punjabi Lokedhara Vishav Kosh*, Delhi, vol. 6, 1992, pp. 1495–6.
26. In sufi symbolism the spinning wheel stands for the physical frame of man; spinning signifies the spiritual practice/meditation; the husband stands for the Lord; the girl's parental home symbolizes the world; the wedding day points to the time of death and when soul is expected to encounter the Lord; and dowry stands for spiritual wealth.
27. For more songs on the spinning wheel composed by Bulleh Shah see: J.R. Puri and T.R. Shangari, eds., *Bulleh Shah: The Love Intoxicated Iconoclast*, Beas, 1986, pp. 333–4 and 383–8.

28. *Hir Waris*, stanza no. 108.
29. Sylvia Walby, *Theorizing Patriarchy*, p. 177.
30. *Hir Waris*, stanza no. 81.
31. I have borrowed this argument from Bhupinder Singh Khera, *Punjabi Mithik Kathawan De Chin Jugat* (in Punjabi), Patiala, 1988, p. 139.
32. *Hir Waris*, stanza no. 84.
33. Ibid., stanza no. 121.
34. Richard Lannoy, *The Speaking Tree: A Study of Indian Cultural and Society*, London, 1971, p. 64.
35. Denis Matringe, 'Hir Waris Shah', p. 222.
36. *Hir Waris*, stanza no. 318.
37. Ibid., stanza no. 32.
38. M. Mujeeb, *The Indian Muslims*, London, 1967, pp. 321–2.
39. *Hir Waris*, stanza nos. 90, 95, and 110.
40. Ibid., stanza no. 110.
41. Ibid., stanza no. 111.
42. Ibid., stanza no. 112.
43. Ibid., stanza no. 113.
44. Abdul Razaq O. Kilani, 'Martyrdom in Islamic Traditions and Its Relevance in Islamic System', *Islamic Culture*, October 1995, p. 77.
45. *Hir Waris*, stanza no. 114.
46. Jeevan Deol, 'Acceptable Poetry: Maqbil's Mystical Qissah Hir Ranjha', *International Journal of Punjab Studies*, vol. 3, no. 2, 1996.
47. Cora Kaplan, 'Language and Gender', in Deborah Cameron, *The Feminist Critique of Language*, London, 1990, pp. 57–69.
48. J.S. Grewal, 'The Qazi in the Pargana', *Miscellaneous Articles*, Amritsar, 1974, p. 39.
49. Ibid., 45.
50. Richard M. Eaton, 'Approaches to the Study of Conversion to Islam in India', in David N. Lorenzen, ed., *Religious Movements in South Asia, 600–1800*, New Delhi, 2004.
51. J.S. Grewal, *Miscellaneous Articles*, p. 46.
52. *Hir Waris*, stanza no. 199.
53. Sant Singh Sekhon, *The Love of Hir and Ranjha*, Ludhiana, 1978, p. 71.
54. Ibid., p. 77.
55. *Hir Waris*, stanza no. 200.
56. Ibid., stanza no. 201.

57. Ibid., stanza no. 202.
58. *Hir Waris*, stanza no. 203.
59. Ibid., stanza no. 204.
60. Ibid., stanza nos. 207 and 211.
61. Ibid., stanza no. 212.
62. See Shafqat Tanveer Mirza, *Resistance Themes in Punjabi Literature*, Lahore, n.d., Acknowledgment, 1991, p. 9.
63. *Hir Waris*, stanza no. 106.
64. Ibid., stanza no. 128.
65. Najm Hosain Syed, *Recurrent Patterns in Punjabi Poetry*, Karachi, 2003, p. 45.
66. *Hir Waris*, stanza nos. 175–6.
67. Ibid., stanza no. 597.
68. Ibid., stanza no. 600.
69. Ibid., stanza no. 602.
70. Ibid., stanza no. 604.
71. Bina Agarwal, 'The Idea of Gender Equality: From Legislative Vision to Everyday Family Practice', in Romila Thapar, ed., *India Another Millennium?* New Delhi, 2000, p. 36.
72. M. Athar Tahir, *Qadir Yar: A Critical Introduction*, Lahore, 1988, p. 68.
73. Harjeet Singh Gill, 'The Semiotics of Discourse in Traditional Indian Culture', in Harjeet Singh Gill, ed., *Parole and Language*, Patiala, 1992, p. 108.
74. *Hir Waris*, stanza no. 215.
75. Ibid., stanza no. 108.
76. Syed Abdul Quddus, *Punjab: The Land of Beauty, Love and Mysticism*, Karachi, 1992, p. 6.
77. Shemeem Burney Abbas explains: 'Generally, it is the woman who professes divine love, particularly *doha* and *git* . . .'. *The Female Voice in Sufi Ritual*, pp. 108–28.
78. Attar Singh, *Secularization of Modern Punjabi Poetry*, Chandigarh, 1986, p. 33.
79. Ibid.
80. Ibid.
81. R.C. Temple, *The Legends of the Panjab*, Patiala, vol. II, 1963, p. 508.
82. About Hir's tomb, Temple writes: 'Hir's tomb is about half a mile from the civil station of Jhang, and is marked on the survey map as 'Mookurba Heer', which stands for 'Maqbara-i-Hir' or Hir's

monument. It is a brick building, resembling in style the ordinary Musalman tomb of the sixteenth century, with the exception that instead of being covered by a dome it is open to the sky. There are niches or windows on the four sides. That on the west is closed, while the other three are open, the reason assigned being that the wind should blow on Hir from every direction except that of her home, where she had been murdered. A *mela* or fair, of some local celebrity, is held at the tomb in the month of *Magh* (February)'. R.C. Temple, *The Legends of the Panjab*, vol. II, pp. 177–8.

83. The 'sacred' (secular) status of *Hir* led Udham Singh to procure a copy of *Hir Waris.* Tanveer Mirza writes: 'On April 6, 1940, Udham Singh wrote a letter to the secretary of a London gurudwara, Jahal Singh, asking him to send a copy of Heer written by Waris Shah. Udham Singh was in Brixton's Jail facing a murder trial. Earlier, after gunning down O'Dwyer in a London hall he voluntarily surrendered to the police and confessed that he had avenged the massacre of Jallianwala Bagh. It was O'Dwyer who imposed Martial Law in the Punjab and handed over all power to Gen. Dyer who was responsible for butchering hundreds of unarmed people in the Jallianwala Bagh, Amritsar, on April 13, 1919.' To the trial court, Udham Singh, who gave his name as Ram Mohammad Singh, said he had a sacred book, *Hir* by Waris Shah, on which to take his oath. Shafqat Tanveer Mirza, *Resistance Themes in Punjabi Literature*, pp. 210–11.
84. Attar Singh, *Secularization of Modern Punjabi Poetry*, p. 33.
85. Ibid.
86. Amarjit Singh Kang, ed., *Punjabi Kissei* (in Punjabi), New Delhi, 1997, p. 25.

CHAPTER 9

Conclusion

My analysis of the qissa, *Hir Waris*, an important part of the folklore of Punjab, explodes certain notions about medieval Punjabi society, particularly with regard to the profile of its Muslim segment. My conclusions are neither startling nor radical, but categorically suggest a revision and re-evaluation of the character of Punjabi Muslims. *Hir Waris* evokes a syncretic socio-cultural life pattern that had evolved historically. It was well-knit, integrated, and holistic Punjabi Muslim society, and in no way can it be compared with that which was, in the colonial period, presented as a segregated community. In this society, with patriarchy and the kinship network as two prominent features, an individual could move and act only within the social parameters of the collectivity (clan or tribe), irrespective of social position. The multi-layered relationships between different social segments were governed by kinship and the *jajmani* system. Inter- and intra-clan relationships were developed on egalitarian lines, while relationships within a rural settlement were hierarchical. Caste in terms of hierarchy and purity-pollution did not function as a major criterion. The joint family was a fundamental unit of the whole social structure.

The point I have emphasized through the study is that the economically dominant segments of the rural Punjab, represented by the chaudharis and sardars, were not identified with a 'single religion' (Islam) and hence had not projected themselves as 'Muslim' on criteria accepted later in colonial Punjab. Punjabi Muslim society had various layers of religious belief and practice, and people did not perceive inner contradictions in such a mixture. If they performed a *nikah* as prescribed by the Islamic codes, they also consulted a Brahman for the fixation of an auspicious date for such occasions. They were not backward in comparison to 'modern' people who are controlled and managed by the numerous forces of science and technology, religion, and politics. They had their own wisdom or commonsense world-view expressed in the form of legends and myths, and with which they regulated their social conduct. The myths were drawn from various religious traditions, and show that the differentiation of the Punjabi Muslims did not go beyond a certain level. Religious fanaticism and orthodoxy were not integral to medieval rural culture. All participated in a historically evolved common culture, which was a people's culture but not a popular culture that prevails upon the masses at the level of consumption and consumerism. People had not yet learnt to assert themselves culturally and religiously on the basis of the exclusion of 'others'.

Waris Shah was versifying the legend of Hir during a period when, politically, dusk had descended on the Mughal Empire and the dawn of the Khalsa Raj could be seen clearly. Nevertheless, cultural and social sectarianism had not yet erupted. It had to wait for a century. The kinds of boundaries that are now drawn by the state, religion, and nationalism, had not yet appeared. Punjabi Muslims represented a fusion of several Islamic and pre-Islamic traditions, i.e. liminality.[1] Their cultural space was neither purely Islamic nor dominated and hegemonized by non-Islamic elements. Certainly, it was not a chaotic space but one for *Punjabi* Muslims. Cultural fusion at the level of people as narrated in *Hir Waris*—a fusion which liberated eighteenth-century Punjabis from communitarian nomenclatures—may be further understood in historical perspective when one reads the following observation of Romila Thapar:

> The fusion of Islamic culture with existing Indian culture achieved its most positive expression in the activities of the artisan classes of the towns and amongst the cultivators, as is evident from the socio-religious ideas of the time, and also in primarily artisan activities such as building monuments, the fusion being evident in the architecture of the period. The pattern of living in both these classes came to be interrelated to a far greater degree than amongst the nobility. Domestic ceremonies and rituals such as those connected with birth, marriage, and death became mingled. The converted Muslims were also heir to long-standing

rituals practiced by the Hindus. New ceremonies which had come with Islam, and which were regarded as auspicious, crept into Hindu ritual.[2]

Rooted in their own land of cultural fusion, the Punjabi Muslims, as described by Waris Shah, were not the 'other'. Waris Shah demolishes the myth of communal antagonism constructed by political, religious, and academic professionals who presented the regional struggle against the central imperial power as one between Sikhs and Muslims. Keeping in view the holistic nature of the Sikh movement, its institutions, and its holy Book, could it be possible for staunch votaries of Guru Gobind Singh to transform their counter-hegemonic struggle into a religious struggle? For whom did the Khalsa-Singhs fight and sacrifice their lives? They were engaged in an armed struggle for native Punjabi rule, just as on the literary front Punjabi poets like Bulleh Shah and Waris Shah were communicating their Punjabi identity in contradistinction to what was being propagated by the orthodox priesthood. It is significant that the political forces that imposed their domination and hegemony had to face the resistance of Punjabis, sometimes represented by Jasrath Khokhar and Hir Siyal, and sometimes by the Sikh gurus, Nanak, Arjan Dev, Tegh Bahadur, and Gobind Singh, and sometimes by Banda Bahadur and sometimes by Shah Husain, Bulleh Shah and Waris Shah.

Waris Shah, as a Punjabi Muslim qissa-kar, continues to offer to the Punjabi Muslims, irrespective of the 'boundaries', their own legacy. In presenting the vast canvas of the social and cultural life of Punjabi Muslims in a single text, Waris Shah is still to be surpassed. The closed boundary constructed around the Muslims as a single identity crumbles down when one discerns in *Hir Waris* a particularly complex culture that had grown from interactions between tribal, Hindu, and Islamic traditions. The Punjabi Muslims in *Hir Waris* are not 'highly' Islamic. At core they are a semi-tribal agrarian population; at the middle level, they are indigenously oriented with interaction between the Punjab 'roots' and Islamic 'routes'; and on the surface they are Islamic. Nevertheless, the form and the nature of their society was neither an incongruous amalgam, nor a blend but a synthetic fusion of these three strands which made it unique in itself. Such might be true also of the other two religious communities of Punjab, Hindu and Sikh.

Hir Waris helps us appreciate Islam as a localized historical reality, a practical religion capable of adapting to its space and soil. Waris Shah may be said to be the first to talk about Muslim diversity. He is different from those who do not take into account the divergent shades of Islam in its local contexts. Ignorance or an underestimation of the vernacular or local character of Indian Muslims has led many scholars to characterize them as 'half Muslims', 'imperfect Muslims' or 'partly converted'.[3] This is in keeping with the ideology of the middle classes who spearheaded the reform movements of the later nineteenth century. With regard to Punjabi literature like *Hir*, which embraces a rich cultural context, it is interesting that at the time when it was propagated and circulated at the mass level with the advent of the printing industry, there was also, simultaneously, a flood of communal and communitarian tracts authored by the elite of Punjab. In the process of printing, in the permanent culture of 'black and white', the oral voice of the bards, who were organically and historically linked with the masses, was lost.

Another significant point that emerges from the present study is the compatibility between literature and political struggle. The nature of eighteenth-century Punjabi literature, in the form of qissa, or heroic ballads, *kafis*, or other poetic genres, was compatible with the people's participation under the leadership of the Khalsa in the struggle against oppression and external aggression. In other words, historically Punjabi literature has accompanied the Punjab struggle for political autonomy.

A similar compatibility can be discerned in the communitarian literature of the Punjabi middle classes and their struggle against British imperialism. Hindu, Muslim, and Sikh literary discourses were compatible with communitarian demands for constitutional concessions and administrative reform. Pre-colonial Punjabi literature never allowed socio-cultural *diversities* to be transformed into *differences*. What is being suggested is that while medieval literature, written by the intellectuals like Waris Shah and Bulleh Shah, integrated the people in political struggles, the colonized middle classes and their literature played a historic role in compartmentalizing political, cultural, and social praxis.

NOTES

1. For the concept of liminality see Shail Mayaram, 'Beyond Ethnicity? Being Hindu and Muslim in South Asia', in Imtiaz Ahmad and Helmut Reifield, eds., *Lived Islam in South Asia: Adaptation, Accommodation and Conflict*, Delhi, 2004, pp. 25–6.
2. Romila Thapar, *A History of India from the Discovery of India to 1526*, New Delhi, 1992, pp. 289–300.
3. Such a characterization of Muslims may be read in Jafar Sharif, *Qanun-i-Islam*, tr. G. Herklot, ed. William Crooke; M. Ayub Khan, *Friends Not Masters*, p. 187; Muhammad Mujeeb, *The Indian Muslims*, p. 22 as quoted in Asim Roy, *Islam in South Asia*, New Delhi, 1996, p. 38; Murray T. Titus, *Indian Islam: A Religious History of Islam in India*, New Delhi, 1979, pp. 147–206.

Plate 1: Waris Shah

Plate 2: Dargah of Waris Shah at Jandiala Sher Khan

Plate 3: Gate of Waris Shah's Tomb

Plate 4: Tomb of Hir–Ranjha at Jhang Siyal

SOCIAL AND RELIGIOUS REBELS OF THE PUNJAB

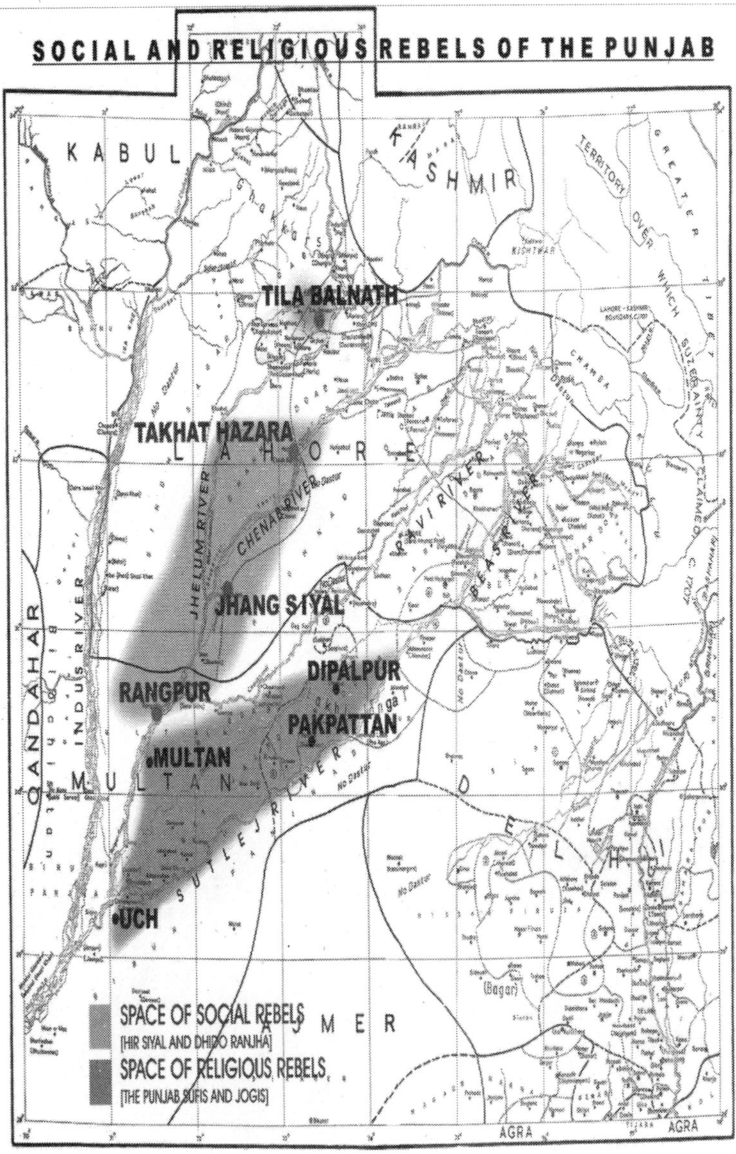

Bibliography

PRIMARY SOURCES

PERSIAN

Ahmad, Khwajah Nizamuddin, *Tabaqat-i-Akbari*, vol. I, tr., B. De, rpt., Calcutta, The Asiatic Society, 1973.

Das, Ganesh, *Char Bagh-i-Panjab* (Early Nineteenth Century Panjab), tr. and ed. J.S. Grewal and Indu Banga, Amritsar: Guru Nanak Dev University, 1975.

Farishta, Muhammed Qasim Hindu Shah, *Tarikh-i-Farishta*, tr. John Briggs (History of the Rise of the Mahomedan Power in India), vol. I, rpt., New Delhi: Low Price Publications, 1990.

Hujweri, Al bin Usman, *Kashf ul-Mahjub*, tr. Reynold A. Nicholson, New Delhi: Taj Company, 1959.

Sirhindi, Yahiya bin Ahmad bin Abdullah, *Tarikh-i-Mubarakshahi*, tr. H. Beveridge, rpt., New Delhi: Low Price Publications, 1990.

Suri, Sohan Lal, *Umdat-ut-Tawarikh,* Daftar III, pts. I-V, 1831–9, tr. V.S. Suri, Chandigarh: Itihas Prakashan, 1974.

QISSAS (PUNJABI/GURMUKHI AND SHAHMUKHI)

Amol, S.S., ed., *Hir Sayad Waris Shah*, Amritsar: Punjabi Book Shop, 2nd edn., 1949.

Nijjar, Bakhshish Singh, ed., *Heer Waris Shah*, Jalandhar: Mehtab Singh New Book Company, 1994.

Padam, Piara Singh, ed., *Sohni Hashim*, Patiala: Sahit Bhawan, 1957.

Padam, S.S., ed., *Hir Ahmad*, Barnala: Punjabi Sahit Sabha, 1960.

Sekhon, Sant Singh, *Heer Waris Shah*, 1969, rpt., Delhi: Sahitya Akademi, 1998.

Shan, Harnam Singh, ed., *Sassi Hashim*, Jalandhar: Dhanpat Rai and Sons, 1959.

Singh, Jagtar, *Hir Damodar*, Patiala: Punjabi University, 2000.

Singh, Mohan, ed., *Hir Waris* (in Shahmukhi), Lahore: Lahore Book Shop, 1947.

Singh, Ujagar, ed., Ahmadyar, *Sassi-Punnun*, Ludhiana: Punjab Sahitya Akademi, 1961.

Sital, Jit Singh, *Hir Waris*, Delhi: Navyug Publishers, 2nd edn., 1973.

PUNJABI SUFI POETRY/QISSA (RENDERED INTO ENGLISH)

Puri, J.R. and Kirpal Singh Khak, *Sultan Bahu*, ed. Maqsood Saqib, Lahore: Suchet Kitab Ghar, 2004.

Puri, J.R. and T.R. Shangari, *Bulleh Shah: The Love Intoxicated Iconoclast*, Beas: Radha Soami Satsang, 1986.

Rafat, Taufiq, *Bulleh Shah*, Lahore: Vanguard, 1982.

Sagar, Brij Mohan, *Hymns of Sheikh Farid*, Amritsar: Guru Nanak Dev University, 1997.

Sekhon, Sant Singh, *The Love of Hir and Ranjha*, Ludhiana: Punjab Agricultural University, 1978.

OFFICIAL PUBLICATIONS

Ibbetson, Denzil, Edward MacLagan and H.A. Rose, *A Glossary of the Tribes and Castes of the Punjab and North-West Frontier Province*, rpt., Patiala: Languages Department, 1883, rpt., 1990.

Ibbetson, Denzil, *Panjab Castes*, 1916, rpt., Delhi: Low Price Publications, 1993.

Secondary Sources

BOOKS (ENGLISH)

Abbas, Shemeem Burney, *The Female Voice in Sufi Ritual: Devotional Practices of Pakistan and India*, Karachi: Oxford University Press, 2003.

Ahmad, Aziz, *Studies in Islamic Culture in the Indian Environment*, 1964; rpt., New Delhi: Oxford University Press, 1999.

Ahmad, Imtiaz and Helmut Reifeld, eds., *Lived Islam in South Asia: Adaptation, Accommodation and Conflict*, Delhi: Social Science Press, 2004.

Ahmad, Rashid and Muhammad Afzal Qarshi, eds., *Islam in South Asia* (Proceedings of International Seminar on Islamic History, Art and Culture in South Asia), Lahore: Institute of Islamic Culture, 1995.

Ahmed, Ishtiaq, *State, Nation and Ethnicity in Contemporary South Asia*, London: Printer, 1996.

Ahmed, Rafiuddin, ed., *Understanding the Bengal Muslims: Interpretative Essays*, New Delhi: Oxford University Press, 2001.

Ahluwalia, M.L., *Landmarks in Sikh History: A Fully Researched and*

Document History: 1699–1947 Dedicated to the Great Khalsa, New Delhi: Ashoka International Publishers, 1996.

Aksari, S.H., *Khusrau's Works as Sources of Social History* (Amir Khusrau Memorial Volume), New Delhi: Publications Division, 1975.

Alam, Muzaffar, *The Crisis of Empire in Mughal North India: Awadh and the Punjab, 1707–1748*, New Delhi: Oxford University Press, 1986.

———, *The Languages of Political Islam in India c. 1200-1800*, New Delhi: Permanent Black, 2004.

Alavi, Seema, ed., *The Eighteenth Century in India*, New Delhi: Oxford University Press, 2002.

Ali, Mubarak, *The Ulema, Sufis and Intellectuals*, Lahore: Fiction House, 2005.

Ali, M. Athar, *Mughal India: Studies in Polity, Ideas, Society, and Culture*, New Delhi: Oxford University Press, 2006.

Ansari, M.T., *Secularism, Islam and Modernity: Selected Essays of Alam Khundmiri*, New Delhi: Sage Publications, 2001.

Arnold, T.W., *The Preaching of Islam*, 1913; rpt., Delhi: Low Price Publications, 1997.

Ashraf, K.M., *Life and Conditions of the People of Hindustan*, 2nd edn., New Delhi: Munshiram Manoharlal, 1988.

———, *Indian Historiography and other Related Papers*, tr. Jaweed Ashraf, New Delhi: Sunrise Publications, 2006.

Auj, Nurul Zaman Ahmad, *Harappan Heritage*, Multan: Caravan Book Centre, 1998.

Bakhtin, Mikhail Mikhailovich, *The Dialogic Imagination*, Austin: University of Texas Press, 1983.

Banerjee A.C., *The Khalsa Raj*, Delhi: Abhinav Publications, 1985.

Barker, Chris, *The Sage Dictionary of Cultural Studies*, New Delhi: Sage Publications, 2004.

Baskerville, Geoffery, *English Monks and the Suppression of the Monasteries*, 1937; rpt., London: Jonathan Cape, 1965.

Bauman, Zygmunt, *Culture as Praxis*, rpt., New Delhi: Sage Publications, 2000.

Bayly, C.A., *Indian Society and the Making of the British Empire* (The New Cambridge History of India), Hyderabad: Orient Longman, 1990.

Berger, Arthur Asa, *Cultural Criticism: A Primer of Key Concepts*, London: Sage Publications, 1995.

Berkey, Jonathan P., *The Formation of Islam: Religion and Society in the Near East, 600–1800*, Cambridge: Cambridge University Press, 2003.

Bilgrami, Fatima Zehra, *History of the Qadiri Order in India (16–18th Century)*, Delhi: Idarah-i Adabiyat-i Dilli, 2005.

Bingley, A.H., *Sikhs*, Shimla, Government of India Central Printing Office, 1899; rpt., Patiala: Languages Department, 1970.

———, *History, Caste and Culture of Jats and Gujars*, 2nd edn., New Delhi: Ess Ess Publications, 1978.

Blackburn, Stuart, *Print, Folklore, and Nationalism in Colonial South India*, Delhi: Permanent Black, 2003.

Brass, Paul R., *Language, Religion and Politics in North India*, Delhi: Vikas Publishing House, 1975.

Bullough, Vern L., *The Subordinate Sex: A History of Attitudes towards Women*, Urbana: University of Illinois Press, 1973.

Chakravarti, K.C., *Ancient Indian Culture and Civilization*, Bombay: Vora and Co., 1961.

Chapekar, Nalinee M., *Ancient India and Greece: A Study of their Cultural Contacts*, Delhi: Ajanta Publishers, 1977.

Chandra, Bipan, *Communalism in Modern India*, rpt., New Delhi: Vikas Publishing House, 1992.

Chandra, Satish, *Medieval India: Society, the Jagirdari Crisis and the Village*, rpt., New Delhi: Macmillan, 1986.

———, *Historiography, Religion and State in Medieval India*, New Delhi, Har-Anand Publications, 1996.

———, *Medieval India: From Sultanat to the Mughals, Part one, (Delhi Sultanate (1206–1526)*, New Delhi: Har-Anand Publications, 1997.

———, *Medieval India: From Sultanate to the Mughals, Part Two, Mughal Empire (1526–1748)*, Delhi: Har-Anand Publications, 2000.

———, *Essays on Medieval Indian History*, New Delhi: Oxford University Press, 2003.

Chattopadhay, Bhaśkar, *The Kushanas: A Numismatic Study*, Calcutta: Punthi Pustak, 1967.

Chattopadhyaya, Brajadulal, *Representing the Other? Sanskrit Sources and the Muslims (Eighth to Fourteenth Century)*, New Delhi: Manohar, 1998.

———, *The Making of Early Medieval India*, New Delhi: Oxford University Press, Indian paperbacks, 2006.

Chaudhuri, Tapan Ray and Irfan Habib, ed., *The Cambridge Economic*

History of India, vol. I, c. 1200–c. 1750, Hyderabad: Orient Longman, 1984.

Clifford, James and George Marcus, ed., *Writing Culture: The Poetics and Politics of Ethnography*, New Delhi: Oxford University Press, 1990.

Culler, Jonathan, *On Deconstruction: Theory and Criticism after Structuralism*, London: Routledge and Kegan Paul, 1983.

Cunningham, Alexander, *The Ancient Geography of India*, Varanasi: Indological Book House, 1963.

Cunningham, Joseph Davey, *A History of the Sikhs from the Origin of the Nation to the Battle of Sutlej*, London, 1849; rpt., New Delhi: S. Chand, 1985.

Currie, Mark, *Postmodern Narrative Theory*, London: Macmillan, 1998.

Dhanagare, D.N., *Themes and Perspectives in Indian Sociology*, rpt., Jaipur: Rawat Publications, 1998.

Dua, J.C., *British Historiography on the Eighteenth Century Punjab*, New Delhi: Radha Publications, 1992.

Duggal, K.S., compiled and transcreated, *Select Sikh Scriptures I: Guru Nanak*, New Delhi: UBS, 1977.

Dumont, Louis, *Religional/Politics and History in India*, Paris: Mouton Publishers, 1970.

Eaton, Richard M., *The Rise of Islam and the Bengal Frontier, 1204–1760*, Berkeley: University of California Press, 1993.

———, *Essays on Islam and Indian History*, New Delhi: Oxford University Press, 2000.

———, *India's Islamic Traditions, 711–1750*, New Delhi: Oxford University Press, 2003.

Engineer, Asghar Ali, ed., *Islam in India: The Impact of Civilization*, Delhi: Shipra Publications, 2002.

Ernst, Carl W., *The Shambhala Guide to Sufism*, New Delhi: Rupa, 2000.

———, *Eternal Garden: Mysticism, History, and Politics at a South Asian Sufi Centre*, New Delhi: Oxford University Press, 2004.

Farid, Arifa, *Muslim Woman in World Religions' Perspective*, Karachi: Bureau of Composition, Compilation & Translation, University of Pakistan, 1994.

Findly, Banks Ellison, *Nur Jahan: Empress of Mughal India*, New Delhi: Oxford University Press, 1993.

Foltz, Richard C., *Mughal India and Central Asia*, Karachi: Oxford University Press, 2001.

Fox, Richard G., *Lions of the Punjab: Culture in the Making*, Delhi: Low Price Publications, 1990.

Friedmann, Yohanan, *Shaykh Ahmad Sirhindi: An Outline of his Thought and a Study of his Image in the Eyes of Posterity*, Montreal and London: McGill-Queen's University Press, 1971.

Gilmartin, David and Bruce B. Lawrence, ed., *Beyond Turk and Hindu: Rethinking Religious Identities in Islamicate South Asia*, New Delhi: India Research Press, 2002.

Goel, Sita Ram, *Story of Islamic Imperialism in India,* New Delhi: Voice of India, 1982.

Goldziher, Ignaz, *Muslim Studies*, tr. C.R. Barber and S.M. Stern, London, George Allen & Unwin, 1971.

Gommans, Joss J.L., *The Rise of the Indo-Afghan Empire c. 1710–1780*, New Delhi: Oxford University Press, 1999.

Gramsci, Antonio, *Selections from the Prison Notebooks*, ed. and tr. Quintin Hoare and Geoffrey Nowell Smith, London: Lawrence and Wishart, 1971.

Grewal, J.S., *Miscellaneous Articles*, Amritsar: Guru Nanak Dev University, 1974.

———, *Guru Nanak in History*, rpt., Chandigarh: Panjab University, 1979.

———, *Sikh Ideology: Polity and Social Order*, New Delhi: Manohar, 1996.

Grewal, J.S. and Indu Banga, eds., *Maharaja Ranjit Singh and His Times*, Amritsar: Guru Nanak Dev University, 1980.

Grunebaum, Gustave E. Von, *Medieval Islam*, Chicago: The University of Chicago Press, 1946.

Habib, Mohammad, *Sultan Mahmud of Ghaznin*, 2nd edn., Delhi: S. Chand, 1951.

Habib, Mohammad and Khaliq Ahmad Nizami, eds., *A Comprehensive History of India, The Delhi Sultanate (AD 1206–1526)*, vol. V, rpt., New Delhi: People's Publishing House, 1982.

Gupta, Hari Ram, *History of the Sikhs*, 5 vols., New Delhi: Munshiram Manoharlal, 1978–91.

Habib, Irfan, *The Agrarian System of Mughal India 1556–1707*, rpt., New Delhi: Oxford University Press, 2000.

Habibullah, A.B.M., *The Foundation of Muslim Rule in India*, 2nd edn., Allahabad: Central Book Depot, 1976.

Halim, Abdul, *Essays on History of Indo-Pak Music*, Dacca: Hai Asiatic Press, 1962.

Hardy, P., *The Muslims of British India*, Cambridge: Cambridge University Press, 1972.

Hasan, Mushirul and Asim Roy, ed., *Living Together Separately: Cultural India in History and Politics*, New Delhi: Oxford University Press, 2005.

Hasan, S. Nurul, *Religion, State and Society: Collected Works of S. Nurul Hasan*, ed. Satish Chandra, New Delhi: Oxford University Press, 2005.

Hasrat, Bikrama Jit, *Life and Times of Ranjit Singh: A Saga of Benevolent Despotism*, Nabha (Punjab): Hathikhana, 1977.

Husain, Yusuf, *Glimpses of Medieval Indian Culture*, rpt., Bombay: Asian Publishing House, 1962.

———, *Indo-Muslim Polity (Turko-Afghan Period)*, Shimla: Indian Institute of Advanced Study, 1971.

———, *Two Studies in Early Mughal History*, Shimla: Indian Institute of Advanced Study, 1976.

Islam, Riazul, *Sufism in South Asia: Impact on Fourteenth Century Muslim Society*, Karachi: Oxford University Press, 2003.

Jackson, Peter, *The Delhi Sultanate: A Political and Military History*, Cambridge: Cambridge University Press, 1999.

Jenkins, Keith, ed., *The Post Modern History Reader*, London: Routledge, 1997.

Jones, Kenneth W., *Arya Dharma*, New Delhi: Manohar, 1976; rpt. 2006.

———, *Socio-Religious Movements in British India* (The New Cambridge History of India); rpt., New Delhi: Cambridge University Press, 1999.

Joshi, L.M. and Fauja Singh, eds., *History of the Punjab*, vol. I, Patiala: Punjabi University, 1997.

Jotwani, Motilal, *Sindhi Literature and Society*, New Delhi: Rajesh Publications, 1979.

Kaufmann, Walter, *The Ragas of North India*, Calcutta: Oxford & IBH, 1968.

Kaushik, Devendra, *Central Asia in Modern Times: A History from the Early 19th Century*, ed. N. Khalfin, Moscow: Progress Publishers, 1970.

Khan, Gulfishan, *Indian Muslims Perceptions of the West during the Eighteenth Century*, Karachi: Oxford University Press, 1998.

Khan, M.A. Saleem, *Early Muslim Perception of India and Hinduism*, New Delhi: South Asian Publishers, 1997.

Khan, Mohammad Ishaq, *Kashmir's Transition to Islam: The Role of Muslim Rishis (Fifteenth to Eighteenth Centuries)*, New Delhi: Manohar, 1994.

Khan, Yar Muhammad, *Studies in the History of Indo-Pakistan Subcontinent*, Lahore: University of the Punjab, 1991.

Khubchandani, Lachman M., *Language, Culture and Nation-Building: Challenge of Modernization*, Shimla: Indian Institute of Advanced Study and New Delhi: Manohar, 1991.

Kohli, Surindar Singh, *Bulleh Shah*, 1987; rpt., New Delhi: Sahitya Akademi, 1990.

Kosambi, D.D., *The Culture and Civilization of Ancient India in Historical Outline*, Delhi: Vikas Publications, 1970.

Kumar, Narendra, *An Encyclopaedic Dictionary of Indian Culture*, Delhi: Agam Kala Prakashan, 1992.

Krishna, Lajwanti Rama, *Panjabi Sufi Poets AD 1460–1900*, rpt., New Delhi: Ashajanak Publications, 1973.

Lal, Kishori Saran, *Twilight of Sultanate: A Political, Social and Cultural History of the Sultanate of Delhi from the Invasion of Timur to the Conquest of Babur 1398–1526*, rev. edn., New Delhi: Munshiram Manoharlal, 1980.

Lannoy, Richard, *The Speaking Tree: A Study of Indian Culture and Society*, London: Oxford University Press, 1971.

Lapidus, Ira M., *A History of Islamic Societies*, Cambridge: Cambridge University Press, 1989.

Latif, Syad Muhammad, *History of the Punjab: From the Remotest Antiquity to the Present Time*, New Delhi: Eurasia Publishing House, 1964.

Lawrence, Bruce B., *Shattering the Myth: Islam Beyond Violence*, Karachi: Oxford University Press, 2000.

———, *Notes from a Distant Flute*, Tehran: Imperial Iranian Academy, 1978.

Lehtonen, Mikko, *The Cultural Analysis of Texts*, tr. Aija-Leena and Kris Clarke, London: Sage Publications, 2000.

Levi, Scott C., ed., *India and Central Asia: Commerce and Culture 1500–1800*, New Delhi: Oxford University Press, 2007.

Lévi-Strauss, Claude, *Structural Anthropology*, tr. Claire Jacobson and Brooke Grundfest Schoepf, 1963; rpt., Harmondsworth: Penguin Books, 1972.

———, *The Savage Mind*, Chicago: The University of Chicago Press, 1969.

Linschoten, J.H.V., *The Voyage of East Indies*, ed. Arthur Coke Burnwell, New Delhi: Asian Educational Society, vol. I, 1988.

Mahil, U.S., *Antiquity of Jat Race*, Ludhiana: Asia Visions, 2005.

Maini, Darshan Singh, *Studies in Punjabi Poetry*, New Delhi: Vikas Publishing House, 1979.

Malik, Jamal and Helmut Reifeld, eds., *Religious Pluralism in South Asia and Europe*, New Delhi: Oxford University Press, 2005.

Malik, Zahir Uddin, *The Reign of Muhammad Shah 1719–1748*, Bombay: Asia Publishing House, 1977.

Manzoor, Ahmed Manzoor, *The Pakistan Problem, Historical Backwardness of Punjab and Consolidation of Pakistan*, Lahore: The Frontier Post Publications, 1993.

Manger, Leif, ed., *Muslim Diversity: Local Islam in Global Contexts*, London: Curzon Press, 1999.

Marshall, P.J., ed., *The Eighteenth Century in Indian History: Evolution or Revolution?*, New Delhi: Oxford University Press, 2003.

McLeod, W.H., *Exploring Sikhism: Aspects of Sikh Identity, Culture, and Thought*, New Delhi: Oxford University Press, 2000.

Merquior, J.G., *The Veil and the Mask: Essays on Culture and Ideology*, London: Routledge, 1979.

Metcalf, Barbara D., *Islamic Contestations: Essays on Muslims in India and Pakistan*, New Delhi: Oxford University Press, 2004.

Mirza, Mohammad Wahid, *The Life and Works of Amir Khusrau*, 1935; rpt., Delhi: Idarah-i Adabiyat-i-Dilli, 1974.

Mirza, Shafqat Tanveer, *Resistance Themes in Punjabi Literature*, Lahore: Sang-e-Meel Publications, 1991.

Mujeeb, M., *The Indian Muslims*, London: George Allen & Unwin, 1967.

Mukerji, K.K., *Rose-Garden of the Punjab*, ed. Gurbachan Singh Talib, Patiala: Punjabi University, 1973.

Murthy, K. Krishna, *Mirrors of Indian Culture*, Delhi: Ajanta Publishers, 1982.

Naim, C.M., *Zikr-i-Mir: The Autobiography of the Eighteenth Century Mughal Poet: Mir Muhammad Taqi 'Mir' (1723–1810)*, New Delhi: Oxford University Press, 2002.

Naqshbandy, Sheikh Parvaiz, *The Saints of Punjab*, Lahore: Umar Publications, 1998.

Narang, A.S., *Ethnic Identities and Federalism*, Shimla: Indian Institute of Advanced Study, 1995.

Nasr, Seyyed Hossein, *Sufi Essays*, London: George Allen and Unwin, 1972.

Nayyar, Gurbachan Singh, *Sikh Polity and Political Institutions*, New Delhi: Oriental Publishers & Distributors, 1979.

Nazim, Muhammad, *The Life and Times of Sultan Mahmud of Ghazna*, rpt., New Delhi: Munshiram Manoharlal, 1971.

Nigam, S.B.P., *Nobility under the Sultans of Delhi, AD 1206–1398*, New Delhi: Munshiram Manoharlal, 1968.

Nizami, Khaliq Ahmad, *Religion and Politics in India during the Thirteenth Century*, 1961; rpt., New Delhi: Oxford University Press, 2002.

———, *The Life and Times of Shaikh Farid-ud-Din Ganj-i-Shakar*, 1955; rpt., Delhi: Idarah-i-Adabiyat-i-Delli, 1973.

———, ed., *Politics and Society during the Early Medieval Period: Collected Works of Professor Mohammad Habib*, vols. I and II, Delhi: People's Publishing House, 1974 and 1981.

———, ed., *Medieval India: A Miscellany*, vol. II, Delhi: Asia Publishing House, 1972.

———, ed., *Shah Wali Ullah Ke Siyasi Maktubat*, Nudwat-ul-Musannifin, Delhi, 1969.

Oberoi, Harjot, *The Construction of Religious Boundaries: Culture, Identity and Diversity in the Sikh Tradition*, New Delhi: Oxford University Press, 1997.

Panikkar, K.N., *Culture, Ideology, Hegemony: Intellectuals and Social Consciousness in Colonial India*, New Delhi: Tulika, 1995.

Parekh, Bhikhu and Thomas Pantham, eds., *Political Discourse: Explorations in Indian and Western Political Thought*, New Delhi: Sage Publications, 1987.

Phadnis, U., *Ethnicity and Nation-building in South Asia*, New Delhi: Sage Publications, 1989.

Pillai, S. Devadas, *Indian Sociology through Ghurye: A Dictionary*, Mumbai: Popular Prakashan, 1997.

Prakash, Buddha, *Aspects of Indian History and Civilization*, Agra: Shivlal & Aggarwal Co. Pvt. Ltd., 1965.

———, *Glimpses of Ancient Panjab*, Patiala: Punjabi University, 1983.

———, *Political and Social Movements in Ancient Punjab*, Delhi: Motilal Banarsidass, 1964.

Propp, Vladimir, *Theory and History of Folklore*, tr. Ariadna Y. Martin and Richard P. Martin, Manchester; Manchester University Press, 1984.

Quddus, Syed Abdul, *Punjab: The Land of Beauty, Love and Mysticism*, Karachi: Royal Book Company, 1992.

Qureshi, Ishtiaq Husain, *The Muslim Community of the Indo-Pakistan Subcontinent (610–1947)*, rpt., Delhi: Renaissance Publishing House, 1985.

———, *A Short History of Pakistan*, rpt., Karachi: University of Karachi, 2000.

Radcliffe-Broun, A.R., *Structure and Function in Primitive Society*, London: Routledge and Kegan Paul, 1979.

Rahman, Fazlur, *Islam*, London: Weidenfeld & Nicolson, 1966.

Rashid, Abdur, *History of the Muslims of Indo-Pakistan Subcontinent 1707–1806*, vol. I, Lahore: University of Punjab, 1997.

Rastogi, T.C., *Sufism: A Dictionary with Profiles of Saint-poets*, Delhi: Sterling Publishers, 1990.

Reetz, Dietrich, *Islam in the Public Sphere: Religious Groups in India, 1900–1947*, New Delhi: Oxford University Press, 2006.

Rizvi, S.A.A., *The Wonder That Was India: A Survey of the History and Culture of the Indian Sub-continent from the Coming of the Muslims to the British Conquest 1200-1700*, 1987; rpt., Calcutta: Rupa and Co., 1993.

———, *Muslim Revivalist Movements in Northern India in the Sixteenth and Seventeenth Centuries*, New Delhi: Munshiram Manoharlal, 1993.

———, *A History of Sufism in India*, vol. I, 1978; rpt., New Delhi, Munshiram Manoharlal, 1986.

———, *Iran: Royalty, Religion and Revolution*, Canberra: Marifat Publishing House, 1980.

Rodinson, Maxime, *Islam and Capitalism*, tr. Brian Pearce, London: Allen Lane, 1974.

Roy, M.N., *The Historical Role of Islam*, 1939; rpt., Delhi: Ajanta Publications, 1981.

Roy, Asim, *Islam in South Asia*, New Delhi: South Asian Publishers, 1996.

———, ed., *Islam in History and Politics: Perspectives from South Asia*, New Delhi: Oxford University Press, 2006.

Ruskin, John, *Sesame and Lilies*, London, George Allen, 1879.

Saleemkhan, M.A., *Early Muslim Perceptions of India and Hinduism*, New Delhi: South Asian Publishers, 1997.

Sarkar, Jadunath, *Mughal Administration*, New Delhi: Orient Longman, 1972.

———, *Fall of the Mughal Empire*, vol. I, 1739–1754, Hyderabad: Orient Longman, 1997.

Saunders, J.J., *A History of Medieval Islam*, London: Routledge and Kegan Paul, 1965.

Schimmel, Annemarie, *Mystical Dimensions of Islam*, Lahore: Sang-e-Meel, 2003.

———, *Islamic Literatures of India*, Wiesbaden: Otto Harrassowitz, 1973.

———, *Islam in the Indian Subcontinent*, Lahore: Sang-e-Meel, 2003.

Sekhon, Sant Singh, *A History of Panjabi Literature*, 2 vols., Patiala: Punjabi University, 1993; rpt. 1996.

Serebryakov, I., *Punjabi Literature: A Brief Outline*, rpt., Chandigarh: Lokayat Prakashan, 2000.

Shackle, Christopher, ed., *Urdu and Muslim South Asia: Studies in Honour of Ralph Russel*, New Delhi: Oxford University Press, 1991.

Shail, Mayaram, *Against History, Against State: Counter Perspectives from the Margins*, New Delhi: Permanent Black, 2004.

Sharma, R.S., *India's Ancient Past*, New Delhi: Oxford University Press, 2006.

Sharma, Sri Ram, *Studies in Medieval Indian History*, Poona: Aryabhushan Press, 1956.

Sharma, Sunil, *Persian Poetry at the Indian Frontier: Masud Sad Salman of Lahore*, Delhi: Permanent Black, 2000.

Shushtery, A.M., *Outlines of Islamic Culture: Historical and Cultural Aspects*, Bangalore: Bangalore Press, 1954.

Singh, Attar, *Secularization of Modern Punjabi Poetry*, Chandigarh: Punjab Prakashan, 1988.

———, ed., *Socio-Cultural Impact of Islam on India*, Chandigarh: Panjab University, 1976.

Singh, Bhagat, *Sikh Polity: In the Eighteenth and Nineteenth Centuries*, New Delhi: Oriental Publishers & Distributors, 1978.

Singh, Chetan, *Region and Empire: Panjab in the Seventeenth Century*, New Delhi: Oxford University Press, 1991.

Singh, Darshan, *Indian Bhakti Tradition and Sikh Gurus*, Ludhiana: Lyall Book Depot, 1968.

Singh, Ganda, *Life of Banda Singh Bahadur*, Amritsar: Khalsa College, 1935.

———, *A Brief Account of the Sikh People*, Delhi, Sikh Gurdwara Board, 1971.

Singh, Gurcharan, *Studies in Punjab History and Culture*, New Delhi: Enkay Publishers, 1990.

Singh, Harbans, *The Heritage of the Sikhs*, Bombay: Asia Publishing House, 1983.

Singh, Khushwant, *A History of the Sikhs*, 2 vols., Princeton: Princeton University Press, 1963; rpt. 1966.

Singh, Mohan, *An Introduction to Panjabi Literature*, Amritsar: Nanak Singh Pustak Mala, 1951.

———, *Order of Siddha-Yogins*, Amritsar: New Suraj Printing Press, n.d.

———, *A History of Panjabi Literature,* 2nd edn., Amritsar: Kasturi Lal & Sons, 1956.

Singh, Nikky-Guninder Kaur, *The Feminine Principle in the Sikh Vision of the Transcendent,* Cambridge: Cambridge University Press, 1993.

Singh, Vir, ed., *The Jats: Their Role and Contribution to the Socio-Economic Life and Polity of North and North-West India,* vol. I, Delhi: Originals, 2004.

Singh, Yogendra, *Modernization of Indian Tradition,* rpt., Jaipur: Rawat Publications, 1988.

Sinha, N.K., *Rise of the Sikh Power,* 1936; rpt., Calcutta: A. Mukherjee, 1973.

Subhan, John A., *Sufism, Its Saints and Shrines: An Introduction to the Study of Sufism with Special Reference to India and Pakistan,* New Delhi: Indigo and Cosmo, 2002.

Srivastava, A.L., *Medieval Indian Culture,* Jaipur: Shiva Lal Agarwala, 1964.

Steinbach, Lieut-Colonel, *The Punjab,* Patiala: Languages Department, 1970.

Swynnerton, Charles, *The Adventures of the Punjab Hero Raja Rasalu,* Calcutta: W. Newman & Co., 1884.

Syed, Najm Hosain, *Recurrent Patterns in Punjabi Poetry,* 1968; rpt., Karachi: City Press, 2003.

Tahir, M. Athar, *Qadir Yar: A Critical Introduction,* Lahore: Pakistan Punjabi Adabi Board, 1988.

Taneja, Anup, ed., *Sufi Cults and the Evolution of Medieval Indian Culture,* Delhi: Indian Council of Historical Research in association with Northern Book Centre, 2003.

Temple, R.C. *The Legends of the Punjab,* 3 vols., Bombay, 1884–6; rpt., Patiala: Languages Department, 1962–3.

Thapar, Romila, *A History of India: From the Discovery of India to 1526,* 1966; rpt., New Delhi: Penguin Books, 1992.

———, *The Penguin History of Early India: From the Origins to AD 1300,* New Delhi: Penguin, 2003.

Thomas, Edward, *The Chronicles of Pathan Kings of Delhi,* rpt., New Delhi: Munshiram Manoharlal, 1967.

Titus, Murray T., *Indian Islam: A Religious History of Islam in India,* 1930; rpt., New Delhi: Oriental Books 1979.

Trimingham, J. Spencer, *The Sufi Orders in Islam,* London, Oxford University Press, 1971.

Troll, Christian W., ed., *Muslim Shrines in India: Their Character, History and Significance*, New Delhi: Oxford University Press, 2003.

Uberoi, J.P.S. *Religion, Civil Society and the State: A Study of Sikhism*, New Delhi: Oxford University Press, 1999.

Umar, Muhammad, *Islam in Northern India during the Eighteenth Century*, New Delhi: Munshiram Manoharlal, 1993.

Vaudeville, Charlotte, *A Weaver Named Kabir*, New Delhi: Oxford University, Press, 2005.

———, *Myths, Saints and Legends in Medieval India*, New Delhi: Oxford University Press, 2005.

Waheed-uz-Zaman and Akhtar, M. Saleem, eds., *Islam in South Asia*, Islamabad: National Institute of Historical and Cultural Research, 1993.

Walby, Sylvia, *Theorizing Patriarchy*, Cambridge: Blackwell, 1994.

Waseem, M., ed. and tr., *On Becoming an Indian Muslim*, New Delhi: Oxford University Press, 2003.

Wikeley, J.M., *Punjabi Muslims*, Lahore: The Book House, n.d.

Williams, John A., ed., *Islam*, London: Prentice-Hall, 1961.

Wink, Andre, *Al-Hind: The Making of the Indo-Islamic World*, vol. I: *Early Medieval India and the Expansion of Islam 7th–11th Centuries*, New Delhi: Oxford University Press, 1970.

———, *Al-Hind: The Making of the Indo-Islamic World*, vol. II: *The Slave Kings and the Islamic Conquest 11th–13th Centuries*, New Delhi: Oxford University Press, 1999.

Young, C., *The Politics of Cultural Pluralism*, Madison: University of Wisconsin Press, 1976.

Yunus, Mohammed and Aradhana Parmar, *South Asia: A Historical Narrative*, Karachi: Oxford University Press, 2003.

Zaehner, R.C., *Mysticism: Sacred and Profane*, London, Oxford University Press, 1971.

ARTICLES (ENGLISH)

Abassi, Lt. Col. Muhammad Yusuf, 'The Transition in Muslim Leadership', in Ahmad Hasan Dani, ed., *Proceedings of the First Congress of Pakistan History and Culture*, vol. I, Islamabad: University of Islamabad Press, 1975.

Agarwal, Bina, 'The Idea of Gender Equality: From Legislative Vision to Everyday Family Practice', in Romila Thapar, ed., *India Another Millennium?*, New Delhi: Viking, 2000.

Ahmad, Aziz, 'India', in Joseph Schacht and C.E. Bosworth, eds., *The Legacy of Islam,* Oxford: Clarendon Press, 1974.

Ahmad, Imtiaz, 'Exclusion and Assimilation in Indian Islam', in Attar Singh, ed., *Socio-Cultural Impact of Islam on India,* Chandigarh: Panjab University, 1976.

———, 'Introduction', in Imtiaz Ahmad, ed., *Ritual and Religion Among Muslims in India,* New Delhi: Manohar, 1981.

Ahmed, Rafiuddin, 'The Emergence of the Bengal Muslims', in Rafiuddin Ahmed, ed., *Understanding the Bengal Muslims: Interpretative Essays,* New Delhi: Oxford University Press, 2001.

Al-Faruque, Muhammad, 'Some Aspects of Muslim Revivalist Movement in India during the 18th Century: The Activities of Shah Wali-Allah of Delhi', *Islamic Culture,* vol. LXIII, no. 3, July 1989.

Alavi, H., 'Politics of Ethnicity in India and Pakistan', in H. Alavi and J. Harris, eds., *Sociology of Developing Societies: South Asia,* London: Macmillan, 1989.

Alavi, Hamza A., 'Kinship in West Punjab Villages', in T.N. Madan, ed., *Muslim Communities of South Asia: Culture and Society,* New Delhi: Vikas Publishing House, 1976.

Allen, Barbara, 'Story in Oral History: Clues to Historical Consciousness', *The Journal of American History,* vol. 79, no. 2, September 1992.

Arberry, J., 'Mysticism', in P.M. Holt, Ann K.S. Lambton and Bernard Lewis, eds., *The Cambridge History of Islam: Islamic Society and Civilization,* vol. 2B, Cambridge: Cambridge University Press, 1970.

Asad, Talal, 'The Concept of Cultural Translation in British Social Anthropology', in James Clifford and George E. Marcus, eds., *Writing Culture: The Poetics and Politics of Ethnography,* New Delhi: Oxford University Press, 1990.

Bal, S.S., 'Presidential Address', *Proceedings of Punjab History Conference,* 1994, Patiala: Punjabi University.

Baloch, N.B., 'Muhammad Ibn al-Qasim: A Study of His Family Background and Personality', *Islamic Culture,* vol. 27, October 1953.

Bajaj, S.K., 'Syad Muhammad Latif', in S.P. Sen, ed., *Historians and Historiography in Modern India,* Calcutta: Institute of Historical Studies, 1973.

Barrier, N. Gerald, 'Sikh Identity in Historical and Contemporary Perspective', in Pashaura Singh and N. Gerald Barrier, eds., *Sikh Identity: Continuity and Change,* New Delhi: Manohar, 2001.

Chandra, Ramesh, 'Sultan Mahmud of Ghazni and the Khokhars', *Proceedings of Punjab History Conference,* 1971.

Chatterji, Suniti Kumar, 'Islamic Mysticism, Iran and India', *Indo-Iranica,* vol. I, no. 2, 1946.

Cronon, William, 'A Place for Stories: Nature, History, and Narrative', *The Journal of American History,* vol. 78, no. 4, March 1992.

Christian, Barbara, 'The Race for Theory', in Linda Kauffmann, ed., *Gender and Theory,* Oxford: Blackwell, 1989.

Davidson, Alastain, 'Gramsci, the Peasantry and Popular Culture', *The Journal of Peasant Studies,* vol. II, no. 4, 1984.

Deplanhol, X, 'The Geographical Setting', in P.M. Holt, Ann. K.S. Lambton and Bernard Lewis, eds., *The Cambridge History of Islam: Islamic Society and Civilization,* vol. 2B, Cambridge: Cambridge University Press, 1970.

Deol, Jeevan, 'Acceptable Poetry: Muqbil's Mystical Qissa Hir Ranjha', *International Journal of Punjab Studies,* vol. 3, no. 2, 1996.

Derrida, Jacques, 'Archive Fever', *Diacritics,* Summer 1995.

Eaton, Richard M., 'The Political and Religious Authority of the Shrine of Baba Farid', in Richard M. Eaton, ed., *India's Islamic Traditions, 711–1750,* New Delhi: Oxford University Press, 2003.

———, 'Approaches to the Study of Conversion to Islam in India', in David N. Lorenzen, ed., *Religious Movements in South Asia, 600–1800,* New Delhi: Oxford University Press, 2004.

Farooqui, Aisha Mahmood, 'Justice in Islam', *Islam and the Modern Age,* February 1989.

Farooqi, N.R., 'The Early Chishti Sufis of India: An Outline of Their Thought and an Account of the Popular Appeal of Their Shrines (1)', *Islamic Culture,* vol. LXXVII, no. I, 2003.

Gardet, Louis, 'Religion and Culture', in P.M. Holt, Ann K.S. Lambton and Bernard Lewis, eds., *The Cambridge History of Islam,* vol. 2B, Cambridge: Cambridge University Press, 1970.

Gill, Harjeet Singh, 'The Semiotics of Discourse in Traditional Indian Culture', in Harjeet Singh Gill, ed., *Parole and Language,* Patiala: Punjabi University, 1992.

Geertz, C., 'The Integrative Revolution', in C. Geertz, ed., *Old Societies and New States,* New York: The Free Press, 1963.

Gellner, E. 'Doctor and Saint', in Nikki R. Keddie, ed., *Scholars, Saints and Sufis: Muslim Religious Institutions in the Middle East since 1500,* Berkelay: University of California, 1972.

Grewal, J.S., 'The Sufi Beliefs and Attitudes in India' in Asghar Ali

Engineer, ed., *Sufism and Communal Harmony*, Jaipur: Printwell, 1991.

Grover, B.R., 'Approach and Methodology to the Study of Medieval Punjab' (Presidential Address, Medieval Section), *Proceedings of the Punjab History Conference*, Patiala: Punjabi University, 1976.

Habib, Irfan, 'Jatts of Punjab and Sind', in Harbans Singh and N. Gerald Barrier, eds., *Essays in Honour of Dr. Ganda Singh*, Patiala: Punjabi University, 1976.

———, 'Classifying Pre-Colonial India', *The Journal of Peasant Studies*, vol. 12, nos. 2 and 3, 1985.

———, 'Exploring Medieval Gender History', *Proceedings of the Indian History Congress*, Calcutta, 2000.

———, 'Non-Agricultural Production and Urban Economy', in Tapan Raychaudhri and Irfan Habib, eds., *The Cambridge Economic History of India*, vol. I: *c. 1200–c.1750*, London: Cambridge University Press, 1982.

Hans, Surjit Singh, 'The Idea of Country in Hir by Waris Shah', *Punjab Journal of Sikh Studies*, vol. XX, no. 2, 1996.

Hasan, S. Nurul, 'Zamindars under the Mughals', in Muzaffar Alam and Sanjay Subrahmanyam, eds., *The Mughal State 1526–1750*, New Delhi: Oxford University Press.

Jaffar, S.M., 'The Arab Administration of Sind', *Islamic Culture*, 1943.

Kaplan, Cora, 'Language and Gender', in Deborah Cameron, ed., *The Feminist Critique of Language: A Reader*, London: Routledge, 1990.

Kapoor, Satish K., 'The Use of Drugs in Indian Tradition', *The Journal of Religious Studies*, vol. XXVII, no. 1, 1997.

Khan, Ahmad Nabi, 'The Tomb of Baba Farid Ganj-i-Shakkar at Pakpattan', *Journal of the Pakistan Historical Society*, vol. XXVII, pt. II, 1979.

Kilani, Abdul Razaq O., 'Martyrdom in Islamic Traditions and its Relevance in Islamic System', *Islamic Culture*, vol. LXIX, October 1995.

Lawrence, Bruce B., 'Islam in India: The Functions of Institutional Sufism in the Islamization of Rajasthan, Gujrat and Kashmir', in Richard C. Martin, ed., *Contributions to Asian Studies: Islam in Local Context*, vol. 17, Leiden: Brill, 1982.

Manchanda, Ram Chand, 'A Punjabi Saint', *Journal of Panjab University Historical Society*, vol. III, pt. I, 1934.

Matringe, Denis, 'Hir Waris Shah', in M. Waseem, ed., *On Becoming an Indian Muslim*, New Delhi: Oxford University Press, 2003.

Maza, Sarah, 'Stories in History: Cultural Narratives in Recent Works in European History', *American Historical Review*, vol. I, no. 5, 1996.

Metcalf, Barbara D., 'The Making of a Muslim Lady: Maulana Thanawi's Bihishti Zewar', in Milton Israel and N.K. Wagle, eds., *Islamic Society and Culture*, New Delhi: Manohar, 1983.

Mohan, Kamlesh, 'Clamping Shutters and Valorizing Women: Tensions in Sculpting Gender-Identities in the Colonial Punjab', in Pritam Singh and Shinder Singh Thandi, eds., *Punjabi Identity in a Global Context*, New Delhi: Oxford University Press, 1999.

Mohammed, Malik, 'Indian Sufism as Harbinger of Inter-Religious Harmony', in Gurbachan Singh Talib, ed., *The Sikh-Sufi Quest for Harmony*, Patiala: Baba Farid Memorial Society, 1980.

Delvoye, Françoise Nalini, 'Revitalization of Dhrupad in the Second Half of the Twentieth Century: Musicological Literature and Patronage', in Indu Banga and Jaidev, eds., *Cultural Reorientation in Modern India*, Shimla: Indian Institute of Advanced Studies, 1996.

Nadvi, Suleyman, 'Literary Relations between Arabia and India', *Islamic Culture*, vol. 6, October 1932.

Nizami, K.A., 'The Delhi Sultanate and the Mughal Empire: Genesis and Salient Features', *Islamic Culture*, vol. 55, July 1981.

Nizami, Khwaja Hasan Sani, 'Sufi Tradition and its Impact on Religious Thought', in Asghar Ali Engineer, ed., *Islam in India: The Impact of Civilization*, Delhi, Shipra Publications, 2002.

Pathan, Mumtaz A., 'Development and Progress of Arabic Literature in Sind during the Arab Period', *Islamic Culture*, vol. 42, April 1968.

Prakash, Buddha, 'People's Struggle against Political Tyranny', in Fauja Singh, ed., *History of the Punjab (1000–1526)*, vol. III, Patiala: Punjabi University, 1972.

———, 'Presidential Address', *Proceedings of the Punjab History Conference*, Patiala: Punjabi University, 1965.

Rafiqi, A.Q., 'India's Interface with Islam', in Asghar Ali Engineer, ed., *Islam in India: The Impact of Civilizations*, Delhi: Shipra Publications, 2002.

Rai, Gulshan, 'The Mughal Province of Multan and its Subsequent History (1707–1849)', *Journal of the Panjab University Historical Society*, vol. II, no. 3, 1933.

Rashid, Shaikh Abdur, 'Decline of Mughal Power', in Ahmad Hasan Dani, ed., *Proceedings of the First Congress of Pakistan History and Culture*, vol. I, Islamabad: University of Islamabad, 1975.

Rineheart, Robin, 'Interpretations of the Poetry of Bulleh Shah', *International Journal of Punjab Studies*, vol. 3, no. 1, 1996.

Rizvi, S.A.A., 'Islamic Proselytization (seventh to sixteenth centuries)', in G.A. Oddie, ed., *Religion in South Asia*, New Delhi: Manohar 1977.

Sachdeva, Veena, 'The Non-Sikh Chiefs of the Punjab Plains and Maharaja Ranjit Singh', *Journal of Regional History*, vol. II, 1981.

Schimmel, Annemarie, 'Reflections on Muslim Poetry', in Richard Martin, ed., *Islam in Local Contexts*, vol. 17, Leiden: E.J. Brill, 1982.

Schwartzberg, Joseph E., 'Caste Regions of the North Indian Plain', in Milton Singer and B.S. Cohen, eds., *Structure and Change in Indian Society*, Chicago: Aldine Press, 1968.

Scott, Rachel Marion, 'Education and Arabism in Damascus at the Turn of the Twentieth Century', *Islamic Culture*, vol. LXXII, no. 3, 1998.

Shackle, Christopher, 'Making Punjabi Literary History', in Christopher Shackle, Gurharpal Singh and Arvindpal Singh Mandair, eds., *Sikh Religion, Culture and Ethnicity*, Richmond: Curzon Press, 2001.

———, 'The Pilgrimage and the Extension of Sacred Geography in the Poetry of Khwaja Ghulam Farid', in Attar Singh, ed., *Socio-Cultural Impact of Islam on India*, Chandigarh: Publication Bureau, 1976.

Shils, E., 'Primordial, Personal, Sacred and Civil Ties', *British Journal of Sociology*, vol. 7, 1957.

Siddiqui, Iqtidar Husain, 'Social Mobility in the Delhi Sultanate', in Irfan Habib, ed., *Medieval India I: Researches in the History of India, 1200–1750*, New Delhi: Oxford University Press, 1999.

———, 'Socio-Political Role of Women in the Sultanate of Delhi', in Kiran Pawar, ed., *Women in Indian History*, Patiala and New Delhi: Vision & Venture, 1996.

Singh, Attar, 'Political Change and Punjabi Literature in the Nineteenth Century', in Indu Banga, ed., *Five Punjabi Centuries, Polity, Economy and Culture, c. 1500–1900, Essays for J.S. Grewal*, New Delhi: Manohar, 1997.

———, 'The Medieval Panjabi Literature', *The Panjab Past and Present,* vol. II, pt. I, sr. no. 3, 1968.

Singh, Fauja, 'The Misaldari Period of Sikh History', *The Panjab Past and Present,* vol. XI, pt. I, sr. no. 21, 1977.

Singh, Ganda, 'Baba Farid: A Real Saint', in Attar Singh, ed., *Socio-Cultural Impact of Islam on India.*

———, 'The Martyrdom of Guru Arjun', *The Panjab Past and Present,* vol. XII, pt. I, April 1978.

———, 'History in Panjabi', *The Panjab Past And Present,* vol. V, no. I, sr. no. 9, 1971.

———, 'The Punjab News in the Akhbar-i-Darbar-i-Mulla', *The Punjab Past and Present,* vol. IV, pt. II, sr. no. 8, 1970.

Singh, Surinder, 'The Life and Times of Miyan Mir', *The Panjab Past and Present,* vol. XX, pt. II, 1986.

Sital, Jit Singh, 'Language and Literature during the Sultanate Period', in Fauja Singh, ed., *History of the Punjab (1000–1526),* vol. III, Patiala: Punjabi University, 1972.

Soze, A.A.K., 'Sheikh Farid, the Missionary of Islam', in Gurbachan Singh Talib, ed., *Baba Sheikh Farid: Life and Teachings,* Patiala: Baba Farid Memorial Society, 1973.

Suri, P., 'Heer Waris Shah as a Document on the Social History of the Punjab in the 18th Century', *Proceedings of Indian History Congress,* 1966.

Syed, Anees J., 'Research in Medieval Indian History', *Indica,* vol. 14, no. 1, March 1977.

Waheed-uz-Zaman, 'Shah Wali Ullah and His Times', in Ahmad Hasan Dani, ed., *Proceedings of the First Congress of Pakistan History and Culture,* March 1975.

Talib, Gurbachan Singh, 'Brief Life Sketch Baba Farid', in Gurbachan Singh Talib, ed., *Baba Sheikh Farid: Life and Teachings,* Patiala: Baba Farid Memorial Society, 1973.

———, 'Guru Nanak's Teaching in Relation to Sufism', *The Journal of Religious Studies,* vol. III, 1971.

Waheed-uz-Zaman, 'Shah Wali Ullah and His Times', in Ahmad Hasan Dani, ed., *Proceedings of the First Congress of Pakistan History and Culture,* vol. I, Islamabad: University of Islamabad Press, 1975.

Waseem, M., 'Introduction', in M. Waseem, tr. and ed., *On Becoming an Indian Muslim: French Essays on Aspects of Syncretism,* New Delhi: Oxford University Press, 2003.

BOOKS (PUNJABI)

Arshi, S.S., *Atharvin Sadi Da Sikh Itihas*, Chandigarh: Arora Publishers, n.d.

Ashok, Shamsher Singh, *Madhkalin Panjab*, Amritsar: Punjabi Sahit Prakashan, n.d.

Azad, Avtar Singh, *Satt Sitarey*, New Delhi: Sikh Publishing House, 1957.

Bedi, Sohinder Singh Wanjara, *Punjabi Lokedhara Vishav Kosh (Panjabi Folklore Encyclopaedia)*, vols. I-IV, Delhi: Lok Prakashan, May 1978, October 1978, November 1979, and March 1981; vols. V–VII), Delhi: National Book Shop, 1991, 1992 and 1994.

———, *Punjab da Lok Sahitya* (A Study of Folk Culture, Language and Literature of Dhan-Pothohar, West Pakistan), Delhi: Navyug Press, 1968.

———, *Panjabi Sahit-Itihas Dian Lok-Roorian*, New Delhi: Lok Prakashan, 1982.

Gasso, Om Parkash, *Punjabi Sabhiachar: Soundria Shaster*, Ludhiana: Chetna Prakashan, 2005.

Gupta, M.G., *Baba Sheikh Farid (Farida Kale Mende Kapde Kala Menda Ves)*, Sirhind: Lokgeet Prakashan, 1996.

Ghuman, Bikram Singh, ed., *Punjabi Qissa Ate Bir Kav*, Amritsar: Guru Nanak Dev University, 1998.

Hoti, Baba Prem Singh, *Punjab Da Samajak Itihas (Khalsa Raj Vekhey)*, ed. Fauja Singh, Patiala: Punjabi University.

Jaggi, Rattan Singh, *Punjabi Sahit Da Itihas, 1701–1850*, vol. II, Patiala: Punjabi University, 1976.

———, *Panjabi Sahit Da Srot Moolak Itihas*, pt. III, Patiala: Punjabi University, 1999.

Kakar, Ajit Singh, ed., *Punjabi Sabhiachar*, Patiala: Bhasha Vibhag, 1998.

Kang, Amarjit Singh, ed., *Punjabi Kisse*, New Delhi: Sahitya Akademi, 1997.

Kang, Jaspal Kaur, *Qissa-Samvad*, Amritsar: Nanak Singh Pustak Mala, 1990.

Kang, K.S., *Sukhan Da Waris*, Amritsar: Waris Shah Foundation, 1990.

———, ed., *Heer Damodar: Ikk Itihasik Te Sahatik Mullankan*, Amritsar: Ruhi Prakashan, 1994.

Kanwar, Tarlok Singh, ed., *Shodh/Parishodh*, Delhi: Arsi Publishers, 1989.

———, *Sanchar Sabhyachar*, Ludhiana: Lahore Book Shop, 1986.

———, ed., *Punjabi Sahit Di Ithaskari*, Delhi: Punjabi Akademi, 1995.

Kaur, Amarjeet, *Kissa Ate Romance*, Amritsar: Nanak Singh Pustak Mala, 1987.

Kaur, Jaswinder, *Heer Waris Shah Da Chehan Vigianik Adhian*, Delhi: Arsi Publishers, 1988.

Kaur, Neelamjit, *Heer Waris Vich Punjabi Sanskriti*, Amritsar: Waris Shah Foundation, 1996.

Khera, Bhupinder Singh, *Punjabi Mithik Kathawan De Chin Jugat*, Patiala: Pepsu Book Depot, 1988.

Kushta, Moula Bakhsh, *Punjab De Heeray*, ed. Gurmukh Singh, Sirhind: Lokgeet Prakashan, 1996.

Nanda, Balbir Singh, ed., *Madh-Kaleen Punjabi Sahit: Punar Nirikhan*, Patiala: Punjabi University, 1994.

Noor, Sutinder Singh, *Sabhiachar Te Sahit*, Delhi: Arsi Publishers, 1994.

———, ed., *Lokyan Sahit Te Sabhyachar*, Delhi: Punjabi Akademi, 1994.

———, *Punjabi Sufi Kaav*, New Delhi: Sahitya Akademi, 1997.

Paul, Amrit Lal, *Sufi Kissa Ate Beer Kav*, Patiala: R.S. Publication, 1999.

Premi, Gurdit Singh, *Waris Shah: Ik Pariche*, Patiala: Punjabi University, 1999.

Padam, Piara Singh, *Punjabi Varan*, Ludhiana: Lahore Book Shop, 1951.

Ravi, Ravinder Singh, *Ravi Chetna*, ed. Gurcharan Singh Arshi, Patiala: Ravi Memorial Trust, 1991.

Randhawa, M.S., ed., *Punjab (Itihas, Kala, Sahit Te Sabhiachar)*, Patiala: Bhasha Vibhag, 1960.

Randhawa, M.S. and Devendra Satyarathi, eds., *Punjabi Lok Geet*, 6th edn., Delhi: Sahitya Akademi, 1999.

Sandhu, Tara Singh, *Heer Vaaris: Lokyanik Adhar*, Ludhiana: Chetna Prakashan, 2005.

Satyarathi, Devendra, *Gidha*, 1936; rpt., New Delhi: Navyug Publishers, 1998.

Shelley, Kuljit, *Punjabi Sufi Kav De Bimb Pattren*, Patiala: Punjab: Bhasha Vibhag, 1992.

Singh, Attar, *Darishtikon*, 2nd edn., Chandigarh: Raghbir Rachna Prakashan, 1991.

———, *Sahit Sanvedna*, Chandigarh: Raghbir Rachna Prakashan, 1984.

Singh, Gulwant, *Islam Ate Sufiwad*, Patiala: Punjabi University, 1994.
Singh, Gurdev, *Punjabi Sufi Kav Da Itihas*, vol. 4, Delhi: Punjabi Akademi, 2005.
Singh, Harbhajan, *Qissa Punjab*, New Delhi: National Book Trust, 1972.
Singh, Harjit, *Punjabi Kissa Kav Da Theme Vigyanik Adhiyan*, Punjab Bhasha Vibhag, 1998.
Singh, Kishan, *Sikh Lehar*, Delhi: Arsi Publishers, 1986.
Singh, Mohan, *Shah Husain*, Amritsar: Kasturi Lal & Sons, 1952.
Singh, Mohinderjit, ed., *Punjabi Sabhiachar: Pehchan Te Shakti*, Ludhiana: Simran Publications, 1998.
Singh, Nahar, *Lok Kaav Di Sirjan Parkiriya*, Chandigarh: Lokgeet Prakashan, 2006.
Singh, Prem Prakash, *Punjabi Bhasha Da Srot Te Bantar*, Patiala: Punjabi University, 1996.
Sital, Jit Singh, *Bulleh Shah Jivan Te Rachna*, 1970; rpt., Patiala: Punjabi University, 1996.
———, ed., *Punjabi Bir Sahit*, Patiala: Languages Department, 1970.
Sital, Jit Singh and Gulwant Singh, eds., *Punjabi Sahit Vich Pramukh Jhakau*, Patiala: Punjabi University, 1976.
Syed, Najm Hosain, *Sedhan Saran ate Hor Lekh*, ed. Purdaman Singh Bedi, Ludhiana: Jaswant Printers, 2005.
Thind, Karnail Singh, *Punjab Da Lok Virsa*, Patiala: Punjabi University, 1996.
———, ed., *Lokyan Adhian*, Amritsar: Guru Nanak Dev University, 1978.

ARTICLES (PUNJABI)

Bhogal, Hirdejit Singh, 'Hir Waris Da Birtant-Shastar', in Bikram Singh Ghuman, ed., *Punjabi Kissa Kav Da Birtant Shastar*, Amritsar: Guru Nanak Dev University, 2001.
Bukhari, Tanvir, 'Waris Da Pind', in Jit Singh Sital, ed., *Waris Shah Jivan Te Rachana* (in Gurmukhi), Patiala: Languages Department, 1970.
Gill, Tejwant Singh, 'Hir Waris Shah: Vichardhara Te Birtant', in Bikram Singh Ghuman, ed., *Punjabi Kissa Kav Da Birtant Shastar*, Amritsar: Guru Nanak Dev University, 2001.
Hans, Surjit, 'Hir Waris Ate Atharvin Sadi Da Punjab', in Bikram Singh Ghuman and Harbhajan Singh Bhatia, eds., *Punjabi Sahit Di Ithaskari*, vol. 2, Amritsar: Guru Nanak Dev University, n.d.

Kang, Jaspal Kaur, 'Qissah Kav Vich Istri Purkh Sambdhan Da Chitran', in Rattan Singh Jaggi, ed., *Khoj Patrika Qissah-Kav-Ank*, Patiala: Punjabi University, 1997.

Kang, Kulbir Singh, 'Hir-Kav Parampara: Kathanak Some', in Rattan Singh Jaggi, ed., *Khoj Patrika Qissa Kav Ank*, Ank 27, 1986, Patiala: Punjabi University.

Singh, Dharam, 'Shah Hussain: Sikh Itihasik Granthan Vich', in Rattan Singh Jaggi, ed., *Khoj Patrika: Sufi Kava Ank*, Patiala, Punjabi University, 1989.

Singh, Gurdev, 'Punjabi Sufi-kav Da Vichardharik Sandrabh', in Balbir Singh Nanda and Inderjit Kaur, eds., *Madh-Kaleen Punjabi Sahit: Punar Nirikhan*, Patiala: Punjabi University, 1994.

Singh, Jagbir, 'Qissa-Kav Da Birtant Vigayanik Adhyan: Seema Te Sambhavana', in Bikram Singh Ghuman, ed., *Punjabi Kissa Kav Da Birtant Shastar*, Amritsar, Guru Nanak Dev University, 2001.

Sital, Jit Singh, 'Waris Di Boli', in Jit Singh Sital, ed., *Waris Jivan te Rachna*, Patiala: Languages Department, 1970.

Shan, Harnam Singh, 'Shah Husain Di Den', *Punjabi Duniya*, nos. 1–2, 1959.

Singh, Pritam, 'Shah Husain Barey Kuj Puranian Kitaban Vichon', *Punjabi Duniya*, nos. 1–2, 1959.

Index